BRITISH AND IRISH DRAMA SINCE 1960

A750
Y/P C
(Ach)

...ks are to be returned on or before
e last date below.

N 1998

WITHDRAWN

- 6 FEB 2008

0333532597

British and Irish Drama since 1960

Edited by

James Acheson

Senior Lecturer in English
University of Canterbury
Christchurch, New Zealand

First published in Great Britain 1993 by
MACMILLAN PRESS LTD
Houndmills, Basingstoke, Hampshire RG21 6XS
and London
Companies and representatives
throughout the world

A catalogue record for this book is available
from the British Library.

ISBN 0–333–53259–7

 First published in the United States of America 1993 by
ST. MARTIN'S PRESS, INC.,
Scholarly and Reference Division,
175 Fifth Avenue,
New York, N.Y. 10010
ISBN 0–312–08046–8

Library of Congress Cataloging-in-Publication Data
British and Irish Drama since 1960 / edited by James Acheson.
p. cm.
Includes index.
ISBN 0–312–08046–8
1. English drama—20th century—History and Criticism. 2. English
drama—Irish Authors—History and criticism. 3. Ireland in
literature. I. Acheson, James, 1947– .
PR737.B675 1993
822'.91409—dc20

92–46047
CIP

10 9 8 7 6 5 4 3 2
04 03 02 01 00 99 98 97 96

Printed in Great Britain by
Antony Rowe Ltd
Chippenham, Wiltshire

Contents

vi   *Contents*

Preface

The fifteen essays in this collection, published here for the first time, survey the work of some of the most major British and Irish dramatists of the past three decades. Its fifteen essayists dwell almost exclusively on British and Irish *theatre*: limitations of space have dictated that cinema screenplay and radio and television drama be treated only tangentially. Included in the collection are four dramatists – Samuel Beckett, Harold Pinter, Peter Shaffer and Peter Nichols – who began writing plays before 1960, and whose work since then has continued to develop in interesting new ways. Most of the dramatists considered here are those who have made their appearance since 1960, and who illustrate some of the distinctive characteristics of British and Irish drama of the past thirty-odd years. I am very grateful to the University of Canterbury for making a research grant available to enable me to complete this collection.

JAMES ACHESON

Notes on the Contributors

James Acheson is Senior Lecturer in English at the University of Canterbury in Christchurch, New Zealand. He is coeditor of *Beckett's Later Fiction and Drama: Texts for Company*, editor of *The British and Irish Novel Since 1960*, and author of two forthcoming books, one on Beckett, the other on John Fowles. A member of the Editorial Board of the *Journal of Beckett Studies*, Dr Acheson has published on Beckett and other modern writers in various essay collections and journals.

Katherine H. Burkman is Professor of English at Ohio State University. She is co-author of *Drama Through Performance*, author of *The Dramatic World of Harold Pinter: its Basis in Ritual*, *Literature Through Performance: 'Shakespeare's Mirror' and 'A Canterbury Caper'* and *The Arrival of Godot: Ritual Patterns in Modern Drama*, and editor of *Myth and Ritual in the Plays of Samuel Beckett*.

Richard Allen Cave is Professor of Drama and Theatre Arts at Royal Holloway and Bedford New College, University of London. He has published extensively in the fields of Renaissance and Modern Drama, Stage Design, Dance, and Anglo-Irish Theatre of the nineteenth and twentieth centuries. Professor Cave is the General Editor of the *Theatre in Focus* series, promoted by the Consortium for Drama and Media in Higher Education, of which he is currently Chairman.

Mary A. Doll is Associate Professor of English at Our Lady of Holy Cross College (New Orleans), where she teaches modern literature. She is author of *Beckett and Myth* and *In the Shadow of the Giant: Thomas Wolfe*, and has published essays on modern drama and fiction in numerous edited collections and journals.

John Fletcher is Professor of Comparative Literature at the University of East Anglia. He is the author or coauthor of many essays on modern drama, and of over a dozen books on contemporary writing, including *The Novels of Samuel Beckett*, *Samuel Beckett's Art*, *New Directions in Literature*, *Beckett: a Study of his Plays*, *A Student's Guide to the Plays of Samuel Beckett*, *Claude Simon and Fiction Now* and *Alain Robbe-Grillet*.

James Gindin is Professor of English at the University of Michigan.

He is author of *Postwar British Fiction: New Accents and Attitudes, Harvest of a Quiet Eye: the Novel of Compassion, The English Climate: an Excursion into a Biography of John Galsworthy, John Galsworthy's Life and Art: an Alien's Fortress, William Golding,* and of numerous essays and reviews.

Frances Gray is Lecturer in English and Drama at the University of Sheffield. She is author of *John Arden* and *Noel Coward,* and is working on a book provisionally entitled *Women and Laughter.* She has written several radio plays and contributes a regular column on radio to *Plays International.*

Romana Huk is Assistant Professor of English at the University of New Hampshire. She is author of a forthcoming book on Stevie Smith, and has published essays on contemporary British and American poets in various collections and journals. Dr Huk is currently writing a book on Tony Harrison, Geoffrey Hill, Jon Silkin, Ken Smith, Jeffrey Wainwright, and the significance of the social context they shared at the University of Leeds.

William Hutchings is Associate Professor of English at the University of Alabama at Birmingham. He is author of both *The Plays of David Storey: a Thematic Study* and a forthcoming book on Alan Sillitoe. In addition, Dr Hutchings has published essays on modern literature in many leading journals.

Anthony Jenkins is Professor of English and Director of Graduate Studies at the University of Victoria. He is author of *The Theatre of Tom Stoppard* and *The Making of Victorian Drama,* and editor of *The Isle of Ladies* and *Critical Essays on Tom Stoppard.* As well as being an academic, Professor Jenkins is a professional actor and director, and hosts a local television programme on the arts.

Andrew Parkin is Professor of English at the Chinese University of Hong Kong. He is author of *The Dramatic Imagination of W.B. Yeats* and a volume of poetry entitled *Dancers in a Web,* and is editor of *Dion Boucicault: Selected Plays* and of Yeats's *The Herne's Egg.* A former Editor of *The Canadian Journal of Irish Studies,* Professor Parkin has published essays on modern drama in numerous journals. He has known Peter Nichols for some years, and has followed his development as a dramatist with considerable interest.

Robert Wilcher is Senior Lecturer in English at the University of Birmingham, where he teaches modern drama and seventeenth century literature. Dr Wilcher is author of *Understanding Arnold*

Wesker and *Andrew Marvell*, and editor of *Andrew Marvell: Selected Poetry and Prose*. He has contributed essays on modern drama to many edited collections and journals.

Ann Wilson is Associate Professor of Drama at the University of Guelph. She has published essays on contemporary British, Canadian and American drama in such journals as *Canadian Theatre Review*, *Modern Drama* and *Theatre Research International*, and is Associate Editor of *Essays in Theatre*.

Katharine Worth is Emeritus Professor of Drama and Theatre Studies in the University of London and currently Visiting Professor at King's College, London. She is author of *Revolutions in Modern English Drama*, *The Irish Drama of Europe from Yeats to Beckett* and *Oscar Wilde*, and is editor of *Beckett the Shape Changer: a Symposium* and of Yeats's *Where There Is Nothing*. Professor Worth has been active in producing plays for radio, television and the theatre.

Hersh Zeifman is Associate Professor of English at York University (Canada), where he teaches dramatic literature. He is author of many essays on modern drama, editor of *David Hare: a Casebook*, and coeditor of *Contemporary British Drama, 1970–90*. Dr Zeifman is President of the Samuel Beckett Society, coeditor of *Modern Drama*, and a member of the Editorial Board of *The Pinter Review*.

1

'The Absolute Absence of the Absolute': the Theory and Practice of Samuel Beckett's Drama

James Acheson

I

Though Beckett is best known for *Waiting for Godot* (1952), he began his career as a writer not with a play but a critical essay.[1] That essay, 'Dante . . . Bruno . Vico . . Joyce' (1929), a defence of Joyce's 'Work in Progress', was the first of a number of occasional essays and reviews he was to write over the next quarter century.[2] Beckett's main ambition during this period was to establish himself as a novelist and poet, not as a literary theorist or journalist. He agreed to write the other essays and reviews either to publicise the work of friends or to supplement a meagre income; he did not set out to develop a literary aesthetic. Nevertheless, there emerges from these occasional pieces a consistent theory about the relationship between art and the limits of human knowledge, a theory he puts into practice both in his early fiction and drama.

As 'Dante . . . Bruno . Vico . . Joyce' makes clear, Beckett finds in Joyce an author preoccupied with the question of whether there are any underlying principles of order in the world at large. 'Work in Progress' draws attention to the existence of various numerical coincidences – to the fact that there are, for example, 'four legs to a table, and four to a horse, and four seasons and four Gospels and four Provinces in Ireland, . . . twelve Tables of the Law, and twelve Apostles and twelve months and twelve Napoleonic marshals and twelve men in Florence called Ottolenghi' – because Joyce is 'conscious that things with a common numerical characteristic tend towards a very significant interrelationship' (32).

If the significance of the interrelationship of things with a common numerical characteristic were to be taken seriously, and could be established with absolute certainty, we might find that the world is governed by some sort of ordering principle. When Beckett claims that Joyce could fashion a definitive account of the coincidences of all the numbers in the number system in a thousand years, however, he is exaggerating for the sake of emphasising Joyce's superiority to the reading public. The problems involved in trying to explain such coincidences are just too vast. Equally daunting are the problems faced by philosophers who wish to establish whether the world is either orderly or random: ultimately, they can say of it only that it is infinitely complex. Despite his admiration for Joyce, Beckett is obliged to admit that he (Joyce) is neither omniscient nor omnipotent, and that he is therefore incapable of fashioning a work as complex and unique as the world at large. Like such earlier figures as Dante, Bruno and Vico, he can only hint at the world's complexity in his writing, and can only be original in a limited, though impressive, sense.

Beckett reminds us in the essay that Dante created a synthetic language from the various dialects of Italy for use in *The Divine Comedy*; that Bruno devised an original theory about the coincidence of contraries; and that Vico argued in a new and interesting way that history is circular. Yet none of these writers worked in a cultural vacuum: Dante made use of the current vernacular in devising his new language, and Vico evolved his theory of history from Bruno, whose own ideas derive from ancient Greek philosophy. The sense in which the three Italians can be said to be original is that each made innovative use of received materials.

Joyce, Beckett emphasises, is original in the same sense. 'Work in Progress' is modelled on Dante in that its language is a multilingual synthesis, and on Vico in that it is structurally circular. Its structure arises from 'an endless verbal germination, maturation, putrefaction', and this, says Beckett, is 'pure Vico, and Vico applied to the problem of style' (29). Yet he is careful to point out that Joyce's interest is in the *shape* of Vico's theory, rather than in its content: 'Work in Progress' is structurally circular because circularity suits Joyce's purposes, and not because it is meant to elucidate or expound Viconian theory. Dante and Vico come together in the 'purgatorial aspect' (29) of 'Work in Progress' – in the fact that it is a work characterised by the 'absolute absence of the Absolute' (33). But whereas Dante's Mount of Purgatory spirals upward, culminating in Paradise, 'Work in Progress' eschews culmination. Its structural circles mirror in language the circular flood of 'movement and vitality' (33) continually issuing from the conflict of two moral extremes.

In Vico the course of history is guided through its recurrent cycle by Providence, a force partly human and partly divine. Providence, Beckett argues, is at the centre of the structural circles in 'Work in Progress'; but here it is merely a 'human institution' (23), a concept men have invented to give meaning to events. Alternations in the predominance of Vice and Virtue are for Joyce strictly representative of trends in human behaviour: his use of Providence in the work as a mere 'structural convenience' (22) is a mark of his scepticism about the existence of God.

Joyce's scepticism is implicitly linked in the essay to the question of whether the world is essentially orderly. In the absolute absence of absolute knowledge of the world around us, Beckett suggests, it is impossible for a writer as intelligent as Joyce to believe either in God or in the notion that God is guiding humanity towards a state of perfection. At another remove, the essay tells us something about the kind of writer Beckett intended to become, and indeed, did become when he started writing novels and plays himself. Asked by Harold Hobson in 1956 why, as a nonbeliever, he was so preoccupied in *Waiting for Godot* with the two thieves crucified with Christ, Beckett replied: 'I am interested in the shape of ideas even if I do not believe them. There is a wonderful sentence in Augustine. . . . "Do not despair; one of the thieves was saved. Do not presume; one of the thieves was damned". That sentence has a wonderful shape. It is the shape that matters'.[3]

Godot mirrors the antithetical shape of the sentence from Augustine in a number of ways. The play is in two acts, and presents two characters – Vladimir and Estragon – awaiting the arrival of the mysterious Godot. They are visited by two other characters: Pozzo, who is blessed with wealth; and Lucky, who is condemned to poverty. The English version of the play is subtitled 'a tragicomedy in two acts', and thereby invites us to ponder the tragedy of the characters' situation and the comedy of their response to it. By way of such dualities as these, Beckett raises the question of whether modern man should or should not believe in divine salvation, and with Godot's nonarrival, strongly hints that he should not.

Beckett's preoccupation with the shape of ideas clearly parallels Joyce's use of Vico for structural purposes in 'Work in Progress': both in Joyce and in *Waiting for Godot* an earlier text provides the basis for an original work expressive of scepticism about the existence and behaviour of God. *Godot* is in this sense typical of much of Beckett's writing. In as early a prose text as *More Pricks Than Kicks* (1934), and in plays as late as *Not I* (1973) and *That Time* (1976), passages from earlier texts serve as points of departure for works that question religious belief.[4]

II

In *That Time*, an old man named Listener attends to memories of the persons he once was: A in middle age, B in youth and C in old age. That he is distanced from all three in time is evident from the fact that he refers to each as 'you' ('tu' in Beckett's French translation).[5] In the opening stage directions, he is said to have an '*Old white face*' and '*long flaring white hair as if seen from above outspread*': the sense we have is that he is on his deathbed, recalling key episodes from his past.[6]

Where the dramatic shape of *Godot* was suggested to Beckett by a passage in St Augustine, the shape of *That Time* derives from another source: Wordsworth's famous poem, 'Lines Written a Few Miles above Tintern Abbey'. Like *That Time*, 'Tintern Abbey' contains a number of structural triads, and deals with three stages in an individual's life. Moreover, of the second stage in his own life, Wordsworth says in the poem:

> That time is past,
> And all its aching joys are now no more,
> And all its dizzy raptures. Not for this
> Faint I, nor mourn nor murmur: other gifts
> Have followed, for such loss, I would believe,
> Abundant recompense.

(ll. 84–9)[7]

'That time' is past for Listener as well: each of the three stages of his life is now behind him and can only be recovered through memory.

But whereas for Wordsworth there are 'other gifts' to compensate for what has been lost, for Listener there is nothing. Beckett adapts the shape of 'Tintern Abbey' to *That Time*, but not its optimistic view of God's presence in nature and benevolence to man, his play being not simply a dramatised version of Wordsworth's poem, but a post-Romantic variation on it instead.

The play opens with the first of Listener's memories of travelling from England to Ireland as a middle-aged man in order to visit the folly where he hid as a child. He finds on his return that he has no friends he can stay with, all the houses having been torn down in the areas where they used to live; he spends only one night away from England because he is anxious to return to the unnamed woman who has been living with him there. The woman may be his mother, though *she* appears to have died earlier ('was your mother ah for God's sake . . . gone long ago' [229]). Alternatively, she may be his mistress, or even his sister, for a woman named 'Dolly' – named, perhaps, after Wordsworth's sister Dorothy – is mentioned in early drafts of the play.[8] Whoever the woman is, she eventually dies or leaves him, and Listener spends the rest of his life as a solitary.

Listener's situation differs radically from Wordsworth's in 'Tintern Abbey', for whereas Beckett's character must live with a haunting awareness of his own solitude, Wordsworth has a source of comfort in the company of his sister:

> For thou art with me, here upon the banks
> Of this fair river; thou, my dearest Friend,
> My dear, dear Friend, and in thy voice I catch
> The language of my former heart, and read
> My former pleasures in the shooting lights
> Of thy wild eyes.
>
> (ll. 116–20)

The phrase 'For thou art with me' is of course an echo of the twenty-third Psalm, and suggests that Dorothy is, in effect, an agent of Providence. For Dorothy supplies the poet not only with the reassurance that his experience of nature is shared by someone else, but with the further implicit assurance that God exists and provides the companionship of fellow man as a balm to the indifference or unpleasantness of strangers, and to our fear of the 'valley of the shadow of death'.

In contrast to Wordsworth, Listener must face death alone: there is nothing in 'Tintern Abbey' as chilling as his final intimation of mortality, which occurs one day when he enters the Public Library to shelter from the winter rain. He sits down and drifts off to sleep; when he opens his eyes, he sees 'from floor to ceiling nothing only dust and not a sound only what was it it said come and gone . . . come and gone . . . come and gone in no time gone in no time' (235). As various critics have observed, this passage is an echo of Genesis 3.19 – ' . . . dust thou art, and unto dust shalt thou return' – and conveys not only that Listener's life is nearly ended, but that life in general comes and goes 'in no time' relative to eternity.

Listener ends the play with an enigmatic smile. 'Is it', asks James Knowlson, ' . . . a smile of satisfaction at the restoration of . . . old times? A smile of relief and contentment that at last all the torment is nearly over? A wry reflection on the insignificance of the individual human existence in the context of infinity? Or a smile indicating that even capitulation to the void can still be endured with serene acceptance?'[9] Surely the smile is all these things and more. In the light, however, of Beckett's 'shape of ideas' approach to dramatic structure – his use of 'Tintern Abbey' as a point of departure for the structuring of *That Time* – it is certain that the smile does not arise from a Wordsworthian sense that God is good and can be relied upon to confer meaning and value on life. Beckett's post-Romantic variation on 'Tintern Abbey' promotes a much darker view altogether.

Not I, a play Beckett once described as 'brother' to *That Time*,[10] takes its title from St Paul's repeated comment in his epistles that it is 'not I' who write, 'but Christ [who] liveth in me'.[11] In accordance with Beckett's 'shape of ideas' approach to drama, that comment becomes the thematic basis for the play: through the I/ not I duality, Beckett offers us the choice of interpreting his play in either religious or psychological terms, while raising questions about the existence and benevolence of God, and about the absolute absence of absolute knowledge.

The main character of *Not I*, an old woman named Mouth, is troubled by the repeated experience of speaking with an involuntary voice – a voice she does not recognise as her own. Conscious of Beckett's longstanding interest in Jung (and of Jung's interest in St Paul), Enoch Brater has suggested that the voice may be that of her Jungian 'shadow'.[12] Jung believed the shadow to be one of a number of inner personalities that come to the fore during the process of individuation – the process by which an individual becomes aware of certain unconscious elements in his psyche, and ultimately achieves a more complete understanding of himself. In Jung's own words, individuation is a matter of "coming to selfhood" or "self-realisation",[13] which involves coming to terms with such personalities as the shadow, the anima and the ego.

The shadow is 'the character that summarises a person's uncontrolled emotional manifestations':[14] it is the unconscious Hyde lurking within the conscious Jekyll, the Caliban within Ariel. Mouth, argues Brater, has yet to reach the end of the individuation process; she is still at the stage of having to contend with her shadow.[15] Her anguish is nowhere more evident than in her descriptions of the occasions on which the voice starts to speak. There is, she tells us, 'no stopping it . . . she who but a moment before . . . could not make a sound . . . now can't stop . . . imagine! . . . and the whole brain begging . . . the mouth to stop . . . and no response . . . like maddened . . . ' (220). It is arguable, given this passage, that Mouth *has* been taken over by her shadow – the sum of her 'uncontrolled emotional manifestations' – for it is clear that the maddened voice is quite out of control; moreover, we discover later in the play that the voice has on at least one occasion been associated with involuntary weeping.

But although it is consistent with the text to suggest, as Brater does, that Mouth's involuntary voice belongs to her shadow, other possibilities also present themselves. It may be, for example, that the involuntary voice in *Not I* is that of Mouth's animus, a personality Jung describes as being a purveyor of opinions – 'opinions scraped together more or less unconsciously from childhood on, and compressed into a canon of average truth, justice, and reasonableness . . . ' (206). Mouth is 'coming up to . . . seventy' (216), and has for many years refused to believe in a 'merciful . . . God' (217). Nevertheless, her childhood belief that 'God is love' (221) has returned with her experiences of the voice: these have all but persuaded her that she has sinned, and the voice is capable of saying the words that will occasion divine forgiveness. The words she needs to say may well be unrecognisable to her when they are uttered, because they are rooted in her unconscious; yet she has an obscure and naive faith that once she has hit on them, they will find favour with the just and merciful God of her childhood.

Still another possibility, however, is that she has come almost to the end of the individuation process – almost to the emergence of the Self – but has not yet attained complete self-realisation. A balance of conscious and unconscious has not yet been struck, and thus the Self – the 'I' not altogether consciously her own – has yet to take full control. This is evident from Jung's description of the final stage of individuation, where the person concerned is meant to experience 'a change of feeling similar to that . . . [of] a father to whom a son has been born, a change known to us from the testimony of St Paul: "Yet not I, but Christ liveth in me". The symbol of "Christ" as "son of man" is an analogous psychic experience of a higher spiritual being who is invisibly born in the individual, a pneumatic body which is to serve us as a future dwelling, a body which, as Paul says, is put on like a garment'.[16]

Mouth experiences neither the joy of a father to whom a son has been born, nor the retrospective joy of a St Paul aware of the presence of Christ within himself. Rather, her experience is of the shock and momentary loss of sight of Saul on the road to Damascus – of Saul who found it hard to 'kick against the pricks'.[17] In describing the endpoint of the individuation process, Jung emphasises that his comparison of self-realisation to the discovery of Christ or God within is merely a convenient way of indicating how profound this experience is. Elsewhere he suggests that God may not even exist – that He may be only 'an historical and intellectual bogey or a philosophical sentimentality' (237). Similarly, it may be that Mouth's vision is devoid of any religious significance; however, the Pauline quality of the play's title and the peculiar nature of Mouth's suffering oblige us to consider the possibility that she has undergone a mystical conversion.

Certainly there is a marked similarity between St Paul's conversion and what Mouth experiences: like the saint, she hears a voice sounding in her ears, and is subjected both to a lapse of vision and a sense of being bathed in an unaccountable light. But she also resembles other mystics who have described hearing voices – voices that have broken abruptly in upon their ordinary everyday activities. Julian of Norwich and St Catherine of Sienna, for example, describe not only hearing the voice of God, but replying to it; St Teresa and Ana de la Encarnacion tell of writing under God's dictation.[18] Their experiences have obvious relevance to *Not I*, where the 'buzzing' (217) in Mouth's head transforms itself into an uncontrollable voice not consciously her own, a voice which sometimes raises questions to which she replies. This involuntary voice works independently of her brain, as though her brain were disconnected from the 'machine' (220) – the body – it usually controls. When it speaks, it is of 'nothing she could tell' (222); in other words, it speaks of an ineffable experience like the mystic's of union with God.

Yet, in spite of all this, and in spite of the fact that the character who listens to her outpourings, Auditor, is reminiscent of a priest in confessional, it is by no means certain that Mouth's experience is necessarily the mystic's of union with God. The possibility remains that it may also be that of a spurious mystical experience, or, quite simply, of madness. Mouth's dalliance with the idea that she has sinned, and that the voice that speaks through her may finally hit on the words to procure God's forgiveness, is an interpretation of her sufferings that offers hope for the future, and is therefore attractive to her. But it is not necessarily the correct interpretation, as her bitter laughter at the thought of the existence of a merciful God testifies. Through her laughter, Beckett urges us to consider the two alternative possibilities raised in his other 'shape of ideas' plays: either there is no God, and our suffering is purely a matter of chance; or God exists and is inexplicably cruel to His creatures.

III

Beckett's interest in what psychology can tell us about the limits of human knowledge is evident in several of the critical essays he wrote after 'Dante . . . Bruno . Vico . . Joyce'. In 'Three Dialogues' (1949), for example, he argues that art is expressive of the artist's 'natural experience, as revealed to the vigilant coenaesthesia'.[19] By 'natural experience', Beckett means the artist's experience of sense-data; 'coenaesthesia' is a term experimental psychologists use to refer to our total bodily consciousness.[20] Despite the vigilance of the coenaesthesia, the artist is, Beckett implies, limited in what he can hope to learn about the world around him.

He is limited by the fact that he is human. Early this century, psychologists established that the world we know through perception is merely a simplification of the infinitely complex world of undifferentiated sense-data. Edgar Rubin, in particular, found by examining 'his own and others' experiences in the presence of meaningless black contours on a white background', that we make sense of sense-data by distinguishing perceptually between 'the figure, the substantial appearance of objects, and the ground, the . . . environment in which the [objects are] placed'.[21]

Experiments performed by some of Rubin's contemporaries show that the figure-ground distinction is invariably a simplification of what is perceived.[22] It follows, then, that the world we know through perception is merely a simplification (because a series of simplifications of sense-data in different situations) of the world as it really is. We are guilty of simplifying not only the world at large, but also the world within – the world of our minds. Unlike the world at large, the mind is not available for perceptual investigation; theories about what it is like must therefore be based partly on the investigator's own experience of introspection, and partly on his observation of the behaviour and inner experience of other people.

Obviously, both sources of information are unsatisfactory, because they are not as direct as perception, and because in the process of interpreting the information, the investigator is obliged to assign some of it the prominence of 'figure', while treating other material as 'ground'. Beckett examines the implications of this for the practice of drama in a number of his plays, including *Endgame* (1957) and *Ohio Impromptu* (1981). Here, as elsewhere, he demonstrates that our experience is characterised by an absolute absence of absolute knowledge of either the world or the mind.

Endgame is an extended chess game with the audience – a game in which the four red- or white-faced characters (red and white being the same side in chess) are pitted against the darkened faces of the audience in the theatre. The game's purpose is to frustrate our attempts to interpret *Endgame* definitively; checkmate occurs when we recognise that the play is meant to be a counterpart both to the infinitely complex world around us and to the equally complex human mind – a counterpart that resists even the most ingenious of explications.

Throughout this game, Beckett as White is on the offensive, and thus requires us to develop defences against his attack. The most obvious defence is to assume that *Endgame* is essentially naturalistic – that it presents us with ostensibly real people enacting a real-life situation. Initially, the action might seem to take place in a bomb shelter in the aftermath of a nuclear war. Yet there is no explicit evidence that this is the situation the play presents; moreover, comments in the dialogue to the effect that there is '[n]o more nature',[23] that there are 'no more tide[s]' (41), and that the seeds

Clov plants will 'never sprout' (17) suggest that a disaster of a quite different kind has taken place.

Beckett is vague both about the setting of *Endgame* and about the identity and relationships of its characters. Their names (all first names, apparently) suggest a bewildering array of nationalities in a family in which it is clear that Nagg and Nell are Hamm's parents, but only implied that Clov is Hamm's adoptive son. We learn next to nothing about the characters' past – about their occupations and living conditions prior to entering the shelter – and are never quite certain about the factors that motivate their behaviour.

Why Clov continues to serve Hamm, for example, is a question the play never answers definitively. One explanation seems to be that Hamm is the only character who knows the combination to the food cupboard, and that he retains Clov's loyalty by threatening him with starvation. Yet Hamm is blind: Beckett perplexes us with the question of how it is possible for a blind man to operate a combination lock. Moreover, we are told time and again that things are running out, the implication being that all four characters are living in any case on a starvation diet. Why, then, does Clov stay? Where does he get the energy to climb up and down ladders, and to push Hamm around the stage? Why do he and the other characters not show more signs of increasing physical decrepitude?

All these questions and more would be answered by a conventional naturalist in order to create and maintain an illusion of reality. It is, however, part of Beckett's strategy in his chess game against the audience that they be left unanswered. Beckett not only fails to create an illusion of reality through his vagueness about details; he undermines, in Brechtian fashion, whatever illusion the play might fortuitously create, by insisting on *Endgame* as theatre. Thus, in answer to Clov's repeated question, 'What is there to keep me here?', Hamm at one point says, 'The dialogue' (39); elsewhere, he speaks of delivering both 'an aside' and his 'last soliloquy' (49). These insistent disruptions of our suspension of disbelief are not just playful bits of comedy; they are deliberately included to make us abandon our attempts to interpret *Endgame* naturalistically.

The next defence that suggests itself, the expressionistic, is based on the assumption that the set of *Endgame* is a reflection not of the world at large, but of the interior of a skull. The play's allusions again suggest a number of different interpretative possibilities. David Hesla and Ross Chambers, for example, find in Hamm's desire to be at the centre of the skull-like set evidence for a Cartesian interpretation:[24] Hamm, says Hesla, is meant to be 'unextended thinking substance, [and] Clov the Body-Sensory apparatus which is extended and unthinking'.[25]

Similarly, Martin Esslin suggests that *Endgame* may allude as a whole to Evreinov's *Theatre of the Soul*, in which, as in Beckett's play, one of the characters represents the rational half of a personality, and the other the emotional.[26] Colin Duckworth sees in the play's relationship to the story of the Flood the possibility of a Jungian interpretation: Jung, he reminds us, considers Noah's ark to be a 'kind of giant uterus'. Hamm, having attained in his womb-like rotunda something resembling the timeless peace of the embryonic existence, refuses to be reborn, to go out'.[27] Like G.C. Barnard before him, Duckworth regards Hamm and Clov as two halves of a schizophrenic personality.[28]

One important difficulty with expressionistic interpretations of *Endgame* is that of trying to find a psychological theory to fit the play exactly. Another difficulty is that of finding mental equivalents for the various on-stage props: critics are quick to identify the *characters* with various elements of the mind, but neglect to assign expressionistic significance to the biscuits, wheel-chair, rat, flea and flea-powder that also appear in the play. It could be argued, of course, that these items are meant to be memories of an earlier life; but there are other problems as well. For example: if Hamm and Clov are meant to be two of the constituents of a mind, what significance are Hamm's confinement to a wheel-chair and Clov's limp meant to have? Or again: if *Endgame* is not altogether expressionistic, but is instead meant to portray two naturalistic characters, Hamm and Clov, and their shared projection of mind – Nagg and Nell – why is it that Hamm and Clov have this projection in common? Why should it be the case, in other words, that they suffer from exactly the same sort of madness?

Human ingenuity being what it is, answers to each of these questions can probably be found. Beckett, however, pre-empts our critical efforts in one of Hamm's speeches. 'Imagine', says Hamm, 'if a rational being came back to earth, wouldn't he be liable to get ideas into his head if he observed us long enough. (*Voice of rational being.*) "Ah, good, now I see what it is, yes, now I understand what they're at"' (27). Here we are being teased: *Endgame* is clearly too complex to yield either to a straightforward naturalistic or expressionistic interpretation on the one hand, or to some combination of such interpretations on the other. Its range of allusions and interpretative possibilities is simply too vast. In no matter what direction we move as audience, we are in check.

Like *Endgame*, *Ohio Impromptu* is a puzzle – though not a chess puzzle. On stage are two characters, Reader and Listener: in the absence of dialogue we are concerned with the story that the one reads to the other. Though Listener says nothing while the story is being read, he occasionally knocks on the table to signal that certain passages are to be re-read. Since there are no other words spoken, the play invites us to consider the kind of relationship that exists between the on-stage characters on the one hand and the story's characters on the other. That relationship has an important bearing on the relationship Beckett establishes in the play between art and the limits of human knowledge.

The story concerns a nameless character who for some time has been grieving over the death of his lover or mistress (the sex of the departed is not specified). 'In a last attempt to obtain relief', Reader tells us, he has moved 'from where they had been so long together to a single room on the far bank. From its single window he could see the . . . Isle of Swans. . . . Day after day he could be seen slowly pacing the islet. . . . [in] his long black coat no matter what the weather and old world Latin Quarter hat' (285–6).

Neither Reader nor the silent Listener comments on the story as it is being read: the only clues we have to its meaning lie within the story itself. Thus, we may find it significant that the Isle of Swans is an island in Paris that features, at its downstream extremity, 'a much reduced replica of . . . the Statue of Liberty'.[29] This information, when imported from outside the play, may suggest to us that the Isle of Swans represents a 'new world' to its grieving character, a world to which he brings memories of the 'old world' he knew in the company of the person he loved.[30]

'At the tip he would always pause to dwell on the receding stream', Reader continues. 'How in joyous eddies its two arms conflowed and flowed united on' (286). Here, in the absence of comment from either Reader or Listener, we might infer that the sight of the two confluent arms of the Seine recalls happy memories to the nameless character's mind; however, as Reader subsequently makes clear, it does not afford him the relief he seeks.

For the character to move back to where he formerly lived is, however, out of the question, and in his new room, away from once-familiar surroundings, he is extremely unhappy. When Reader goes on to tell how one night a stranger appeared to the story's character and said, 'I have been sent by – and here he named the dear name – to comfort you' (287), it might seem that we are being told a story about the benevolence of God. Yet this is not the only way of accounting for the stranger's arrival: it is equally possible that he is a figment of the character's imagination, created to provide psychological comfort for himself. S.E. Gontarski has argued, accordingly, that '*Ohio Impromptu* finally brings to the fore the elemental creative process . . . suggested in *That Time*, where the protagonist of narrative A would hide as a youth, "making up talk breaking up two or more talking to himself being together that way", or in *Endgame*, where Hamm speaks of "the solitary child who turns himself into children, two, three, so as to be together in the dark".'[31]

One of the most puzzling things about *Ohio Impromptu* is the very crucial relationship between the characters in the story and the two characters on stage. The fact that one of the on-stage characters is reading and the other listening, like the two men in the story; and that Reader and Listener are, as the stage directions tell us, as '*alike in appearance as possible*' (285), where the story's characters '[grow] to be as one' (287), suggests that Reader's story is about the two characters who appear before us in the play. But to accept this too readily is to be a 'gentle skimmer': there is simply not enough evidence for us to be certain that Reader and Listener are to be identified with the story's two characters so neatly.

What Beckett is offering us in *Ohio Impromptu* is a play that resembles the figures used in the psychological experiments early this century to establish the principle of closure.[32] In effect, the play is like a triangle with only two vertices joined together, or a circle whose circumference is flawed by a gap. Just as the people who participated in the experiments felt impelled to fill in the gaps for the sake of forming an intelligible whole, so we do, too; yet in the process we run the risk of simplifying or distorting our experience of what is happening on stage.

The fact that the costumes and set of *Ohio Impromptu* are exclusively black and white calls to mind Rubin's figure-ground experiments. When we read *Ohio Impromptu* or see it performed on stage, the way we interpret the play will vary depending on the details we assign either greater or lesser importance. If the resemblance between the two on-stage characters and the two in the story strikes us especially forcibly, we will conclude that the story is about Reader and Listener. But it is equally possible that the story is quite unrelated to the characters on stage: Listener may well be a writer of fiction and Reader his amanuensis, seen reading back the work the former has just completed. Moreover, if we bring to *Ohio Impromptu* the knowledge that Beckett served for a time as Joyce's amanuensis; that the two men used to walk together on the Isle of Swans during the thirties; and that Joyce used to wear a Latin Quarter hat, we may find an autobiographical dimension to the play.[33]

A further possibility, however, is that Listener is not a writer at all, but simply a man who likes to be read to: he may be a perfectly harmless figure, or he may, like the madman at the end of Waugh's *A Handful of Dust*, be a tyrant who demands that Reader devote his life to entertaining him. But again, there is no compelling reason to assume that there *are* two characters on stage, for the presence of a single hat on the table suggests that one of the characters may be the other's projection of mind.[34]

In *Ohio Impromptu*, on a smaller scale than in *Endgame*, Beckett presents us with a puzzle analagous to what one of his favourite philosophers, Arthur Schopenhauer, refers to as the 'riddle' posed by our infinitely complex world.[35] Such are the limits of human knowledge that neither the puzzle nor the riddle will ever be definitively solved: *Ohio Impromptu* resists our attempts to interpret it definitively, just as the world at large does. Absolute knowledge lies beyond human reach.

IV

While the five plays discussed in this essay are only a small proportion of Beckett's dramatic canon, they serve to illustrate how he put his theories about the limitations of human knowledge into practice in his drama. In *Waiting for Godot, That Time* and *Not I* he presents us with three 'shape of ideas' plays – highly original works that owe something to earlier sources, but go beyond them to demonstrate that traditional certainties about the existence and benevolence of God may be unfounded. In *Endgame* Beckett plays a chess game against the audience to show that both the world and the mind are infinitely complex, while in *Ohio Impromptu* he plays a slightly different game to achieve the same end. That end, of course, is to show that we live our lives in the absolute absence of absolute knowledge, for nothing incontrovertible is ever revealed to the 'coenaesthesia', however 'vigilant' it may be.

Notes

1. For a complete list of the plays of Samuel Beckett (1906–89) see *Contemporary Dramatists*, ed. D.L. Kirkpatrick (London: St James Press, 1988).
2. All quotations from 'Dante . . . Bruno . Vico . . Joyce' are from Samuel Beckett, *Disjecta: Miscellaneous Writings and a Dramatic Fragment*, ed. Ruby Cohn (London: John Calder, 1983); page numbers will be given in the text.
3. Harold Hobson, 'Samuel Beckett: Dramatist of the Year', *International Theatre Annual*, No. 1 (London: John Calder, 1956) p. 153. Earlier in the interview Beckett reveals that, although raised a Protestant, he lost his faith 'after leaving Trinity [College]'.
4. It is well established that the title of *More Pricks Than Kicks* derives from Acts 9.5. I shall argue that the titles of *Not I* and *That Time* derive from the Bible and Wordsworth, respectively.
5. See Samuel Beckett, *Cette fois* (Paris: Minuit, 1978).
6. *That Time*, in Samuel Beckett, *Collected Shorter Plays* (London: Faber & Faber, 1984) p. 228. All quotations from *That Time, Not I* and *Ohio Impromptu* are from this edition; page numbers will be given in the text.
7. William Wordsworth, 'Lines Written a Few Miles above Tintern Abbey', in William Wordsworth and Samuel Taylor Coleridge, *Lyrical Ballads* (1798, 1800; rpt. London: Methuen, 1963) p. 116. All quotations from the poem are from this edition; line numbers will be given in the text.
8. S.E. Gontarski, '"Making Yourself All Up Again": the Composition of Samuel Beckett's *That Time*', *Modern Drama*, 23 (June 1980) 114.
9. James Knowlson and John Pilling, *Frescoes of the Skull: the Later Prose and Drama of Samuel Beckett* (London: John Calder, 1979) p. 210.
10. Quoted in Knowlson and Pilling, p. 206.
11. Galatians 2.20. See also 1 Corinthians 7.10 and 1 Corinthians 15.10.
12. Enoch Brater, 'The "I" in Beckett's *Not I*', *Twentieth Century Literature*, 20 (1974) 189–200. See Bair, pp. 174–93 and *passim* for an account of Beckett's interest in Jung.
13. C.G. Jung, 'The Relations of the Ego and the Unconscious', in *Two Essays on Analytical Psychology*, trans. R.F.C. Hull (London: Routledge & Kegan Paul, 1953) p. 171. Hereafter, page numbers of quotations from this work will be given in the text.
14. C.G. Jung, *The Integration of the Personality*, trans. Stanley Dell (London: Routledge & Kegan Paul, 1940) p. 20.
15. Brater, p. 196.
16. C.G. Jung, 'Commentary on "The Secret of the Golden Flower"' (1929) in *Alchemical Studies*, trans. R.F.C. Hull (London: Routledge

& Kegan Paul, 1953) p. 52.
17. Acts 9.5.
18. See Evelyn Underhill, *Mysticism* (1911; rpt. London: Methuen, 1967) p. 227 and pp. 294–5.
19. 'Three Dialogues', in *Disjecta: Miscellaneous Writings and a Dramatic Fragment*, p. 138.
20. For a discussion of the term 'coenaesthesia' (or 'coenaesthesis') see John Herbert Parsons, *An Introduction to the Theory of Perception* (Cambridge: Cambridge University Press, 1927) pp. 10–11 and 31–41.
21. George W. Hartmann, *Gestalt Psychology* (NewYork: Ronald Press, 1935) pp. 23–4; Robert I. Watson, *The Great Philosophers from Aristotle to Freud* (Philadelphia: J.B. Lippincott, 1968) p. 439.
22. See Solomon E. Asch, 'Gestalt Theory', in *The International Encyclopedia of the Social Sciences*, ed. David Sills (London: Macmillan and the Free Press, 1968) VI, 168.
23. Samuel Beckett, *Endgame* (London: Faber & Faber, 1965) p. 16. All quotations are from this edition; hereafter, page numbers will be given in the text.
24. See Ross Chambers, 'An Approach to *Endgame*', in *Twentieth Century Interpretations of* Endgame, ed. Bell Gale Chevigny (Englewood Cliffs, N.J.: Prentice-Hall, 1969) pp. 72–3.
25. David Hesla, *The Shape of Chaos* (Minneapolis: University of Minnesota Press, 1971) p. 154.
26. Martin Esslin, *The Theatre of the Absurd* (Harmondsworth, Middlesex: Penguin, 1968) pp. 64–5.
27. Colin Duckworth, *Angels of Darkness: Dramatic Impact in Beckett and Ionesco* (London: George Allen & Unwin, 1972) p. 89.
28. See G.C. Barnard, *Samuel Beckett: a New Approach* (London: Dent, 1970) pp. 101–9.
29. Pierre Astier, 'Beckett's *Ohio Impromptu*: a View from the Isle of Swans', *Modern Drama*, 25 (Sept. 1982) 337.
30. Astier, 338, comments, similarly, that the story's character 'remains a hopeless prisoner of his "old world" thoughts, unable ever to open his mind to a "new world" of ideas'.
31. S.E. Gontarski, *The Intent of Undoing in Samuel Beckett's Dramatic Texts* (Bloomington: Indiana U.P., 1985) p. 178.
32. See Hartmann, p. 184.
33. See Richard Ellmann, *James Joyce* (London: Oxford U.P., 1966) pp. 661–2.
34. Bernard Beckerman makes this point in 'Samuel Beckett and the Art of Listening', in *Beckett at 80/ Beckett in Context*, p. 165. Similarly, in 'Beckett's Auditors: *Not I* to *Ohio Impromptu*',in *Beckett at 80/Beckett in Context*, p. 188, Katharine Worth argues that the two characters are different aspects of a single writer.
35. See Arthur Schopenhauer, *The World as Will and Idea*, trans. R.B. Haldane and J. Kemp (London: Kegan Paul, Trench, Trübner & Co., 1909) II, 392.

2
Pinter and the Pinteresque
John Fletcher

1. The 'Vivien Merchant Factor'

Harold Pinter was born in London in 1930, became a professional actor, and wrote his first play in 1957.[1] He married an actress, Vivien Merchant, in 1956; they were divorced in 1980 and she died in 1982. She had performed in many of his works; although he did not write parts specifically for her, 'she has . . . proved to be very good in my plays' (he said in 1971), because she had what he called 'a wonderful instinct for [the] roles'.[2] Since their partnership ended he has not written a good play, indeed no play of any length or substance: his great period extends from 1960, when *The Caretaker* was produced, to 1978, the year when *Betrayal* was put on. *Betrayal*, a play about marital infidelity, contained the first major female role not created for Vivien Merchant, and this happened to coincide with public knowledge that Pinter had left his wife for another person. Future biographers will no doubt either confirm or invalidate the assumption made by audiences at the time that the two events were connected; my present purpose is not to speculate about this, but rather to note that Pinter's greatness as a dramatist rests on the production of the last eighteen years or so he spent under the influence of the wife-muse Vivien Merchant.

That Pinter is the greatest British playwright since Shaw cannot be seriously doubted. Like Shaw's, his surname has been turned into an adjective in his own lifetime: ' . . . his work is so singular that the word "Pinteresque" has entered the language to describe those situations fraught with menacing ambiguity which are the hallmark of his plays'.[3] The play which first brought Pinteresque ambiguity to the public's attention was *The Birthday Party*, but it was a spectacular flop when it was put on in London in May 1958 after a brief provincial try-out in Cambridge where, as a second-year

18

undergraduate, I saw it. I will never forget that matinée performance at the Arts Theatre. The auditorium was virtually empty, but I happened to be sitting next to the novelist Andrew Sinclair, who took it upon himself to explain to me – it was his right, he had done his national service before coming up, whereas I hadn't, so this made him a couple of years my senior – that any apparent ambiguity resolved itself once one realised that Pinter was Jewish. As a Jew – Sinclair pointed out – Pinter was acutely conscious of the reality of persecution, so Stanley is duly persecuted in the play. Sinclair did not explain, to the callow youth that I then was, what the Jew Goldberg was doing as the persecutor of the Gentile Stanley: should it not rather, I wondered innocently, have been the other way round? It was only much later that I realised how characteristic Sinclair's neat 'explanation' of the play was of much Pinter criticism: a flawed solution to a puzzle which existed only in the critic's mind.

For Pinter is at once a more mysterious and a more straightforward person than is commonly realised. In many respects he is 'a very traditional dramatist . . . [whose] plays are conceived for an orthodox proscenium stage; they are conventionally based on speech and dialogue with only a marginal inference of physical action',[4] and the text is fully written out, leaving no scope whatever for improvisation, a theatrical fad which Pinter views with distaste.[5] His settings are concrete, firmly located in time and place (mid-century London for the most part), and the social milieu is precisely defined (British middle or lower-middle class society, exclusively). His mentors are Chekhov, Pirandello and Beckett, all dead masters, avant-garde perhaps in their own day, but established classics of the stage now. Moreover, much of his dialogue is straight out of Noel Coward, who was hardly avant-garde when alive; and that most conservative of institutions, the British stand-up comic, provides him with the inspiration for much of his patter. Ken Dodd, for example:

> I had a marvellous childhood, yes, a marvellous childhood. We never stopped laughing, my brother and sister, my mother and father. We were a very funny, very laughter-conscious sort of family. My father was probably the funniest man that I have ever known. He was a very, very funny man.[6]

The professional comedian's patter, which Pinter steeped himself in when he trod the boards of seaside theatres himself in the 1950s, with its repetitions and reformulations within a severely restricted lexis and range of ideas, is here exemplified by one of its greatest living practitioners, the hugely successful Ken Dodd. But the interesting thing about this quotation from the self-styled King of the Diddymen is that it comes not from a live act but from an interview. As the interviewer Russell Miller points out, the protestation about Dodd's childhood does not ring quite true: 'behind the façade of the ebullient, fast-talking comedian, the "master of mirth", [is] an enigmatic, lonely, vulnerable, almost tragic figure, still living in the ramshackle house where he was born, measuring his success by bundles of money hoarded in the attic. . . . '[7] Almost a Pinter character, in fact.

Moreover, Pinter's mental universe seems largely innocent of Marx and Freud, let alone of Lacan, Derrida, Irigaray or of other currently fashionable *maîtres à penser* of whom he has probably never heard. In this too he is very British: 'I'm not a theorist', he unashamedly confessed as long ago as 1962 to an audience of students,[8] and he has frequently repeated the disclaimer in interviews since.[9] But this anti-theorist is not anti-intellectual: far from it. He discovered Beckett long before the great Irishman became culturally respectable.[10] He adapted Proust to the screen without hope or prospect of seeing the film made (*The Proust Screenplay*, 1978). He read and was moved by the study of Oliver Sacks MD on *encaphalitis lethargica*, a kind of sleeping sickness, and in 1982 wrote *A Kind of Alaska* about it.[11] And if Pinter is a close reader of Noel Coward, he is an equally devoted student of Franz Kafka, so that his well-made plays à la Coward are just as nightmarish as the labyrinthine rat-runs of the unquiet mind explored so obsessively by the God-tormented genius of Prague.

It is this extraordinary amalgam of Coward and Kafka which characterises Pinter's best work. He not only has, like Coward, a finely-tuned ear for what people actually say – a prerequisite in any competent writer for the stage – he also picks up what is not being said, in other words the Kafkaesque dimension of social intercourse. 'So often', he points out, 'below the word spoken, is the thing known and unspoken . . . under what is said, another thing is being said', and he goes on: 'we communicate only too well, in our silence, in what is unsaid, . . . what takes place is a continual evasion, desperate rearguard attempts to keep ourselves to ourselves' (*PI* 13–15). This makes Pinter's plays hyper-realistic, to borrow a term from art criticism, where it is applied to works that copy reality so effectively that they can be confused with it (an example would be the life-size figure of a male cleaner in the Milwaukee Museum of Modern Art). 'We have to react to a Pinter play more as we have to react to real life than as we do with conventional drama', writes Anthony Suter; 'the audience is forced to see a total area of experience and, as in life, to have only exterior signs of behaviour (language in all its forms) as interpretative guide-lines'.[12] This is the source of the famous 'menace' which is universally recognised as Pinter's hallmark: what we hear spoken is bound to sound threatening if we simultaneously intuit a subtext which fails to square with what is explicitly stated. The *locus classicus* of this is the well-known moment in *The Caretaker* when Aston says that he cannot drink Guinness from a thick mug, whereas what really troubles him is the fear that he will be recalled to mental hospital to undergo electroconvulsive therapy once again (*PII* 28).

The 'desperate rearguard attempts to keep ourselves to ourselves' which Pinter concentrates on his drama are not mere verbal skirmishes: they frequently become 'strategic campaigns in the "battle for positions", in the struggle for "dominance and subservience" which . . . is a repeated theme in his plays'.[13] In *The Caretaker* the intruder Davies is outmanoeuvred by Mick and expelled from the relative Eden of the house into the inhospitable winter weather outside; in *Night School* Walter forces his aunt's lodger Sally to go so that he may recover his bedroom (*PII* 87, 238). No wonder Pinter cannot see 'anything very strange' about these plays, which he considers 'very straightforward and simple' (*PII* 10). 'What goes on in my plays is realistic', he adds, even if 'what I'm doing is not realism' (*PII* 11). True enough. All human relationships in Pinter are based on power struggles, be they the individual's struggle to appropriate or hold on to a loved one as in *The Caretaker* (Mick loves his brother Aston; Davies represents a threat to the stability of the relationship), the couple's struggle to exclude rivals/outsiders as in *Old Times* (where the couple could be lesbian – Kate/Anna – just as much as it could be the married pair), or the clan's struggle to close ranks, as in *The Homecoming*. A particularly insistent theme is that of male solidarity against women: in *The Lover* Max says to Sarah of her husband, 'After all, he's a man, like me. We're both men. You're just a bloody woman' (*PII* 183), and in *Betrayal* Robert, who married Emma for conventional reasons, actually dislikes women, whom he sees as a threat to male supremacy, and chooses instead to privilege his relationship with her lover Jerry, whom he dominates:

he makes sure that it is *this* union which will survive what he sees as a wilful female's attempt to spite him by taking his friends as her lovers. The cards are laid on the table when Robert launches on a 'brutally honest' tirade about male intimacy in the squash courts (*PIV* 209–10), a good example of the 'mug of Guinness' kind of transparent metaphor I alluded to earlier.

Language – as in this example – is used to dominate other people. There is little physical violence in Pinter's plays. Instead, characters browbeat others through linguistic fluency. Once again, the *locus classicus* is to be found in *The Caretaker*, where Mick uses the clichés of the glossy magazine home-decorating column to attack Davies at his most vulnerable point, his sensitivity over his vagrant status (*PII* 81).

Likewise, the articulate Lenny outflanks the reticent Teddy in *The Homecoming* and detaches his wife Ruth from him; Anna comes close to taking Kate away from Deeley in *Old Times*; Hirst outguns Spooner in the decisive verbal engagement in the second act of *No Man's Land*; and Robert defeats Emma in the battle of the sexes in *Betrayal* through his linguistic dominance of Jerry. It is in these verbal tussles that Pinter's music-hall humour is used to best effect, from the funny if coarse 'to put the old tin lid on it, you stink from arse-hole to breakfast time', to the groan-provoking rhyme 'I killed a man with my own hands, a six foot ten lascar from Madagascar . . . Alaska? Madagascar!' (*PII* 83, 213).

The sense of menace is reinforced too by the palpable feeling of suspense Pinter's best plays generate through the use of fades and blackouts. The structure of *The Caretaker* is articulated around sudden extinction of the lights, and the same device is used at the end of the first act of *No Man's Land*. This is what Pinter meant when he said that what goes on in his plays is realistic, but what he is doing is not realism (*PII* 11). In looking more closely at the way non-realistic devices like startling blackouts contribute to the heightened realism which is Pinter's hallmark, I shall concentrate on the stage plays of his mature 'Vivien Merchant period', although it needs to be borne in mind that Pinter has written more for radio, television and cinema than for the theatre; nevertheless, his finest as well as his most substantial works (*The Caretaker*, *The Homecoming*, *Old Times* and *Betrayal*) were written for the live medium.

2. Old Times in No Man's Land

In *The Caretaker* (1960), a grim nightmare (complete with gallows humour) of a play, three people, all to a greater or lesser extent sick in mind, feed off each other's psychological inadequacies. Aston is recovering, slowly and painfully, from electroshock treatment. His way of coming to terms with this is to stress that he likes working with his hands. He fantasises about getting the shed up in the garden (after clearing the ground, since it is completely overgrown) so that he can start work on renovating the house. To that end he compulsively accumulates junk, most of it useless, in the room. Pinter says he always starts with a room, and then peoples it with appropriate characters (*PII* 10). Soon Aston adds to his collection a new acquisition: this time it is a human being, a tramp whom he has rescued in a punch-up at the all-night café where Davies is employed. Aston is pathetic and gentle, and it is not long before Davies starts taking advantage of him, especially as he imagines that he has an ally in Aston's vicious brother Mick. But, like most cunning people, Davies is in certain key respects obtuse, and so fails to pick up the signals of complicity between the brothers (such as the famous 'faint smile' which they exchange).[14] When he attempts to play the one off against the other (*PII* 77) he alienates his benefactor, and the play ends on a note of great sadness when the gentle Aston turns his back on Davies and forces him to leave. 'Thank God they got rid of the bastard' was Pinter's revealing comment to the actor Donald Pleasence at rehearsal,[15] and yet the play is so finely balanced that the audience feels sorry for the foul-mouthed racist who every night suffers from troubled dreams.

It is evident from this summary that the story of the play is perfectly plausible: an outsider is invited in, fails to get on with the occupant, and is asked to leave. The décor is realistic too, even down to the gas-stove which worries Davies so much because he thinks it can come on accidentally. The use of lighting (from the unobtrusive fade-down when Aston is confiding in Davies about the hallucinations which resulted in his hospitalisation, to the sudden blackouts used to indicate nightfall in the middle of each act) is a non-naturalistic device which has however become such a common feature of theatrical shorthand – as well as being widely used in film and television – that its artificiality is no longer remarked. Such visual clichés do not undermine the naturalism; at most they reinforce the theatricality. Back to Noel Coward again . . .

So firmly rooted in contemporary reality is Pinter's dramaturgy that a critic has been led to suggest, perfectly seriously, that *The Caretaker* 'could be read as a social, or even a political satire' on the grounds that 'Harold Pinter, due both to his experiences as a member of an unpopular ethnic minority and his desire for integration, was more receptive than most to the ambivalent attitudes that the vast majority of British people were only just beginning to discover in themselves' as the first violent clashes in Nottingham and Notting Hill drew their attention to the issue of race.[16] Without going that far, I am pleased Pinter's relevance is noticed in this way. The 'rootedness' of his best plays becomes, indeed, more evident with the passage of time. A recent revival of *The Homecoming* (1965) highlighted the fact that 'this most cruel of family plays' shows 'a Jewish family closing ranks against a *shicksa* (dismissive term for a female Gentile) being brought into the household by the returning successful son' and drew attention to the vein of Jewish comedy that runs through the play, particularly in Max's eulogy of his dead wife at the beginning of Act II.[17] According to Pinter, the play is straightforwardly 'about love and lack of love',[18] by which I take him to mean the love binding the Jewish family together and the lack of it cementing the relationship between Ruth and Teddy, which helps explain why the family manages to detach her from him so easily. For me, it is a black comedy constructed along traditional lines: the setting is homely and familiar (a living room complete with sideboard and radiogram) and the action is continuous, Act I taking place before lunch and Act II after it, the (unseen) meal in the interval representing temporary reconciliation and calm before the final struggle in which the details of the deal – that the *shicksa* shall operate as a call-girl in their employ – are worked out between Ruth and the family to the exclusion of Teddy, who is sent home to America empty-handed. Although this comedy is a lot coarser and less whimsical than Noel Coward, is it really all that different in essence from *Private Lives*?

Naturalism of a more cinematic kind – and we are reminded that Pinter has written ably for the screen, beginning with his fine script for Joseph Losey's masterpiece *The Servant* (1962) – marks *Old Times* (1971). The three characters are all on stage at the outset, but Anna is not involved in the action for ten minutes or so; she stands, dimly lit, looking out of the window while Kate and Deeley discuss her imminent visit, particularly the dinner they plan to serve her. She then moves centre stage and begins reminiscing about the past as

Kate pours coffee and Deeley offers brandy. This jump-cut erasing the meal itself would seem perfectly natural in the cinema. Once again, too, the setting is naturalistic: a converted farmhouse in the country of the sort which the British professional classes began to move into in increasing numbers in the late 1960s. If Harold Pinter is not a reader of the glossy magazine *Homes and Gardens* he has an uncanny nose for the trendy and the modish in home decoration, as can be seen from Mick's DIY fantasies in *The Caretaker* (*PII* 69), and Deeley's converted farmhouse sounds a tellingly authentic note in this play, especially as there is one-upmanship between him and Anna over her obviously much more luxurious villa above Taormina (*PIV* 36; where her remarks could have come straight out of the pages of *Vogue*).

Film construction, particularly the use of short scenes (like 'takes'), is brilliantly used in *Betrayal* (1978), the other 'triangle' play, although this time the suggestion of a lesbian past between two women is replaced by more conventional adultery between a wife and her husband's best friend. What redeems the play from banality is the 'reverse' construction: we start with the lovers meeting in one of their old pub haunts in order finally to bury their liaison ('It's all all over', says Emma, *PIV* 176), and then we move progressively, through all stages of the affair, *backwards* in time to the lovers' first embrace with the 'husband . . . at the other side of th[e] door' (*PIV* 266) nearly ten years earlier. The device is brilliantly effective in rendering both the misery and the ecstasy of illicit love, set against a backdrop of the London of publishers and literary agents sketched in convincingly and with great economy of means. As so often in Pinter, this is a play about loneliness, about love, and about male friendship which goes deeper than love. Of the Sam Spiegel movie version, which he wrote and David Jones directed, with Jeremy Irons brilliantly incarnating the lover, and Patricia Hodge an Emma who bore a disturbing physical resemblance to (the by then dead) Vivien Merchant, Pinter suggested that the theme was 'various different kinds of betrayal', that it was a story in which all three characters betray one another in separate ways.[19]

Since *Betrayal*, as I said at the outset, Pinter has not written anything nearly as good. About his embarrassing attempts at political drama – *One For the Road* (1984), about torture in Turkish prisons, and *Mountain Language* (1988), a playlet about a people (the Kurds) forbidden to use their mother tongue – the less said the better. Noting, as I have done, that 'something essential went from his work in the 1980s', Benedict Nightingale put the problem of Pinter's latest plays in these terms: 'Subtext has become text. Fear, suspicion and anger are out in the open. Troubling strangers and sinister intruders have turned into sadistic policemen and nasty prison guards. Subtle, amorphous dangers have become obvious, political ones', with the result that the 'comedies of menace' and the 'dramas of paranoia' – the post-1960 masterpieces, in other words – 'have given way to propaganda for Amnesty International: worthy, no doubt, but far less original'. Nevertheless, Nightingale praised Pinter for having in the past 'found such striking ways of dramatising some of the deepest human dreads and desires'.[20] As Hirst says in *No Man's Land*, 'I'll drink to that' (*PIV* 153).

3. The Landscape of Silence

In a tone of mild exasperation, the critic Nigel Andrew recently asked of the characters in a radio adaptation of *Betrayal*: 'why, come to that, can they never finish a sentence, or answer a question, or say what they mean?'[21] This was a surprising question to ask in 1990. A competent undergraduate, set a practical criticism exercise consisting of almost any dozen pages chosen at random, could have told him that Pinter's characters do finish sentences, answer questions, and even say what they mean, provided that the sentences are devoid of emotive charge, the questions uninquisitive, and the avowals of no personal significance. As soon as sentences look like getting them into deep water, they abandon them; and once they are asked a question which they prefer not to answer, they pretend not to have heard it and reply instead to a different one; and when saying what they mean would be to say what they *really* mean, they take refuge in irrelevance and evasion. (One is entitled to wonder what circles Nigel Andrew moves in: has he never had to deal with a salesman who cannot be pinned down to a delivery date, or a mechanic who is incapable of answering a straight question about a fault in the clutch?). As Almansi and Henderson put it, 'one has to reach into the subtext of the unspoken' with Pinter in the same way as one does with Chekhov, 'for rarely is there the comfort of a stated unequivocal fact' (though they imply, and I agree, that no intelligent spectator has difficulty 'reading' the subtext, completing the unfinished sentences, answering the evaded questions, or divining the concealed meaning).[22]

Such cunning on the part of the characters notwithstanding, there 'invariably' does come a moment when a player says something 'irrevocable', something which 'he in fact means', and this can then 'never be taken back' (*PI* 15). Examples of this 'snatched truth among lies'[23] would be Davies blurting out that he thinks Aston is off his head (*PII* 76), Teddy admitting it was he who stole Lenny's cheese roll, thus bringing the unspoken struggle with his brother out in the open (*PIII* 71), or Emma breaking it to Robert that she and Jerry are lovers (*PIV* 222). Often a character tests out the reception his/her idea will receive and then repeats the word to hold on to the common ground when it is agreed with; and Pinter is always careful to listen to the particular 'voice' of a character, so that he does not put words into his or her mouth which the character would be unlikely to say. It is incorrect of some critics to suggest that all Pinter's people use the same kind of 'Pinterspeak'. Davies the tramp speaks ungrammatically, for instance, while Teddy the philosophy professor does not; Teddy's father-in-law Max, a retired butcher, has a working-class voice, whereas Anna in *Old Times* talks exactly like the ex-secretary-who-has-married-well that she is. Similarly, Pinter's famous silences are never incomprehensible, arbitrary pauses but rather moments when words can no longer disguise the real thought or emotion being experienced. They are, not infrequently, moments of real reckoning. One of the most dramatic silences is found right at the end of *The Caretaker* when Aston refuses to allow Davies to stay. Such a powerful rejection could not have been achieved through words.[24]

No critic fails to note that Pinter's language is at once 'banal and bizarre', 'pitched somewhere between the comic and the creepy',[25] and the science of linguistics has ways of describing what he does. 'Illocution' is the technical term used to refer to what is communicated unsaid, that is, the extra meaning conveyed over and above the overt linguistic message (example: 'It's very hot in here, isn't it?' is a way of asking 'Would you mind if we opened the window?'); and 'implication' is the implied meaning over and above the purely linguistic message (example: 'You weren't born in a barn' is a way of saying 'Shut the door').[26] Illocution and implication explain many of Pinter's finest touches, such as the astonishing casualness of Ruth's farewell to her husband, 'Don't become a stranger' (*PIII* 96), where the context turns a polite cliché into a shocking cruelty.

I began by stressing that Pinter is a realistic, even a naturalistic writer. In the field of language, where at first he seems so strange, he is careful to stick to the concrete and familiar. Here is a Blackburn tramp, Frank Bennett, talking to Jeremy Seabrook:

> From fourteen to seventeen I was buried twice in Clifton pit. I was buried there twice. So I joined the Army for twelve years, and I went all over the world, every country you can mention. I fought for my country and I was a prisoner of war in Italy, in Syria, and I met the best people in the world when I was taken prisoner. I escaped out of that camp, and I come back, and my friend shot himself, a fellow called Tommy Aspic, he shot himself, definitely . . . [M]y buddy Tommy, one of the best pals in the world, and I'm a real professional – machine-guns, anything. Them Germans wanted to kill us, but I killed them, and that was it. And I'll kill any German that comes on this foreign country, England, because I've fought for it, and I'll die for it again, and I'll say this, and I'll say it again, on my life: . . . I'm an Englishman, I'm Frankie Bennett, definite, a real tough sergeant . . . I'm the toughest, roughest boy in the world.[27]

The repetitions are characteristic of Davies' speech, as are the disingenuous evasions (the 'friend' mentioned was probably a homosexual lover), the xenophobia, and the pathetic boastfulness (like Davies, Bennett deludes himself that he is 'tough'). Obviously Pinter shapes and edits what his characters say, whereas Seabrook the sociologist does not; but otherwise Pinter is faithful to the words contemporary British people actually speak.

4. To Conclude

After a truly great playwright drama is never quite the same again. 'Pinter's outrage has become the norm of respectability',[28] and what made *The Birthday Party* a commercial flop in 1958 has become virtually *de rigueur* in British theatre today.[29] The 'Pinteresque' (words of great banality concealing menace) has become as much part of our cultural consciousness as the 'Kafkaesque' (often used to describe the citizen's impotence in the face of bureaucracy), the 'Proustian' (buried memories resurrected by a chance sight or smell) or the 'Beckettian' (mind and body out of sync). Only the literary genius has this power to so alter our perception of the world, and Pinter is probably a genius.

I say 'probably', not out of Pinteresque foot-shuffling, but because he is very much alive and so the jury is still out. There are a number of indications that he may be. For one thing, he is not an academic, even less a product of university creative writing courses, but someone whose degrees are all honorary. For another, he appears a case of the right hand not knowing what the left is doing: his finest writing seems to erupt from a zone of which the author knows little and which he cannot explain, but which helps account for the occasional vulgar excess of language in the later works which is not always justified by the context.[30] It may also be that Pinter (like Mozart, who was a genius), is in some ways a shallow, even immature person, not 'deep' at all.[31] This would explain the occasional disconcerting lapses of taste and the inconsistency of achievement (even Mozart has been known to lock on to autopilot, after all).[32]

So I come back to the 'Vivien Merchant factor'. Pinter does appear to have depended on her, not only for definitive performances in the role of Ruth and of Anna, of Sarah and of Sally, but as the muse. Since the muse deserted him around the mid-seventies he seems to have run out of inspiration, a latter-day Rimbaud whose Abyssinia is Holland Park, W8. The Vivien Merchant years, by contrast, saw the production of work, which drew on a hallucinatory vision expressed in unique language and which exploited a rich vein of popular culture.[33] That seam appears now to have been worked out, but fortunately the masterpieces remain: *The Caretaker, The Homecoming, Old Times* and *Betrayal*.

Notes

1. For a complete list to 1988 of the plays of Harold Pinter (b. 1930), see *Contemporary Dramatists*, ed. D.L. Kirkpatrick (London: St James Press, 1988). Since *Mountain Language* (1988), Pinter has published *The Heat of the Day* (1989; adapted from the novel by Elizabeth Bowen), *The Comfort of Strangers and Other Screenplays* (1990), and *Party Time* (1991).
2. 'Pinter's Pains', *The Listener*, 5 August 1971, p. 176.
3. 'Radical Departures', *The Listener*, 27 October 1988, p. 4.
4. Guido Almansi and Simon Henderson, *Harold Pinter* (London/ New York: Methuen, 1983) pp. 14–15.
5. See Almansi and Henderson, p. 102, n. 4.
6. 'What's So Funny?', *Sunday Times Magazine*, 28 April 1991, pp. 33–4.
7. Ibid., p. 33.

8.   Harold Pinter, *Plays: One* (London: Eyre Methuen, 1976; New York: Grove Press, 1977) p. 9. All quotations from the plays are taken from the four volumes, *Plays: One, Plays: Two, Plays: Three* and *Plays: Four.* Page numbers will be given in the text, preceded by *PI, PII, PIII* or *PIV.*

9.   For a list of interviews, see Stephen Grecco, 'Harold Pinter', in *British Dramatists Since World War II*, ed. Stanley Weintraub (Detroit: Gale, 1982), Part 2, p. 413 (*Dictionary of Literary Biography*, Vol. 13).

10. See Harold Pinter, 'Beckett', in *Beckett at 60: a Festschrift* (London: Calder & Boyars, 1967) p. 86.

11. *The Proust Screenplay* (New York: Grove Press, 1978; London: Eyre Methuen/Chatto & Windus, 1978); *A Kind of Alaska* (London: Methuen, 1982).

12. Anthony Suter, 'A Psycho-Aesthetic Approach to the Plays of Pinter', *Etudes anglaises*, 32, 4 (1979) 417.

13. Almansi and Henderson, p. 26.

14. Almansi and Henderson, p. 57; see *PII* 84.

15. Quoted on BBC Radio 3, 7 October 1990. See also Peter Lewis, 'Tramp's Progress', *Sunday Times*, 16 June 1991, section 5, pp. 1–2.

16. Graham Woodroffe, 'Taking Care of the "Coloureds": the Political Metaphor of Harold Pinter's *The Caretaker*', *Theatre Journal*, 40, 4 (December 1988) 508.

17. Press comment from the *Sunday Times*, 13 January 1991, section 7, p. 7, and *The Times*, 31 December 1990, p. 17.

18. Almansi and Henderson, p. 58.

19. Virgin Films Press Release, 1983.

20. Benedict Nightingale, 'Caretaker of Subtle Paranoia', *The Times*, 17 November 1990, p. 21. Nightingale shares my view that Pinter's golden period was 1958 to 1978 (the dates are his).

21. Nigel Andrew, 'No Laugh Lines', *The Listener*, 18 October 1990, p. 47.

22. Almansi and Henderson, pp. 28–9.

23. Almansi and Henderson, p. 29.

24. I have used here some formulations by two students in my seminar on modern drama at the University of East Anglia, Elisabeth Mears and Selina Ayers; my thanks to them both. See too Almansi and Henderson, p. 12: 'pauses and silences . . . become the natural repositories of meaning'.

25. Peter Kemp, 'Pinter's Longest Pause', *Sunday Times*, 30 September 1990, section 8, p. 4.

26. I am grateful to Roger Greaves of the British Institute in Paris for drawing my attention to these terms.

27. *The Listener*, 13 August 1970, p. 207.

28. Almansi and Henderson, p. 72.

29. Two recent BBC commissions confirm this. In 'A Kind of Arden', Martin Crimp (Radio 3, 7 January 1989) used several Pinteresque techniques in the dialogue, such as cliché and evasion. In 'Joseph Dintenfass' David Mamet (Radio 3, 7 October 1989) showed Pinter's influence in seemingly aimless dialogue, unfinished sentences,

silences and hesitations, all pregnant with unexpressed meaning, and in having no climax or real conclusion. It is only fair to say, though, that both plays were sub-Pinter rather than emulations of the master: like T.S. Eliot in verse, Pinter is more frequently pastiched than equalled.

30. Note Pinter's unconvincing defence, during an interview with Anna Ford (*The Listener*, 27 October 1988, p. 4), of the young female character's obscene question near the end of *Mountain Language*.

31. There is some evidence for this in the way the separation scandal in the mid-seventies was handled.

32. Margaret Walters, a sound reliable commentator, described Pinter's script for the film *The Handmaid's Tale* as 'often perfunctory' (*The Listener*, 1 November 1990, p. 42).

33. Noel Coward is pastiched in *No Man's Land* (*PIV* 130ff.), and snatches of songs by Jerome Kern, Gershwin and Rogers and Hart are sung by Deeley and Anna in *Old Times*.

3

Revitalised Ritual and Theatrical Flair: the Plays of Peter Shaffer

William Hutchings

Among post-1960 British dramatists, Peter Shaffer is in many ways a theatrical contrarian, a playwright who has consistently gone against the current, achieving tremendous popular success and considerable critical acclaim with plays whose subjects, strategies, and style are often quite the opposite of prevailing theatrical trends.[1] While such playwrights as Samuel Beckett, Harold Pinter, and David Storey explored the dramatic eloquence of the unspoken and understated (and perfected its theatrical potential), Shaffer created characters who speak with rhetorical flourish, articulating their concerns through frequently poetic images in soliloquies that are as emotionally intense and dramatically effective as any on the modern stage. Yet, in an age when theatrical discourse has often been dominated by angry outbursts of class-based frustration with the here-and-now, by anti-capitalist agitprop, and by various milder forms of social protest, Shaffer's plays avoid such topical sociopolitical commentary. They have, in fact, often depicted the not-here and not-now, with subjects that are as diverse and *seemingly* as remote from contemporary issues as Pizarro's conquest of the Incas and Antonio Salieri's rivalry with Mozart. Even when his plays are set in modern English society, they are often fundamentally concerned with history, juxtaposing now-lost values of an intensely-lived (if idealised) past against the mundane exigencies of modern life. Consistently, his major characters resist – or at least rail against – the ordinary, the 'average', the 'normal', the 'mere'. His plays are remarkable for their carefully balanced dialectical (and dialogic) structure, their revitalisation of on-stage ritual, and their uniquely theatrical flair.

Among these characteristics, it is primarily the dialogical structure that is most noteworthy about his first play, *Five Finger Exercise* (1958), an otherwise Rattiganesque family drama that Shaffer has himself characterised as having been written 'in order to be pitied in public'.[2] However, its particular strengths become readily apparent when it is contrasted with John Osborne's *Look Back in Anger* (1956) – another first play about which Shaffer's observation is especially *à propos*, despite the manifest differences in the social class of their respective central characters. Although each is a five-character play rife with generational conflict and social alienation, the working-class household of Osborne's characters is far removed (by both geography and socioeconomics) from the weekend cottage in Suffolk that is Shaffer's setting. Each protagonist is a disaffected young man whose values collide with those of his (or, in Osborne's play, his wife's) parents, who are stolid and conventionally respectable – though personally scorned – embodiments of the social *status quo*. Osborne's play is 'monological' in Mikhail Bakhtin's sense of the term: its characters are all subordinated to (and function primarily as targets for) the single point of view expressed in the harangues of its central 'angry young man', Jimmy Porter.[3] Shaffer's play, however, tends to be more 'polyphonic' or truly 'dialogical', presenting multiple points of view sympathetically and insightfully, allowing four of the five characters relatively lengthy speeches in which they rather eloquently set forth their particular perspectives on events transpiring in the plot. Although the elder Harringtons' shortcomings are unmistakable (the father's philistinism, the mother's protectiveness and overbearing coquettishness), they are not mere sounding-boards for the Sensitive Youth's amply voiced frustrations and rage; the parents prove themselves quite capable of articulating such emotions of their own. That such rival points of view are so equally and sympathetically articulated in an author's first work is particularly unusual, and the dialectical pattern that is thus formed recurs throughout Shaffer's later works.

Shaffer's next works, the one-act plays *The Private Ear* and *The Public Eye*, were produced together in London in 1962; they too are dramas of contemporary domestic life with well-made plots and polished dialogue. *The Private Ear* concerns two contrasting male friends in their early-to-mid-twenties, Bob and Ted (an introvert and extrovert, respectively), as the latter seeks the former's advice on getting a date with a co-worker, Doreen. Although the plot and character types are formulaic, the play contains a relatively daring innovation in theatrical form: a six-minute wordless sequence during which, as the love duet from *Madame Butterfly* is played on a gramophone, the romantic tensions between Bob and Doreen are resolved. The scene is alternately tender and clumsy, poignant and comic; meticulously detailed in Shaffer's stage directions, it anticipates the use of mime and other aspects of 'total theatre' that he would develop in subsequent plays. *The Public Eye*, though deftly plotted, is a less significant play; as in Pinter's *A Slight Ache* (1961), a husband and an 'outsider' exchange roles, though here the latter is a detective whom the former has hired to follow his wife.

With *The Royal Hunt of the Sun* (1964), however, Shaffer abandoned the contemporary settings and domestic realism of his earlier plays, creating instead a work that is epic in scope, highly stylised in production, opulent in its spectacle and ambitious in its themes. 'My hope', Shaffer wrote in a prefatory note,

> was always to realise on stage a kind of 'total' theater, involving not only words but rites, mimes, masks, and magics. . . . [The play] is a director's piece, a pantomimist's piece, a musician's piece, a designer's piece, and of course an actor's piece, almost as much as it is an author's. (244)

He particularly acknowledged John Napier's set design for the National Theatre production: a bare stage with an upper acting/observatory area, dominated by a twelve-foot aluminium ring with twelve petals hinged around the circumference, each with a gold overlay. When opened, these formed the rays of a golden sun, a symbol sacred to the Incas; when closed, they comprised a giant medallion bearing the emblem of the conquistadors, a circle 'quartered by four black crucifixes, sharpened to resemble swords' (247). The play flexibly utilises the bare stage space(s) to represent locales from Spain and Panama to the town of Cajamarca in the mountains of the Incan Empire's Upper Province (now southern Ecuador and northwestern Peru). Marc Wilkinson's musical score (which Shaffer considers 'an integral part of any production') includes not only traditionally religious plainchant and organ music but also exotic bird calls, 'freezing sounds' that accompany the soldiers' ascent of the Andes, and a 'Chant of Resurrection, to be whined and whispered, howled and hooted' during the climax of the second act (244).

Like Chinua Achebe's novel *Things Fall Apart* (1958), *The Royal Hunt of the Sun* depicts the fatal consequences that result from the historic collision of European and non-European civilisations. Set between June 1529 and August 1533, it portrays the encounter between Spanish explorer Francisco Pizarro and Atahuallpa, the Sovereign Inca of Peru; theirs is, as Shaffer remarked, 'the confrontation of two totally different ways of life: the Catholic individualism of the invaders and the complete communist society of the Incas.'⁴ Though their cultures are diametrically opposite in many ways, their spokesmen are fundamentally alike, making them carefully balanced adversaries; as Shaffer notes, 'they are both bastards, both usurpers, both unscrupulous men of action, both illiterate'.⁵ Nevertheless, each is a surprisingly eloquent exponent of his culture's central ideologies, both secular and sacred – the representative of his state as well as the emissary of his religion. Pizarro's mandate includes a Church-sanctioned mission to Christianise the natives while their culture is violently subjugated and plundered; Atahuallpa is not only the head of state but the earthly incarnation of his culture's sun-god, whose bodily resurrection is expected (though unachieved) as the play ends. Their epoch-making, mutually destructive *agon* is observed and abetted by Pizarro's young page Martin who, as an old man, provides the play's retrospective frame narrative and functions as the chorus to the unfolding tragedy. Directly addressing the audience, he recounts his story of 'ruin and gold', of 'how one hundred and sixty-seven men conquered an empire of twenty-four million' (247).

Although the savage nature of imperialism and cultural hegemony is evident throughout *The Royal Hunt of the Sun*, they culminate in Atahuallpa's degrading forced conversion to Christianity immediately before his execution, a final act of carnage in the name of Christ. However, all three major characters are preoccupied by the need for and nature of worship as well as the consequences of its absence – recurrent themes throughout Shaffer's later works. Thus, as he explained,

the theme which lies behind their relationship is the search for God – the search for a definition of the idea of God. . . . In fact, the play is an attempt to define the concept of God.⁶

Pizarro soon becomes disillusioned as a result of the ferocity and bigotry of the expedition's Dominican Chaplain, who not only sanctions 'tak[ing] from [the natives] what they don't value [i.e., gold] and giv[ing] them instead the priceless mercy of heaven', but also willingly absolves the soldiers of 'all crimes [they] ever committed' (250) or may commit in accomplishing their goals. Atahuallpa's forced conversion to Christianity is juxtaposed against Pizarro's voluntary acceptance of Atahuallpa's religion, making confession 'in the Inca manner' although 'none heard what he said except the King, who could not understand it' (308). The audience does, however, hear Pizarro's reflections on the possibilities inherent in the religion that Atahuallpa incarnates as Son of the Sun, God of the Four Quarters:

What if it's possible, here in a land beyond all maps and scholars, guarded by mountains up to the sky, that there were true gods on earth, creators of true peace? . . . It's the only way to give life meaning! To blast out of Time forever, *us*, in our own persons! This is the law: die in despair or be a god yourself! (306)

For Martin, the consequences of the loss of worship are more dire. In his retrospective monologue that begins the play, he characterises himself as having been, at the outset of the expedition, a callow teenager who would 'have died for him [Pizarro] *or for any worship*' (247; emphasis mine); disillusioned by the immorality, treachery, ruthlessness, and excesses of the expedition as the play proceeds, he later acknowledges that it was to be during this expedition that '[I] dropped my first tears as a man. My first and last. That was my first and last worship too. Devotion never came again' (297). Like the modern-day audience whom he addresses in the theatre, old Martin is an inhabitant of what Mircea Eliade has termed a 'desacralised' world – one from which the archaic 'sense of the sacred', here embodied in the Incan worship of the incarnate Sun, has been irretrievably lost.[7]

In contrast to the Christian rituals in the play, which tend to be drab, stationary, and primarily verbal (e.g., the blessing of the conquistadors' expedition and the consecration of their weaponry), the Incan rituals of church and state are literally spectacular – colourful, motion-filled processionals and ceremonies conducted by masked figures adorned in ornate gold and attired with parrot-bright feathers. The first act contains two such processionals (255, 276) before concluding with 'The Mime of the Great Massacre' (277), while the second act includes two 'Gold Processions' during which a large room is filled with gold artefacts intended to ransom Atahuallpa from captivity. Those events culminate in an event designated 'The Rape of the Sun' (291), during which even the Incan emblem that dominates the stage is pillaged by Pizarro's men, and the play's climax – the execution of Atahuallpa on a stake (in various ways a counterpart of the crucifixion of Christ) – is itself a ritual that leads to an expected resurrection that does not come. Not since the elaborate masques designed by Indigo Jones in the early seventeenth century had a new English play so extensively relied on spectacle, ritual, and symbolic ceremonies (both sacred and secular).[8]

Black Comedy (1965) is a deftly plotted one-act contemporary farce which, though quite unritualistic and certainly unspectacular in comparison to its predecessor, relies on a simple but ingenious and purely theatrical premise that was adapted from conventions of Chinese drama: it reverses the perception of light and darkness, so that when the characters are 'able to see' the stage is in fact in total darkness, but when they are 'unable' to see (during a power failure) the stage is fully lit. When it opened in New York in 1967, it was paired with *White Liars*, a one-act drama for three characters, a sham fortune-teller and two male friends; the plot, which involves multiple deceptions, is cleverly constructed and includes a more direct disclosure of homosexuality than that in *Five Finger Exercise*, but it remains a relatively minor work.

The Battle of Shrivings (1970, unpublished; rewritten as *Shrivings* and published in 1974, though the later version remains unproduced) was a critical failure that closed after two months in London and was never staged in the United States. As Shaffer conceded in 1982, the play was marred by the 'danger in [his] work of theme dictating event', and by his 'strong impulse to compose rhetorical dialectic [that] was beginning to freeze [his] characters into theoretical attitudes' (xiv). Even in its revised form, it is Shaffer's most self-consciously erudite and conspicuously allusive play, with historical references ranging from ancient Nineveh to modern Nuremburg. Comprised of five scenes in three acts, it is (like *Five Finger Exercise*) a 'well-made' domestic drama that is set in a country house; the plot, which involves a pacifist who is goaded into an act of violence, was inspired in part by student protests of the 1960s and in part by Mahatma Gandhi's renunciation of sex (the impulse for which he considered a form of aggression and therefore incompatible with his doctrine of nonviolence). As in George

Bernard Shaw's 'metabiological Pentateuch', *Back to Methuselah*,
ideas about evolution that ostensibly 'transcend' Darwin's theories
provide a prominent theme; Shaffer's central character proclaims
that '*You* are the link between the animals and what must appear
if we are not to be sucked back into annihilation', since human
beings possess 'Powers to symbolise, to imagine, . . . to help free
[mankind] from the violent circular force that dominates all other
life' (340). With Shavian ardour, he attacks 'conventional wisdom'
and supposedly shared values, namely

> Mangerism, or worship of family; Flaggism, or worship of Tribe;
> Thingism, or worship of Money. In our theatres and on our
> screens, you are taught to find the act of killing men exciting,
> and the act of creating them obscene. You can go to church, and
> respect the stopped mind. You can go to war memorials, and
> respect the stopped body. What more do you want? (340)

Such eloquence notwithstanding, *Shrivings* demonstrates primarily
that Shavian dramaturgy – whether 'metabiological' or not – is not
Shaffer's theatrical forte.[9] The characters' often abstract, allusive
talk is virtually unrelieved by any of the theatricality that com-
plements the dialogue in his better-known plays, and the sole
semblances of meaningful ritual in the play are mundane and
certainly unspectacular: (1) a bit of psychological gamesmanship
at the climax of which an apple is smashed on stage and (2) a
husband's prayers at a family shrine containing the ashes of his
dead wife.

   With *Equus* (1973), Shaffer returned to the theatrical paradigm
of *The Royal Hunt of the Sun*: a two-act structure within which
consecutive (numbered) scenes are performed without pause or
interruption; a dialectical opposition of incompatible world-views
that ends with the joyless destruction of one of them; a retrospective
chronology, facilitated by soliloquies and dramatic monologues;
a stylised and non-representational set; the eloquent presentation
of multiple characters' conflicting points of view; and re-enacted
onstage rituals which bring to the fore issues about the nature
(and necessity) of worship and the desacralisation of modern life.
Unlike *The Royal Hunt of the Sun*, however, *Equus* was based on a
contemporary incident in which a 'highly disturbed young man'
had blinded six horses in a stable – an act that 'had deeply shocked
a local bench of magistrates' but had 'lacked, finally, any coherent

explanation', as Shaffer has noted. Never learning any details of the actual incident, he became increasingly concerned 'with a different kind of exploration' as he sought 'to interpret it in some entirely personal way', creating 'a mental world in which the deed could be made comprehensible' (398). Accordingly, *Equus* is a *'why*-done it' rather than a 'who-done-it'.

Although its 'investigator' is a psychiatrist rather than a detective and the setting is a psychiatric hospital, the play carefully and cleverly *subverts* the conventional hierarchies (binary oppositions) that such a locale connotes. In order to enable his two central characters (the teenager Alan Strang and the psychiatrist Martin Dysart) to function as worthy dramatic adversaries and credible exponents of alternate but mutually incompatible world-views, Shaffer deconstructs – and induces the audience to suspend – conventional attitudes that 'privilege' the psychiatrist over the patient, the 'adult' over the adolescent, 'sanity' over 'insanity', and the 'normal' over the 'abnormal'. These subversions are accomplished in part through an avoidance of literalism throughout the play – a strategy embodied in the stylised horses that are the best-known symbols of the play. As designed by John Napier (perhaps inspired by the 'man-horse' of Jean Cocteau's 1959 film *Le Testament d'Orphée*), the horses are represented by actors who ceremonially don skeletal metal horse- masks in full view of the audience; the human faces remain visible behind the mask, however, and the actors – 'wear[ing] tracksuits of chestnut velvet' – are to avoid any semblance of 'the cosy familiarity of a domestic animal' (400). Through this *uniquely theatrical* effect, the audience can simultaneously accept the 'horse' thus portrayed as a literal animal (the 'normal' view) *and* see the physical form of the man-god that Alan so ardently believes is there. Similarly, the play's minimalist set – a railed 'square of wood set on a circle of wood' with rows of seats at its perimeter where all of the actors and some audience members are seated – 'resembles . . . a boxing ring' (399). As such, it is designed to avoid any suggestion of a literal hospital ward, wherein the superior knowledge and refined skills of the doctors ('heavyweights', culturally sanctioned and empowered) would give an unquestionable technical superiority over their patients ('lightweights', culturally unsanctioned and unempowered) in an obviously unfair fight. Throughout *Equus*, the main characters – like equally weighted competitors – struggle for (ideological) dominance, and Shaffer avoids such terms as 'sanity' and 'insanity', using the latter only once during the play (455). Instead, Alan's actions and motives are repeatedly described in non-technical terms: the fact that he is 'in pain' has led him to commit a 'shocking' act by which even less experienced psychiatrists than Dysart will be 'disgusted' and 'revolted' (403). Significantly, Alan's 'condition' is never precisely diagnosed; the phrase 'advanced neurotic', used once, occurs in a context which may or may not include him (436).

Strategically, the first act establishes a surprising but crucial *parity* between doctor and patient. Thus, in scene five, Dysart vividly describes his nightmare of presiding at a ritual sacrifice of children (407); in scene six the nurse discloses that Alan wakes up screaming as a result of equally vivid nightmares (408–9), and he is seen doing so in scene eight (416). In scene nine, despite the obvious disparity in their formal education and other experience, each of the central characters functions as the other's psychiatrist; as they take turns asking and answering each other's questions, Alan probes Dysart's passionless marriage as cunningly and incisively as Dysart examines the motives behind Alan's crime. Each is empowered (and equalised) by his knowledge of the other's 'area of maximum vulnerability', as Dysart later terms it (436); furthermore, each such 'area' is eventually disclosed to be the product of a sexual dysfunction (Alan with Jill Mason in the stable, Dysart with his wife Margaret). Because the characters are so carefully balanced, it is a mistake to regard either as 'the' clear protagonist of the play. Alan is (or can certainly be played as) a rebellious and clever anti-hero who has defied societal norms, notwithstanding the obvious pain that he, like a typical romantic 'outcast', endures for having defied his gods; Dysart, though compassionate, is stolid and dyspeptic, passionate only about his passionlessness. Each audience member must decide which character is the play's protagonist – and whether either's plight is a tragedy by any definition of the term.

Divided into two acts containing a total of thirty-five scenes, *Equus* consists of three distinct sequences of discovery, each of which develops a different aspect of Alan's complex attitude toward horses and concludes with the re-enactment of a private ritual epitomising the relationship that the sequence has made clear. Following Dysart's prologue and exposition describing Alan's crime and his behaviour in the courtroom, the first sequence (scenes three to fourteen) establishes childhood influences and experiences that contribute to his abject adoration of horses. Images of noble and mighty horses from religion, myth, fiction, and history predominate in this section, which culminates in a secret act of devotion in which Alan furtively bridles, binds, and flogs himself after repeating the genealogy that he has devised for the god Equus, a Christ-like 'suffering servant'. Whereas the first sequence concludes with a ritual of self-willed bondage and worshipful obeisance, the second sequence (scenes fifteen to twenty-one) ends in a triumphant union of the worshipper and his god. During the exultant, clandestine ride across night-darkened fields, horse and rider are unencumbered by the restraints that are imposed on them by 'normal' propriety and social conventions of the daylight world (the horse's bridle, bit, harness, and saddle, the boy's clothing). Together, they return to the wholly 'natural' state that allies man and beast, conjoining them in a primal, pre-rational, intensely physical way. Accordingly, scenes in this sequence emphasise Alan's contact with 'real' horses during the year preceding the blinding incident.

The third sequence of discovery constitutes the play's second act (scenes 22–35, including Dysart's epilogue), revealing Alan's relationship with Jill and the events that led him to blind the horses in the stable. Attending a 'skinflick' with Jill at her suggestion, the boy is found there by his father, who for the third time interrupts an experience that Dysart recognises as a crucial part of Alan's sexual development (the previous incidents occurred during the ride on Trojan along the beach and during Alan's secret bondage-rite, which his father accidentally observed, making his presence known by a cough). Eager to consummate his relationship with Jill, Alan panics when she leads him to the stables for that purpose; he realises intuitively that such an act would profane his temple of Equus as he 'worships with his body' someone other than his god. Overcome by his divided allegiance and compounded guilt and therefore unable to fulfill his desire, he feels certain that his gods have literally *seen* his attempted profanation of their temple and will, in revenge for his defiance and betrayal of faith, taunt him forever with their knowledge of his failure to perform. Feeling himself a dual failure, incapacitated in his attempted relationship with Jill and unfaithful in his devotion to Equus, Alan strikes back at the horses' eyes with the hoof-pick, blinding them in the final stylised, bloodless, quasi-balletic ritual that provides the play's climax.

Underlying the central thematic conflict of *Equus* is the profound and fundamental change in man's perception of the natural world, which Susanne Langer eloquently summarised in *Philosophy in a New Key*:

> Nature, as man has always known it, he knows no more. Since he has learned to esteem signs above symbols, to suppress his emotional reactions in favour of practical ones and *make use of nature* instead of holding so much of it sacred, he has altered the face, if not the heart, of reality . . . He thinks of human power as the highest power, and of nature as so much 'raw material'! . . . With his new outlook on the world, of course the old symbolism of human values has collapsed.[10]

Like the sun (Langer's example), the horse has therefore become much

> too interesting as an object, a source of transformable energies, to be interpreted as a god, a hero, or a symbol of passion. . . . [W]e take a realistic, not a mystical attitude toward it[,] . . . the 'practical vision' that sees sun and moon and earth, land and sea, growth and destruction, in terms of *natural law and historical fact.*[11]

No longer a mystical symbol as in the Book of Revelation nor a mighty and valiant steed for combat, the horse has been wholly 'domesticated', to be mounted by masterful riders in bowler hats and jodhpurs for equitation – the refinement and artifice of which Alan particularly detests, and the utter antithesis of which he becomes in his naked night-ride across the fields alone.

With virtually the same dialectical structure as its predecessor, *Amadeus* (1979) also juxtaposes the idiosyncratic and passionate life of its teenaged protagonist (Mozart) and the stolid 'normal' world of Antonio Salieri, his older adversary, the more mundane and uninspired composer who is his rival for court favours. The issues here are more complicated than those in *Equus*: artistic inspiration, inexplicable creative genius, and the envious resentments secretly harboured by the workaday but mediocre when in the presence of the truly exceptional. As in Shaffer's earlier plays, fundamental religious issues recur: why, the conventionally stolid and decorous Salieri wonders, has God so favoured the irreverent, sexually unrestrained, foul-mouthed man-child Mozart by giving him the gift of easily achieving the musically sublime, which Salieri's own compositions never approximate? Although Shaffer's depiction of Mozart appalled a number of early reviewers of the play, who deplored the earthiness, coarse behaviour, and crude language of the young composer, the characterisation was carefully based on historical accounts. Like John Osborne's *Luther* (1961), which similarly appalled theatregoers with its torrent of scatological language adapted from its subject's historical documents, *Amadeus* depicts its protagonist in ways that, though accurate, appear far from middle-class expectations of the supposedly familiar historical figure.[12] Substantially rewritten after its successful London run but before opening in New York, the 'American version' of *Amadeus* gives Salieri a far more active role in Mozart's destruction, 'at the wicked center of the action', as Shaffer explains (xvii). The older composer becomes, in effect, Mozart's surrogate father and actively induces him to disclose secrets of Freemasonry in *The Magic Flute*, which allegedly caused him to lose favour with the court. Nevertheless, Shaffer acknowledges that here he 'took certain obvious liberties with this part of the story' (xvii) – as with the visit of

> the Masked Figure who appeared to Mozart to commission a Requiem Mass and whom Mozart in the frenzy of his sick imagination came to regard as the Messenger of Death. In London this figure was actually Salieri's grim manservant Greybig, a religious fanatic dispatched by his murderous master to drive Mozart toward madness. . . . I finally replaced the mask on Salieri's face, but by this time he was not a crudely melodramatic figure – a spooky, improbably Messenger of Death – but a more poetic and dangerous apparition, a Messenger from God stepping out of Mozart's confused dreams. (xvii–xviii)

The similarities to *Equus* here are obvious – the theatricality, the use of masks, the conjunction of psychological and theological crises, the teenaged character whose idiosyncracy and passion are ultimately destroyed by his dialectical adversary and dramatic antagonist. Suffused with Mozart's music, *Amadeus* depicts both the process and the exuberance of artistic creation with virtually unrivalled effectiveness; yet, despite its unorthodox depiction of the composer, the play tends to reconfirm such familiar concepts as the eccentricities of genius and the bitter internecine rivalries of artists – whereas *Equus* more radically subverted conventional notions of madness and 'normalcy'.

Based on an incident from the Book of Daniel in which King David's daughter, Tamar, is raped by her brother, Amnon, *Yonadab*

(1986) was also concerned with 'the theme of divinity – the argument with which Yonadab persuades Amnon that incest, far from being a crime, is the prerogative of the gods',[13] as the ancient Egyptian pharoahs believed. Like *The Royal Hunt of the Sun*, the play featured a fundamentally dialectical structure but three central characters: Yonadab himself, Amnon, and Absalom, the defender of his sister's honour. Nevertheless, the play was not well received when it opened at the National Theatre, has not been produced in the United States, and has not been published.

Shaffer returned to popular success and critical acclaim on both sides of the Atlantic with *Lettice and Lovage* (1987), a contemporary comedy in which, for the first time, the two dialectical adversaries are women and the central issue is history itself. As a tour guide at Fustian House, the least noteworthy country house in England, Lettice Douffet embellishes and (melo)dramatises the past, entertaining the visitors with ever more outrageous tales that have little or no basis in fact. Her boss at the office of the Preservation Trust in London, Lotte Schoen, dismisses Lettice for her outrageous fabrications; she is as strict an advocate of Fact as Thomas Gradgrind in Charles Dickens's *Hard Times*. Nevertheless, the two eventually find themselves united in their preference for the past, and their detestation of the present-day 'mere', 'ordinary', and mundane. For the first time in a Shaffer play, the adversaries become allies against a common enemy and a synthesis of their opposing views is achieved. Less plausibly, they also resolve to strike back against the obtrusive and senselessly destructive present – specifically, against the works of all mutilators of the London skyline, corporate demolishers of historic sites, boorish developers, and shameless profiteers. Lotte discloses that, when young, she and a boyfriend devised the self-styled Eyesore Negation Detachment, which planned to bomb such a site; now, as 'an expert in architecture and an expert in [Elizabethan] weaponry', respectively, the women make a 'formidable combination' against 'the top ten ugliest buildings' in contemporary London.[14] At the end of the play, they point an Elizabethan petard (gunpowder bomb) directly at the audience – and therefore, in the original production, at the National Theatre complex itself, considered by many one of the foremost such architectural offenders, though unnamed in the play.

'I am not aware of the [structural and dialectical] similarities in the plays', Shaffer remarked in a 1986 interview, 'but as the same head is creating them, it is not surprising. After all, the word dialogue, which is what plays largely consist of, is taken from the word duologue, and that means exploring two sides of an argument'.[15] Although his detractors have tended to dismiss his works as 'middlebrow' (and popular) theatre relying excessively on spectacle, the credo proclaimed by Lettice Douffet might well serve as Shaffer's own in the theatre: 'Enlarge! Enliven! Enlighten!' (23). In so doing, he has devised a unique, eloquent, yet accessible form of 'total theatre' that remains inimitably his own – incorporating not only striking visual effects, classical music, and on-stage ritual, but also a provocative, uniquely dialectical 'theatre of ideas' that appeals even to the popular audience. Therein lies his foremost theatrical – and literary – achievement.

Notes

1. For a complete list of Shaffer's plays to 1988, see *Contemporary Dramatists*, ed. D.L. Kirkpatrick (London: St James Press, 1988). Since 1988 Shaffer has published a radio play, *Whom Do I Have the Honour of Addressing?* (1990).
2. Peter Shaffer, 'Preface', *The Collected Plays of Peter Shaffer* (New York: Harmony Books, 1982) p. vii. Subsequent page references to all prefaces and plays except *Lettice and Lovage* are taken from this edition, and have been inserted parenthetically into the text. Readers should be aware, however, that Shaffer has frequently revised his plays and that earlier versions of the text (particularly the early 'acting editions') may differ substantially from the ones quoted herein.
3. See Mikhail Bakhtin, *Problems of Dostoevsky's Poetics*, ed. and trans. Caryl Emerson (1929, rev. 1963; Minneapolis: University of Minnesota Press, 1984), and also Bakhtin's *The Dialogic Imagination: Four Essays*, ed. Michael Holquist, trans. Caryl Emerson and Michael Holquist (Austin: University of Texas Press, 1981).
4. Peter Shaffer, 'In Search of a God', *Plays and Players* (October 1964) 22.
5. Ibid.
6. Ibid.
7. For an overview of Eliade's theories of desacralisation, see particularly *The Sacred and the Profane: The Nature of Religion*, trans. Willard R. Trask (New York: Harcourt Brace & Co., 1959).
8. For a discussion of the influence of Antonin Artaud's theories on Shaffer's use of ritual, see Gene A. Plunka, *Peter Shaffer: Roles, Rites, and Rituals in the Theatre* (Rutherford NJ: Fairleigh Dickinson University Press, 1988) pp. 42–50. Similarities between Artaud's plans for staging *The Conquest of Mexico* and Shaffer's *Royal Hunt of the Sun* are discussed on pp. 110–113.

9.   For more detailed analyses of the play's themes, see Plunka, 127–48
     and also Dennis A. Klein, *Peter Shaffer* (Boston: Twayne, 1979) pp.
     98–112.
10. Susanne K. Langer, *Philosophy in a New Key*, 3rd edition (Cambridge,
     Mass.: Harvard U.P., 1959) pp. 278–9.
11. Langer, pp. 278–9.
12. For further discussion of Shaffer's use of historic detail, see Plunka,
     pp. 175–82.
13. Claire Colvin, 'Quest for Perfection', *Drama: The Quarterly Theatre
     Review*, 159 (First Quarter 1986) 11.
14. Peter Shaffer, *Lettice and Lovage* (London: André Deutsch Ltd., 1988)
     p. 93.
15. Colvin, pp. 11–12.

4

Mirrors of Utopia: Caryl Churchill and Joint Stock

Frances Gray

Two women are looking into a mirror. They wear the clothes of the seventeenth century, the clothes of the poor. The mirror comes from a great house seized by the dispossessed. Its value, for the woman who took it – rather than food or a warm blanket – lies in the fact that a mirror situates you in the material world, granting – literally – self-possession. 'They must know what they look like all the time. And now we do.'[1] Self-creation is a prime activity for the poor and the women in *Light Shining in Buckinghamshire*, Churchill's account of the English Civil War and its impact on the ordinary people.[2] They choose new identities in relation to the hegemony: Saxons taking back their land from the Norman aristocracy; brothers and sisters with equal rights; fellows in Christ entitled to interpret and proclaim the word of God.

The scene prompts a specifically feminist reading, rendering literal as it does the 'mirror stage' of infant development widely discussed by feminist theorists. In Jacques Lacan's post-structuralist reading of Freud, the act of looking in a mirror endows the baby with a unified image of itself; it identifies with the Other in the mirror and indeed with all others. But at this point the father enters the Oedipal triangle; the child defines itself as a separate being and enters into language, into what Lacan calls the Symbolic Order. The female child learns to define herself in terms of lack, as being without a phallus, and is thus alienated from language even as she enters it.[3]

Churchill's image radically subverts this. We see not one being

47

with its first mirror, but a dyad. A woman identifies herself not as alienated but, in solidarity with another woman, as a political being. It is not surprising that throughout *Light Shining in Buckinghamshire* one of the most prominent acts of the female revolutionaries is to seize the language. Jone Hoskins claims the right to preach; though driven out of the church she creates new understanding of sexual politics in Claxton, the man who saves her. Margaret Brotherton, a vagrant beaten from parish to parish, abandons her concept of herself as 'evil', and redefines herself as someone who can be touched without anger. The new England is potentially filled with speaking subjects, not constructed by the language of others.

It is, of course, a thwarted potential. The Cromwellian hegemony invests the government of the country in the propertied classes; the King restores both social and sexual hierarchies. Jone Hoskins sums up: 'I think what happened was, Jesus Christ did come and nobody noticed'.[4] Men speak the last thirty or so lines of the play, while the women keep silent.

Hoskins' diagnosis is political as well as theological. The possibilities for women shown in this historical moment open up in a unique, eschatological, context, the perceived advent of the millenium. The changes shown in the play are by definition temporary; we enter the theatre aware of the ultimate failure of the revolution. Nevertheless, single incidents – like the moment with the mirror – provide a fully concrete image of Utopia.

Churchill's work has always explored alternative worlds, both good and bad, from her first broadcast radio play, *The Ants*, in which an ant colony symbolises for a child both the dangers of the outside world and his disintegrating family, to *Softcops*, written in the mid-eighties, a wildly farcical account of the search of an incompetent authority figure for the perfect system of punishment. In those plays focussed most sharply upon women and their social context, however, notably *Vinegar Tom*, *Cloud Nine*, *Fen* and *Top Girls*, Utopia is always present, as concrete image or speaking absence. Gisela Ecker writes:

[A] myth of non-alienated expression of gender and sexual identity must necessarily lie behind a utopian programme like feminist politics and it is hardly possible not to attach concrete fantasies to it. . . . [W]e have to be sure of a vague utopia in the background, an idea of not only what we want to be liberated *from* but also liberated *to*.[5]

Two women are looking in a mirror. They are actresses with a company called Joint Stock. As such they are committed to a style grounded on the premise that the purpose of theatre is political. As an organisation the company strove for democracy, equal pay and collective control of the budget (Utopia); actors worked with writers before a text emerged, improvising, researching, discussing. A Joint Stock play seldom tried to absorb the audience in a story of 'heroes' with whom they might identify. It focussed upon ordinary members of specific communities, often in a state of flux and change; it sought to demonstrate clearly, through speech, movement and image, the political meaning of each scene – what Brecht called the *gestus*. Its approach made it one of the few companies capable of performing *Light Shining* as opposed to the usual picture of the English Revolution as an all-star shouting match between Charles I and Cromwell.

The effect of working with Joint Stock was to have far-reaching consequences for Churchill's work. The process of creating *Light Shining*, and, simultaneously, of working with the feminist company Monstrous Regiment to create *Vinegar Tom*, shifted the focus of her work from the analysis of private suffering to the political reasons behind it; her plays became, in Howard Brenton's phrase, 'plays for public places', while continuing to explore the personal pain of the characters in a way few political playwrights have matched.[6] It is illuminating to examine in some detail this watershed in Churchill's writing life because it contrasts sharply with the experience of male contemporaries like Brenton and Hare, and throws into relief qualities forged by a career experience common to women of her generation.

The seventies had seen the rise of a powerful political drama written by men, capable of developing from a Brechtian base in varied and interesting ways. Many of these writers showed a common career trajectory of university followed by fringe theatre – often with companies they themselves had founded – followed by entry into mainstream subsidised theatres. The impact of feminism on these male playwrights tended to reflect the impact of feminism on the British Left as a whole. There was certainly a concern to provide women with more and better jobs – i.e., to create 'good parts' for them within the existing framework. 'Good parts' tended to be of two kinds: a central female figure whose politicisation is one of the main themes of the play, as in Red Ladder's *Strike While The Iron is Hot*, John McGrath's *Yobbo Nowt*, (both derived from Brecht's version of Gorki's *The Mother*), or Brenton's *Weapons of Happiness;* or the romantic conscience of a corrupt world, like the Greenham women in Edgar's *Maydays* or the heroines of David Hare. While these plays recognise the oppression of women and redress the weak and insignificant image they present in earlier drama, they are reformist rather than feminist. The women enter into socialist discourse on male terms. It changes them; they do not change it. There is no attempt to find theatrical forms which deconstruct the idea of gender; the assumption seems to be that sexual relations will sort themselves out while male and female comrades struggle side by side – never face to face.

Joint Stock was not a feminist company but a development of the sixties Fringe, now seeking better facilities, bigger audiences and texts of greater complexity. Founded in 1974, it preceded by a year or so the more influential women's companies, such as Monstrous Regiment and the Women's Theatre Group. The gender balance in the company for *Light Shining* – four men, two women – was not atypical. Carol Hayman, a longstanding member, writes:

> I remember . . . [s]uggesting the Board consider more projects by women and being told . . . women had nothing to write about – they hadn't *done* anything in the world.[7]

When Churchill began working with Joint Stock in 1976 she had been writing plays for eighteen years; she had also raised three children. This had a considerable influence on her choice of medium: most of the plays were for radio. In practical terms, this meant less time away from home, for the radio writer works virtually alone till recording. It also meant an apprenticeship in a medium which excels at presenting the interior world and which, being purely aural, demands intense verbal precision. For many women, too, the fact that radio plays work well in small scenic units is a major advantage in a life fragmented by differing responsibilities. Gillian Hanna of Monstrous Regiment comments on the way in which feminist writers often reject the linear structure of the male-authored political plays of the seventies:

> [Men] are born into a world where they can map out life . . . it has to do with a career. Now for a woman, life is not like that. It doesn't have that pattern. For a woman life and experience is broken-backed.[8]

Churchill said the years at home with her children 'politicised' her.[9] Working with Joint Stock and Monstrous Regiment enabled her to place a developed talent for intricate and subtle work into a political frame and gave her the support she needed to paint on a larger canvas. Her stage practice in both *Light Shining* and *Vinegar Tom* was geared to concretising the idea that gender is socially constructed, and to reflect the 'broken-backed' experience of women. In *Light Shining* she developed a powerful image out of what started as a casting problem:

> The main characters were cast and the idea was that everyone would play minor parts in each other's stories. Then Max [Stafford-Clark] and I had the idea, first a joke, then seriously, that perhaps there wasn't any need to write the missing scenes if it wasn't quite clear which character was which and different actors played the same character in different scenes. This . . . gave an effect we liked of many people having the same experiences during the revolution.[10]

Hayman, for instance, eventually shared the roles of Hoskins and Brotherton and played several unnamed women (including one in the mirror scene). Common experience is thus privileged over individual epiphany; in the case of the women, this structure reflects the way they as gendered subjects are shaped by ideologies of family, class and patriarchal theology, fragmenting their sense of themselves. As audience we too experience their sense of fragmentation; the play is a mosaic of data we piece together, not a simple presentation of cause and effect.

Meanwhile, in *Vinegar Tom*, Churchill explored similar pressures on women in a play about the seventeenth century witch craze; it was, as she put it, 'a play about witches with no witches in it', witchcraft being the name given to any alternative female lifestyle.[11] Here the 'logical' structure was broken not by casting but by the use of rock songs between scenes which swung the audience constantly between past and present. Monstrous Regiment, then, as well as Joint Stock, were responsible for giving Churchill what she needed to develop as a political playwright, and it is important not to undervalue their influence. It was to Joint Stock that she returned most frequently in following years, however, and her Joint Stock plays provide in many ways a microcosm of her work: they mark breakthroughs in stage method, they raise issues subsequently developed in other plays, and they crystallise ideas previously explored. For this reason I shall concentrate on the Joint Stock plays as forming the most useful introduction to Churchill.

Churchill returned to work with Joint Stock in 1979 with *Cloud Nine*, which might lay claim to be their first specifically feminist play. *Cloud Nine* uses and develops the stage practices of *Light Shining*. It had both critical and popular success, a fact that has sometimes led to the under-estimation of its feminist power and of its bold attack on conventional theatrical structure. Certainly its subject – sexual politics, in particular the politics of orgasm – drew audiences; but the highly original techniques of casting and structure provide powerful dramatic tools for feminist writers.

In the second act the cast sing the title song. 'Cloud Nine' was the term for orgasm used by the caretaker of the rehearsal room, drawn into the workshops in which actors discussed their own sexual lives. For her, orgasm was a transforming experience; for the characters it represents both personal and political freedom, yet to be realised in day-to-day living. Only outside the narrative can they articulate it fully, as the singers in *Vinegar Tom* articulate the real female strength labelled 'witchcraft'. Within the story, however, are moments which suggest that this Utopia can be seen as aim rather than dream. Betty has left her husband after years of unhappy marriage. She tells us:

> I thought if Clive wasn't looking at me there wasn't a person there. And one night in bed in my flat I was so frightened I started touching myself. I thought my hand might go through space. I touched my face, it was there, my arm, my breast, and my hand went down where I thought it shouldn't, and I thought well there is somebody there.[12]

The seventies saw a rash of novels in which one woman leaves her husband, learns to cope with work and money, and is rewarded with sexual satisfaction – male-, female- or auto-generated. While these may have been empowering for some, they also shut out the notion of social change. Churchill's stage practice, however, strongly resists the reading 'one woman triumphs', and she rejected alterations in the first American production which put Betty's monologue at the end precisely because it encouraged this. What matters is not simply Betty's sexual achievement; it is the way in which recognition of her own sexuality enables her to move in her world from object to subject, and the parallel movement which takes place in our perception of the way women are represented in our culture. Hence Churchill sets the first half of the play in a time and place at which, for the West, racial and sexual roles were polarised – British colonial Africa. The characters are familiar from nostalgic treatments such as *Upstairs, Downstairs* – martial husband, heroic friend, (with whom frail wife is tempted to stray), dragon mother-in-law, hostile natives. But our position in relation to them is subverted. Churchill refuses to permit 'the male gaze' which renders man the subject and woman the (sexual) object. Betty is played by a man. He makes no attempt to disguise his maleness, nor does he make parodic gestures of femininity; rather he incarnates the idea that 'Betty' does not exist in her own right. She is a male construct defined by male need:

> HARRY: Betty, you are a star in my sky. Without you I would have no sense of direction. I need you, and I need you where you are, I need you to be Clive's wife. I need to go up rivers and know you are sitting here thinking of me.
> BETTY: I want more than that. Is that wicked of me?
> HARRY: Not wicked, Betty. Silly.
>
> (23)

Other stage techniques too physicalise the invisibility of female desire. Mrs Saunders, the only woman able fully to articulate her sexual need, is shown describing her desire *for* and dislike *of* Clive while he disappears up her skirts, emerging when he is satisfied and she is not – a comic but also savage image. The trap in which Mrs Saunders finds herself is stressed by casting: a more sympathetic recipient of her desire might be Ellen, the governess with a hopeless love for Betty, but as these parts are played by the same actress the characters are literally invisible to each other. The way in which Victorian patriarchy perceives women is also concretised by non-human casting: Victoria, Betty's daughter, is played by a doll. Ironically, the doll has a doll, in which Betty's son Edward (played by a woman) is interested until his interest in it is beaten out of him; the doll is abused by the black servant, Joshua (played by a white man). It is hard to distinguish the two dolls; when Joshua rips stuffing out of the toy, we are instantly reminded of Victoria; the image powerfully connotes the gap oppression opens up between the colonised and the women they might perceive as allies.

In the second half – set in the present, though the characters have aged only twenty-five years – actors largely play their own gender. The original cross-casting prevented our treating characters as sexual objects: we now accept them as sexual subjects, their subjectivity achieved while they are still struggling with their oppressive heritage. Their personal difficulties are couched in conventions which, after the sometimes cartoon-like first half, seem almost naturalistic. Two scenes, however, open up into Utopian fantasy. Edward, Victoria and her lover Lin attempt to call up the Goddess in the park; the ceremony collapses – first into a giggly orgy, when the stranger they drag into their ceremonies proves to be Victoria's estranged husband Martin; then into a painful reminder of colonial values as the next stranger is the ghost of Lin's brother, a soldier in Northern Ireland. While Churchill's innovative casting resists the essentialist position that biology is destiny, the idea of the 'goddess of fat bellies and babies' has a resonance and beauty that contrasts with Martin's desire for a nineteen-sixties male-controlled orgy or the crude and angry fuck that is all the soldier-ghost is capable of longing for.

The final moment of the play is both more and less optimistic than Betty's soliloquy. Victorian Betty enters and embraces her counterpart: it is a concrete image of the healing of the body-mind split imposed by Clive's world. (Clive loves Betty, fucks Mrs Saunders. Harry loves Clive, fucks Joshua); it is a symbol of our need to accept our history; the fact that what is physically shown is, in real life, impossible, is also a measure of the difficulty of the task. It is, too, an image of Utopian tenderness: two women looking in a mirror. Churchill wrote of *Cloud Nine*: 'For the first time I brought together two preoccupations of mine – people's internal states of being and the external political structures which affect them, which make them insane'.[13] Her next Joint Stock play, *Fen*, partly inspired by Mary Chamberlain's book about women in the Cambridgeshire village of Gislea, *Fenwomen*, used different stage practices to accomplish this 'bringing together'. Chamberlain's book is prefaced by a quotation from the eighteenth century poet Mary Collier: 'Our Toil and Labour's daily so extreme,/ That we have hardly even Time to dream.'[14] But in *Fen* women do dream, and it is through realising their imaginative lives that the stage practice makes concrete social and political possibilities denied them – through language, set, and the breaking of naturalistic boundaries. The play touches on the lives of sixteen women; the linking thread is the story of Val. She is married but loves another man, Frank. Poverty makes it impossible for her to live with both Frank and her children; torn both ways, she asks Frank to kill her.

If this sounds like a folk song it is not coincidental, for in folk songs the personal meets the political. Val's story is set clearly in economic context: a Japanese businessman opens the play, detailing big multinational companies with interests in the fens. Val and Frank's employer, Tewson – who controls their wages, Frank's tied cottage, and thus their lives – settles the future of his land with a representative from the City. Later he smugly comments: 'I've seen women working in my fields with icicles on their faces. I admire that.'[15]

But while men speak a language of individualism – significantly Churchill only used one male actor, so men are never presented in dialogue – women are a community with a richer language. They tell jokes, sing, write poems and testify in chapel. Sometimes this language reveals a cruel impoverishment: Val seeks comfort at the local Baptist church, where a woman sees the words 'more jam, mum' as a sign of divine grace towards her worthlessness; her linguistic and spiritual deprivation are highlighted as Shirley, the hardest worker in the play, sings a snatch of Bunyan's pilgrim hymn. This is the language of *Light Shining*, language that adequately expressed revolution.

But the women are also guardians of more nourishing traditions. Nell, the political activist, is also the community story-teller, and claims fairy-tale terminology for her alternative lifestyle: when the children ask if she is a witch she says, firmly, 'No, I'm a princess' (65). Val's grandmother Ivy tells stories of a radical past and active resistance to the landowners. This more subversive language seems to bubble beneath the talk of hardship and family pain, then suddenly surfaces to reveal its potential power.

The sense of barely contained energy is stressed by the set Annie Smart devised, a field surrealistically planted with domestic objects. It politicised the most personal scenes; for instance, there is an exchange of silly jokes between Val and her daughter, in which the emotional point – that Val is losing her daughter's love – is made subtextually; meanwhile, the set visually embodies the link between the land as a source of profit and the economic constraints underlying Val's domestic situation.

The surreal set also facilitated the movement into a dramatic mode in which the unspoken becomes concrete. A ghost appears to tell Tewson that her child died starving, and that she is angry because he perpetuates the political system that permitted it. Her appearance is a powerful theatrical coup, yet it springs logically out of the set and the women's stories; it prepares us for the final, boldest, theatrical shift into the territory of dreams: Frank kills Val and hides the body in a wardrobe. Val emerges, now empowered to see ghosts from the past – like the woman with the starving child – and also to summon up the dreaming selves of the other women. Shirley, still working, ironing the very field, describes a past when labourers killed the owner's cattle instead of working with icicles on their faces. Nell crosses on stilts, a fully realised Fen tiger instead of the village eccentric. Val says 'My mother wanted to be a singer. That's why she'd never sing' (98). But May sings, beautifully, operatically, as the lights go down on the play. The physical expression Churchill gives these dreams and desires stresses that they are still a real force with the possibility of accomplishing real change.

Powerful in its own right, *Fen* also forms an introduction to a group of plays anatomising the England of the 1980s: *Top Girls*, *Hot Fudge* and *Serious Money* all premiered at the Royal Court and featured members of Joint Stock. All show *Fen*'s concern with language. Here, however, the focus is dystopian: language is not charged with the potential to embody and achieve a better world but a rigid discourse imposing as well as expressing monetary values. *Top Girls*, written just before *Fen*, juxtaposes the life of the rural poor with the values of big business. Marlene, the only character to appear throughout, speaks the language of Thatcherism. 'Anyone can do anything if they've got what it takes'. It is juxtaposed with the far more complex language of the women from history with whom, in a surrealistic opening, she celebrates her success, a language that speaks of achievement but also of its cost in personal pain and struggle: with the socialist discourse of her sister, living a life like that of the Fenwomen, and with the inarticulacy of young people growing up in the world her language has constructed – the pathetic Shona, a feeble echo of Marlene, and Marlene's retarded daughter Angie, who sums up the future for those unwilling or unable to enter Marlene's web of monetarist discourse: 'Frightening'. In the two later plays the element of dialectic disappears. The powerless are invisible and voiceless – to us and to the characters. In *Serious Money*, which deals with the explosion of acquisitiveness following the deregulation of the Stock Exchange, the characters speak verse. Its brisk rhythms simultaneously reflect their energy and their dehumanisation as world events – boom or recession – and commodities – copper or cocaine – are reduced to signifiers with a common signified: profit. For women in all three plays, other than those who are willing to construct themselves through the discourse of patriarchal capitalism, the possibilities are black.

Churchill was to also add to the techniques of *Fen* in making the subconscious concrete by exploring movement and dance; before Joint Stock fell victim to Arts Council cuts, she collaborated with playwright/anthropologist David Lan. The starting point of *A Mouthful of Birds* was Euripides' *Bacchae* but with a significant difference. In Euripides' play the Bacchantes, possessed by Dionysus, tear Pentheus to pieces, then, horrified at what they have done, come down from the mountain to resume their lives. Here seven characters are possessed, but choose to stay on the mountain. Each sex explores extreme feelings usually associated with its opposite, and each gains power from doing so. Their experience is expressed in dance and surrealist images: the Pentheus-figure, Derek, torn to pieces in a dance involving all the characters, is resurrected into a new feminine body, in which he feels great peace and happiness. The woman who has performed the most shocking act, the killing of a child (symbolised by the simple act of washing a shawl) sums up: 'It's nice to make someone alive and it's nice to make someone dead. Either way. That power is what I like best in the world. The struggle is every day not to use it.'[16] A man talking with a hermaphrodite is transformed into her, repeating her words and blessed by her with a kiss. Here the whole stage action concerns what in *Fen* was a momentary possibility, the magical realisation of the imaginative life; the stage itself has become Utopia, a place of transformation.

I should like to conclude this introduction to Churchill by discussing her first play of the 90s, in which the collaborative methods learned from Joint Stock were used with students from the Central School of Speech and Drama. *Mad Forest* returns to the territory of *Light Shining*, a potentially Utopian people's revolution – this time the Romanian uprising. It employs similar techniques – multiple casting, short scenes – to build up a mosaic set within a tripartite structure: the weddings of two sisters, Lucia and Florina, mirror each other on either side of the events of December 1989. The first half shows in densely packed vignettes aspects of Romanian life familiar from the news: queues, shortages, fear of speaking out, Lucia bribing a corrupt doctor to obtain an abortion. Then new characters narrate events preceding the fall of Ceaucescu, with a variety of viewpoints and priorities: one woman remembers getting milk for her dog, another describes the rejoicing, another the details of the bullet wounds she treated in the hospital. The effect is of documentary taking over from the fictitious. But as Churchill resumes the sisters' story it assumes a new complexity.

A patient nursed by Florina begins to ask questions: 'did we have a revolution or a putsch? Who was shooting on the 21st? And who was shooting on the 22nd?'[17] It prompts us to ask questions too: Is he in hospital because he is wounded, or because he asks questions? As events become harder to judge, so do characters: Lucia leaves her American husband, coming home to resume an affair with Janos, a Hungarian. What we saw as romance now seems to be a cynical attempt to get a passport; but this expectation, too, is confounded, as it is she who most strongly rejects Western materialism, describing in disgust dustbins crammed with food. Characters who showed heroism in the uprising, like Gabriel, the brother of the brides, articulate an uglier side of nationalism: an improvised skit on the killing of Ceaucescu acquires disturbing overtones, and as Janos laughs with Lucia, Gabriel says: 'get your filthy Hungarian hands off her' (75). Among the realistically drawn characters are a dog, a vampire, bored with and addicted to killing, and an angel who tells the parish priest, 'I try to keep clear of the political side. You should do the same' (26). At the end, everyone is speaking, opinions, feelings, fears: a society in chaos.

It is impossible to draw simple conclusions from *Mad Forest*, and this makes it entirely representative of Churchill's particular vision. The shapes in which we clothe our spiritual feelings are, like the angel, also constructed by ideology. To love can be a political act, like Lucia's love of the Hungarian Janos. A Churchill play is not a linear argument but a mosaic; each piece, whether concerned with bodily, spiritual or social being, is equally important. It makes up a mirror which does not simply reflect but transforms political and social relations.

Notes

1. Caryl Churchill, *Light Shining in Buckinghamshire* (London: Pluto Press, 1978) p. 14.
2. For a complete list to 1988 of the plays of Caryl Churchill (b. 1938),

see *Contemporary Dramatists*, ed. D.L. Kirkpatrick (London: St James Press, 1988). Since 1988 Churchill has published *Ice Cream* (1989), *Shorts* [includes: *Lovesick, Abortive, Not Not Not Not Not Enough Oxygen, Schreber's Nervous Illness, The Hospital at the Time of the Revolution, The Judge's Wife, The After Dinner Joke, Seagulls, Three More Sleepless Nights, Hot Fudge*] (1990), and *Mad Forest* (1990).

3. See Jacques Lacan, *Speech and Language in Psychoanlysis*, trans. Anthony Wilden (Baltimore: Johns Hopkins, 1968) pp. 159 ff. This work is usefully discussed by Elin Diamond in *Performing Feminisms*, (Baltimore: Johns Hopkins Press, 1990) p. 93.
4. *Light Shining*, p. 38.
5. *Feminist Aesthetics*, ed. Gisele Ecker, trans. H. Anderson (London: Women's Press, 1985) p. 19.
6. Howard Brenton, *Plays for Public Places* (London: Methuen, 1970).
7. Rob Ritchie, *The Joint Stock Book* (London: Methuen, 1987) p. 110.
8. Quoted in Sue Ellen Case, *Feminism and Theatre* (London: Macmillan, 1988) p. 123.
9. Quoted in Catherine Itzin, *Stages in the Revolution* (London: Eyre Methuen, 1980) p. 278.
10. *The Joint Stock Book*, p. 120.
11. *Plays by Women: I*, ed. Michelene Wandor (London: Methuen, 1982) p. 39.
12. Caryl Churchill, *Cloud Nine* (London: Nick Hern Books, 1989) pp. 82–3. All quotations are from this edition; hereafter, page numbers will be given in the text.
13. Quoted in *Stages in the Revolution*, p. 287.
14. Mary Chamberlain, *Fenwomen* (London: Virago, 1975) p. 10.
15. Caryl Churchill, *Fen* (London: Methuen, 1986) p. 79. All quotations are from this edition; hereafter, page numbers will be given in the text.
16. Caryl Churchill and David Lan, *A Mouthful of Birds* (London: Methuen, 1986) p. 70.
17. Caryl Churchill, *Mad Forest* (London: Nick Hern Books, 1990) p. 54. All quotations are from this edition; hereafter, page numbers will be given in the text.

5

Casting the Audience: Theatricality in the Stage Plays of Peter Nichols

Andrew Parkin

Peter Nichols, born 1927, is among that generation of British drama-tists who matured in the late 1960s, having grown up during the second world war on cinema and music hall. Although beginning with plays for television, he aimed always to write for the stage.[1] Although music hall declined after the war (hurt by social change, television, and the rage for Bingo) it taught Nichols a good deal about theatre. And although, as he told me in 1986, many of his plays use cinema techniques, when he writes for the stage he always tries to create 'something special for the theatre'. He is never satisfied with fourth wall realism, because he always finds 'it difficult to ignore the audience'.[2]

Theatre happens when 'the public is let in'; it is then that 'the play becomes interplay'.[3] He sees pre-sixties realism as a form ripe to be taken over by television, as indeed it was, in the 1950s. When writing for the theatre, his rule, therefore, is to seek ways of escaping that old-fashioned realism in order 'to find a role for the spectators'.[4] Another kind of interplay is at the basis of theatre, that between physical being, on stage, appealing to our senses, and verbal images brought to us 'through imagination, evoked through the word', as Max Frisch points out; he explains that 'Their playing together, ... the sphere of tension which is produced between them, ... is what one might designate as being the theatrical'.[5] I believe that Nichols' plays are intensely theatrical in these two ways, as well as in others.

The most damning criticism of Nichols as stage dramatist comes perhaps from Stanley Kauffmann in *Persons of the Drama*. The charge is that Nichols tricks out his situations and characters in such a way as to break a few taboos, but his irreverence never pushes further to the real confrontations: 'He *seems* to bite bullets . . . but he just mouths them for a while before he spits them out, he never really crunches'. Kauffmann demands that Nichols comment seriously: 'We keep waiting for the author's gravity as distinct from the subject's'.[6] This is tantamount to demanding that plays have a message. John Russell Taylor sees, though, that Nichols' *Forget-Me-Not Lane* 'resolutely shows us everything, tells us nothing. That is why we understand so much from it'.[7] Nichols does not moralise; instead, he presents people, things, events, in a theatrical way. My aim is to discuss his theatricality in *A Day in the Death of Joe Egg* (1967), *Forget-Me-Not Lane* (1971), *Passion Play* (1981), and *A Piece of My Mind* (1987). All these family plays, a sub-genre Nichols delights in, push conventional realism offstage by means of theatrical virtuosity.

A Day in the Death of Joe Egg, first performed in Glasgow at the Citizen's Theatre in May 1967, scored subsequent successes in London and New York, was made into a film, has been translated into many languages, and is still performed in professional revivals and by amateurs in different parts of the world. The situation of the play is that Bri and his wife Sheila have a badly brain-damaged child. This terrible misfortune they deal with as best they can, through humorous banter and running jokes. The play opens with Bri's monologue full of the kind of British school teacher rhetoric audiences can instantly recognise. During his speech the audience is cast as a naughty class. He hectors, disciplines, threatens, and orders them to put hands on heads; the audience is by an instant reflex back at school, conscious in their adult laughter of the healthy youngsters they all once were. This of course makes the plight of Bri and Sheila the more affecting. The interplay between actor and audience, stage and auditorium, that Nichols sets up in the opening monologue is a powerful and ancient theatrical device. When Bri remarks 'That characteristic performance from our friend near the window means we return to Go',[8] we are in the grip of a theatricality that has never failed since orators, whether comedians or moralists, discovered it. But the oratorical bubble is fragile. Anyone who has heard enough rhetoric knows how easily it can falter and become absurd. Nichols exploits this too, sure of his laugh lines, when Bri, dreaming of his young wife at home, says to the class 'Yes – eyes front . . . hands on breasts . . . STOP the laughter!' (10).

The very structure of Act I uses symmetrically placed monologues as theatrical foundation stones, as it were, for Bri has a second monologue in the middle of the act followed quickly by Sheila's first monologue, and then followed by her second monologue near the end of the act. Thus we have a series of major speeches directly addressing the audience in the sequence Bri – Bri – Sheila – Sheila, the act closing with a brief speech from the crippled child, Joe herself. This is a climactic *coup de théâtre*.

Bri's second monologue casts the audience as one for a stand-up comic: he prepares them by evoking the image of his wife undressing upstairs, and then goes on to confide in the audience in the manner of comedians like Frankie Howerd or Ronny Corbett: 'No, but she is a wonderful woman, my wife. That girl upstairs. In the bedroom, off in the wings, wherever she is' (25). The text reminds us of another form of theatre, front-cloth comedy in music hall or variety shows. It also reminds us that physically we are in a theatre, watching a play, and that Sheila, the wife, is an actress resting somewhere until her next cue. It is theatre referring to itself – metatheatre.

Sheila's first monologue exploits the audience in the same way. But brilliantly the comic's wife now has the stage and can answer back, something that never happens in the variety show. In appealing to the audience to side with her point of view about Bri's insecurities, Sheila casts them as what they are, the theatre audience, 'a lot of complete strangers' (27). The basis of theatre is frankly revealed as exposure, the exhibition of intimacies in front of strangers. The rest of the act shows the parents coping with their sick joke of a child as if fate were the celestial sick jester; they cope by means of humour, jokes about Joe Egg which help them retain their sanity. From one point of view the play is an extended sick joke, one played by fate upon parents. Sick jokes were very much a sixties phenomenon, but theatrical here because the audience recognises them as part of their frame of reference, just as they recognise and are involved by the references to other sixties household details: guinea pigs, stick insects, natural childbirth and the contraceptive coil, not to mention the catchword of the era, 'swinging'. If Bri's opening monologue is loud and rhetorical, Sheila's at the end of Act I is quiet and explanatory. It gives a vividly poignant vision of the child, demonstrates Sheila's compassion, and demands our own. Nichols then changes the lighting and 'JOE *skips on, using a rope'* (45). Sheila's powerful verbal evocation of the crippled Joe cross cuts as it were to the physical image of Joe as she might have been as a healthy child. It is a *coup de théâtre* gained from tension and conflict between the verbal and visual images, between the tragic fact and the dream of normality. It is a perfect example of theatricality in Frisch's sense.

Another way of casting the audience is as visitors: Bri and Sheila explain about life with Joe and their experience of doctors, hospital, and the vicar. Again the audience are *confidants*, as they are basically for the stand-up comedian.

Besides casting the audience, Nichols also likes to surprise it with the situation of something having unexpectedly gone wrong in the production, as if the play had suddenly given way to a real life event. This happens in the Universal Shafting sequence of Act I. Bri and Sheila have got the audience used to their enacting a number of assumed roles to illustrate officials they have known and would rather have done without. In the persona of a Viennese pediatrician, Bri explains the brain as a kind of telephone switchboard. When Sheila assumes a telephonist's voice and answers 'Universal Shafting' Bri is so amazed by the pun in what he assumes to be a real job Sheila once had, that he comes out of role; the dialogue between the actor and actress talking about their improvisation, with Bri remarking, 'You've never put that in before'. The audience thinks they are out of role and engaged in a real life professional *contretemps*:

> SHEILA (*shrugs*): I thought I would this time.
> BRI: Universal Shafting? Story of your life.
> (*She stares coldly . . .*)
>
> (37)

Audiences of one Broadway production applauded every night at this point, thinking something had happened and the actors were *ad libbing*; one reviewer actually wrote that the actors helped the author with comic asides. Nichols revels in the fact that the moment is planned and scripted but uniquely theatrical.[9]

All these devices in Nichols' first major stage play are theatre in its essence: they depend on the actor's ability to assume roles and step out of them in front of the audience's eyes. They do not depend on machinery. Drawing on the prime resource of theatre, the live actor, they stubbornly affirm the stage for what it offers that television and filmed drama cannot.

Forget-Me-Not Lane explores the kind of family and upbringing someone like Bri escaped from to begin his own family with someone like Sheila. Peter Nichols and his wife and members of their families, as well as some of their friends, often provide situations, jokes, sayings and character traits for Nichols' largely autobiographical plays, but autobiography is only a beginning. Readers of Nichols' autobiography, *Feeling You're Behind*, and of some of his press interviews, may pursue the question of autobiographical drama. What seems more interesting is how Nichols makes theatre, how his exploitation of stage effects proceeds.

As with *Joe Egg*, *Forget-Me-Not Lane* opens with monologue; Frank is playing some music while packing, a process that triggers his memories of his father, Charles, who was a commercial traveller. The family theme is now complicated by having to stage two generations of the family, 'Both my families. The one I was issued with and the one I escaped to'.[10] Nichols avoids the literalism of two sets, one for each family; although his dialogue is realistic, he makes the set, a semi-circular screen with six or perhaps eight doors, an image of the portals of the memory, the stage being Frank's consciousness, in which the primal scenes get played out to create a theatre of family memory. Frank and to a lesser extent his wife Ursula bring the past blundering in through the doors to the arena of consciousness. But memories cannot always be controlled, and Act I ends with the painfully vivid evocation of a homosexual artiste, Mr Magic, after Frank has come to the realisation that he is the unfortunate beneficiary of his father's brand of sexuality, 'A lack of mastery. Dependence' (46). The heterosexual but insecure Frank rounds on his adolescent self, that self's friend, Ivor, Charles, Amy, the mother, and Mr Magic, who have all popped through the doors, and cries out in desperation, 'Can't you leave me alone for ten minutes! [*They all slam the doors together.*] (47). The sudden intensity and pace is that of farce, the emotion that of the problem drama. This complex moment of theatre is further complicated by the realisation that it is also the cue for the interval. Frank is addressing his past; Nichols is addressing his audience.

In this play the audience are cast mainly as *confidants* for Frank's psychodrama, though at one point Charles blithely treats them as the garden on which he sprinkles his nail clippings to do it good.

They are also briefly apprehended by Frank as listeners to be entertained, as when in Act I Amy is going off while Young Frank reads his paper. Brief silence, then Frank things what to give us next: 'I know! [*The air-raid siren sounds the alert*]' (17). That powerful signal, full of dread and, for those who survived, a strange nostalgia, is part of Nichols' theatricality of sound in the play. Frequent snatches of recorded music give instant access through classics, swing, and jazz to the remembered era, the changing sensibilities, and the generation gap that is dramatised. The sounds chart the emotional terrain and remain for Nichols a basic theatrical element in his other plays. They are just as much a part of that theatricality of common allusion as the catch phrases and slang of an era, such as the comic allusions in the play to such things as the Old Codgers of the *Daily Mirror* letters page whose spirited replies to readers were always couched in working-class lingo full of phrases like 'Not 'arf!' and 'Cor Blimey, mate!'.

Nichols' juxtapositioning of present and past results not in the play within the play, but a variant we might call the sketches within the play. Of course this is a very theatrical form because its rapid switching of gears is always drawing the audience's attention to the fact that actors are performing; we never settle into one theatrical time-frame and situation that permits the illusion that we are absorbed in reality. The theatricality goes even further when Frank's past shows us the kind of concert party show he was involved in. This happens in the sequence of Amy and Mr Magic with 'There'll always be an England' (24–6). So we arrive at the concert party item within the sketch within the play. The stage is a space that can accommodate any time, any place, in rapid succession, or simultaneously, as when the present Frank is surrounded by his pasts.

What Nichols achieves, among other things, by juxtaposing two generations of family life, is the enrichment of abiding themes. If Frank inherits his father's sexual nature, he also shares Bri's sexual problem, the feeling that he missed out on a promiscuous youth, whereas his wife fully enjoyed hers. The feeling is the more intense for being the reversal of the usual stereotype of boys being boys and girls being virgins. The depiction of Young Frank and the parents, particularly Charles, helps to explain Frank's problem. It also gives us a primal scene for the formation of the darkly comic sensibility in the plays and its focus on regret and recrimination. Amy feels both in relation to Charles; Young Frank tries to get her to leave so that they might be free of the father's tyranny. But female practicality in Amy always cuts across dreams and aspirations. When Young Frank spouts his social welfare dreams, Amy asks prosaically, 'If everyone's just enjoying themselves, who's going to clear up all the mess?' (17). When Charles thinks of the chances he missed for sexual adventure in his youth, he speculates, 'Vicky Edmunds, for instance, lived in Leytonstone. I wonder what Vicky's doing now'. Amy replies, 'Drawing the old age pension, I should think' (67). Nichols' sense of humour always responds to the balloon of fancy being pricked by the realist's pin. Where Frank's and Bri's painful sexual frustrations issue in the serious desire to divorce or at least commit adultery, Charles's pain finds expression in grotesque imagery of frustration that is so extreme as to be painful and comic: Amy's scorn prompts him to say, 'I shall boil a kettle to fill my hot-water bottle. Once in bed, I shall place it scalding between my thighs'. But Amy is relentless, detecting the old man's remarks as a kind of sexual show for his daughter-in-law: 'AMY: I don't think Ursula's interested in what you do in bed' (67). Ursula feels sorry for him and kisses him as he goes off. Charles is also excluded by his family; his travels take him away for most of the week, and his goings are always reluctant, with the family struggling to get him off and away at last so that they can enjoy a respite from his puritanical hectorings; his homecomings are always dreaded and greeted with gracelessness.

The damage done in childhood by such a family life comes out in Young Frank's bed-wetting at an age when it should have been long outgrown. The father's lack of sensitivity and even his cruelty to the boy are captured in a moment that uses fully the theatrical device of the doors, suggesting the slamming of doors that is often the accompaniment of family rows. Charles makes a joke about the bed-wetting in front of Young Ursula.[11] At the same time, Frank's assessment of his father as a 'pre-Freudian clown' in that scene takes us to another aspect of Charles, his comic vitality. His pompous lower middle-class efforts at correctness of speech and propriety, his ludicrous involvement with the Freemasonry of small businessmen, and his absurdities as a self-appointed watchdog of public standards of decency and clean-living, make him at once a wonderful comic target and somewhat sad. His accounts of his exploits and Amy's deflation of them are richly theatrical in the way that pairs of comedians are. They play on the different facets of our natures. It is the triumph of Nichols' sense of theatre in this play not to discuss the meaning of family or fatherhood, but to present us with its *being*, the comic life of his father character on stage. Theatricality for Nichols is what theatre has always provided, the resurrection of something or its spirit in the living flesh of an actor. That he was able to achieve such a rounded view of the father was doubtless partly a result of his own middle-aged experience. At the end of the play, Frank has recognised his own frustration and that of the father; he also realises they are closer for sharing a sense of missed sexual exploits. At the same time he is old enough, and perhaps still immature enough, to envy his son's easygoing sexuality in the era following the 'swinging' sixties. The bitter complexity of this middle-aged Frank provides the context for all the promise, sensuality, and excitement of young passion remembered, embodied in the simple theatricality of the moment at the end of the play when Young Ursula reveals her nakedness to him. But Ursula the wife crashes in to dismiss past for present.

Because of the theatrical context in which it appears, the moment is very moving, and we recall the beginning of Act II with Frank's decision to leave, and Ursula's confidence that the children will keep him at home. She tells him, 'the family's inevitable', and he replies, 'Then God help us' (49). But we know from Act I that Frank has left her; the play has been a theatrical reconstruction of his two families in an attempt to see what led to the failure of the marriage. But Nichols does not philosophise. He gives us the stage pictures of the death of passion, and it dies laughing.

In *Passion Play* this theme is the whole focus; children do not complicate the issue. The ancient theatre situation of the love triangle is difficult to treat freshly. Nichols finds a way and it is by means of specifically theatrical devices. The play seems to be set in a realistic living-room but there is an ambiguity about the room that makes it suggest also, as a general note to the text explains, 'a fashionable art gallery'.[12] Realistic dialogue can thus switch rapidly between locations and is abruptly punctuated by short bursts of music giving ironic point to the stage situation. After an evening with Kate, the young widow of Albert, their middle-aged friend, James is alone while his wife Eleanor shows Kate out. Mozart's *Requiem* bursts in, reflecting James' sudden intimations of mortality. Later, he wants to make love to Eleanor on the stairs, or failing that, the landing. She wants to go to bed and reminds him as she goes off that they are grandparents. James is alone with his lust and his sense of mortality. Again the *Requiem* bursts in with the *Dies Irae*. The music makes points which need no explanation from the dialogue. The day of wrath and reckoning makes us ponder the meaning of our life. For some it will induce a strict morality. For others, like James, it will sharpen the desire to taste experience, to live fully, and more selfishly, before it is all over. This theatrical method is established in the first beats of the play. The second burst of Mozart makes also a fast transition to a restaurant where James has lost no time in having an assignation with Kate. The speed suggests the urgency of his need to change the priorities of his life. Nichols establishes by the music and the rapid beginning of the affair between Kate and James the two themes of death and love contained in the ambiguity of the word 'passion' in his title. This ambiguity is more to the point than speculations about the play's connexion with medieval passion plays. Nichols' theatrical method is very obviously contemporary and post-sixties. Christ's passion is evoked by the music bursts rather than by medieval theatre reference. The use of music derives as much from Nichols' experience as a television dramatist in the sixties as from earlier theatre practice. Perhaps more deeply, the music is there because Nichols grew up with his father's music always playing; indeed, his father died while listening to music, a significant point made in *Forget-Me-Not Lane*. No wonder his symbol for the moment of recognition of one's own mortality should be musical.

The plot of *Passion Play* works out a fundamental dramatic irony. Eleanor advises her friend, Agnes, to forgive Kate for supplanting her as Albert's wife. Agnes, however, is full of bitterness and cannot forget and forgive, 'Haven't you even grasped that Albert was my life? We not only had four children, we made his career' (12). But a profound dramatic irony begins at this point, for Nichols has the scene played simultaneously against the scene of James paying the bill for lunching with Kate, a lunch that is the start of his adulterous liaison with her. Will Eleanor be able to forgive and forget in her turn? By means of the Chekhovian theatrical device of interlacing dialogue from two different scenes played in different locations represented by different stage areas Nichols achieves sharp dramatic irony in the situation of the two deceived wives. Agnes swears revenge on Kate. What she achieves, again ironically, is no such revenge; instead, she shatters Eleanor's illusions and marriage by finding the evidence to prove James's adultery with Kate.

It is directly after the simultaneous scenes establishing the chain of deception and irony that Nichols splits James into the surface

James, happily married husband, and Jim, the lustful part of him, deceptive, libidinous, and adulterous. This theatrical device pushes the play further from realism in its technique. Similarly, after Agnes has unmasked James's affair with Kate, not without some satisfaction at shattering Eleanor's complacency, Eleanor, poised and civilised, acquires Nell, the part of her that knows now just what betrayal feels like. In this way Nichols dramatises the added complexity that people acquire by living through crises of this sort. With James/Jim and Eleanor/Nell responding to everything that subsequently happens, many ironies and comic moments arise from the contrasts between surface politeness and brute feeling. Eleanor's fall from innocence and the appearance of Nell are powerful moments in themselves, but Nichols adds a further emotional dimension by allusions to the *St Matthew Passion* and Mozart *Requiem* in Kate's love letter Agnes has stolen, and by the burst of the *'dissonant fanfare from the Choral Symphony'* (42) when Eleanor, blinded with emotion, bumps into the waitress as she leaves her meeting with Agnes. Nichols explores another aspect of musicality in the final scene of Act I: the dialogue itself is used musically, Nichols perhaps having learned something in this respect from Shaw. The directions read: *'The rest of the Act works like this – a fugue of voices, the written speeches predominating and improvised dialogue continuing behind'* (53). The post-Shavian element is, of course, the use of improvisation. And at this point Nichols casts the audience as reader-recipients of letters. James, Kate, and Eleanor use direct address to reveal to the audience the letters they are writing to one another about the love triangle, while Nell and Jim add their rudely honest comments.

Act II complicates, develops, and resolves the situation established in Act I, using the powerful theatrical conventions now in place. Nichols provides *en passant* the justification for squaring the hypotenuse of his love triangle with great works of Christian religious music. James points out that 'We still live in the shadow of His death. And His birth, for that matter. A virgin birth' (57). Our carnality as human beings is ironically at odds with the sexual attitudes of Christianity, in which many of us no longer believe, and its central myth of the non-carnal conception and birth of Christ. James desires a pagan sexuality not bound by monogamy. Act II plays with the ideas of group sex that became fashionable between the sixties and the advent of AIDS. But Eleanor asserts that 'It's hard enough to find one person you fancy, leave alone two' (59). James, like Frank in *Forget-Me-Not Lane*, sees that his wife will settle only for monogamy.

Eleanor's nightmare, achieved by theatrical means (pictures of sexual acrobatics, ironic musical accompaniment of the Chorus 'He trusted in God' from *The Messiah*, religious pictures used as icons of lechery, and lascivious actions by James) is an intensely vivid enactment of what the Christian sensibility finds so frightening and destructive about pagan sexuality free of monogamy. James's nightmare is not staged in this melodramatic way. His nightmare is the waking life he leads trapped by his wife's possessiveness. In fact, the conflict turns out not to be based so much on Christian and pagan values but on James's desire to keep his settled marriage and have a fling on the side. He wants a mini-seraglio. Eleanor resists this, she tells him, 'Because I won't be second best' (90). It is a matter of personal pride. Whereas Frank leaves home to pursue his sexual freedom in *Forget-Me-Not Lane*, in *Passion Play* it is Eleanor or Nell (either can leave at the end) because James and Kate have kept up their affair while pretending it is over. James's solution was to fall back on deception in order to have his fling. The dream girl Kate appears at the end wearing only high heels and fur coat. The play ends with James kneeling and kissing her naked body. But there is no poignancy. James has achieved his sexual liberation through adultery. The tableau is not, as with *Forget-Me-Not Lane*, the focus of our sympathy. Our compassion is for the lonely and deceived wife.

In real life, however, Nichols, unlike his heroes, had not broken up his marriage. The fourth family play considered here, *A Piece of My Mind* (1987), envisages the death of the playwright hero, his wife now a widow free to pursue the sexual promiscuity she had known before their marriage. The abiding theme of regret and recrimination recurs, complicated by the subject of a writer's block and the stock-taking of a career in the theatre.

After announcing his disenchantment with commercial theatre and attempting to turn himself into a novelist, Nichols discovered he was no novelist, and wrote himself back on stage in a play which combines the old sexual anxiety with artistic anxiety and corrosive satire of a writer's envy for others with more fame and more critical success. It is a *tour de force* of theatricality deserving a detailed essay in itself. Here I can merely sketch Nichols' virtuoso performance.

Intimations of mortality have now become the Swiftian satirical vision of the imagined death of the author. The satirical mood of the play extends to the casting of the audience as sheep bleating around the old country house of the deceased Ted Forrest. This main character is accompanied by two actors and two actresses who slip in and out of all the other roles. The device is adroitly theatrical and, as the play metatheatrically states, saves the management wages. The four play seventeen roles between them.

The situation is that Forrest's main rival, the younger and more brilliant generation of playwrights (Stoppard, for example), represented by Miles Whittier, will write a play in Forrest's style to give the widow more royalties, at the same time serving her sexual needs. Whittier's play starts with a scene between Ted Forrest and his wife Dinah. The play within the play convention has a new twist, in that the play within is being written as it is played, and Forrest/Nichols is resurrected theatrically by the imagined rival writer within the play *A Piece of My Mind* by Peter Nichols. The theatricality is at its most ingenious. The abiding Nichols theme of sexual jealousy or envy is now seen as growing from a deeper root that sprouts twin shoots, the second being artistic envy. Dinah recognises this when she tells Ted 'It's killing you like unrequited lust'.[13] In this scene Nichols makes things more complicated than anything in Stoppard's *Travesties*. Whittier's play about Ted now reveals that Ted had been trying to write a scene in which he had died and Whittier and Dinah were embracing over his coffin. The opening situation of the main play is the 'real life' of Whittier. Now we see he has used this autobiographical material in the Forrest pastiche he is writing! As the play continues, Ted Forrest emerges as the thread on which all else hangs, theatrical image of the writer's inner world, his obsessions with life and art. But because the character of Ted is being written by the rival Whittier, Whittier's envy comes out in the jaundiced view Ted takes of his own earlier work. The jealousy of each for the other allows Nichols as author of *A Piece of My Mind* to present his overall view of the cut-throat business of the theatre. The play therefore abounds in metatheatrical moments and direct address to the pastoral audience. All Nichols' regrets and recriminations about family, sexuality, career, and the conditions of the West End theatre are summed up in a grand *reprise* of his technical mastery. The fourth wall is the window through which the writer views the world, his study wherever it happens to be, and his eye, examining life and casting the audience to which he presents his vision of life. Whittier's pastiche play ends with a gunshot offstage, perhaps the death of the playwright, as in Chekhov's *The Seagull*. But then the play continues to a different ending – Forrest in his study writing again, the theatrical vision he is writing enacted before us silently: mime, theatre in its ancient form, and the mime is of popular song and dance. It is 'showbiz' and we, the audience, hear only ourselves, the bleating of sheep, and realise that theatre itself is the target.

In the tetralogy that emerges from this discussion of his work, Nichols offers no profound philosophy or discussion of his themes. He remains stubbornly theatrical, finding ways to stage the primal scenes of the family, of *l'homme moyen sensuel* and of *l'artiste moyen sensuel*.

Notes

1. For a complete list of Nichols' plays to 1988, see *Contemporary Dramatists*, ed. D.L. Kirkpatrick (London: St James Press, 1988). Since 1988 Nichols has published *Plays: One* (1991). This is a revised edition of his 1987 *Plays: One*, having only two plays in common with the earlier edition: *Forget-Me-Not Lane* and *Hearts and Flowers*.
2. 'Peter Nichols in Conversation with Andrew Parkin' (unpublished transcript of conversation recorded in Summer 1986) p. 6.
3. Peter Nichols, *Plays: One* (London: Methuen, 1987) p. xi.
4. Ibid., xiii.
5. Max Frisch, 'On the Nature of Theatre', trans. C.R. Mueller, in *Tulane Drama Review*, 6, 3 (1962) 3.
6. Stanley Kauffmann, *Persons of the Drama* (New York: Harper & Row, 1976) p. 243.
7. John Russell Taylor, *The Second Wave: British Dramatists for the Seventies* (London: Methuen, 1971) p. 35.
8. *A Day in the Death of Joe Egg* (London: Faber & Faber, 1967) p. 10. All quotations are from this edition; hereafter, page numbers will be given in the text.
9. 'Peter Nichols in Conversation', p. 10.
10. *Forget-Me-Not Lane*, in *Plays: One*, p. 11. All quotations are from this edition; hereafter, page numbers will be given in the text.
11. See *Plays: One*, p. 55.
12. *Passion Play* (1981; London: Methuen [3rd rev. ed.], 1985) p. [1]. All quotations from the play are from this edition; hereafter, page numbers will be given in the text.
13. *A Piece of My Mind* (London: Methuen, 1987) p. 5.

6

Translations of History:
Story-telling in Brian
Friel's Theatre
Katharine Worth

Translations, one of Brian Friel's most admired plays, has a title that could aptly be applied to his oeuvre as a whole.[1] His characters are deeply engaged in attempts to 'translate' the confused, complicated experiences of their lives into stories with shape and meaning; always in relation to the wider history which helps to form them (and into which they feed). It is an Irish history and the stories are told against a remarkably consistent Irish landscape which Friel has created for the stage, with the imagined Donegal town of Ballybeg as its magnetic centre, but the force and interest of his plays extends far beyond a specific history or the concern with cultural identity of a particular audience in a particular place.

What kind of truth their translations achieve, what sort of future history they might germinate: these are questions that agitate Friel's obsessive story-tellers and their listeners. Gar O'Donnell in *Philadelphia Here I Come* (1964), who splits into two to be his own narrator and listener, uses the word 'translate' in this way. On the eve of emigrating, he bitterly reflects that Ballybeg might have been different if the 'arid' Canon had made some attempt to 'translate all this loneliness, this groping, this dreadful bloody buffoonery into Christian terms that will make life bearable for us all'.[2] At the other end of the *oeuvre*, in *Making History* (1989), a clerical historian, Peter Lombard, is shown actually at work on such a 'translation'. He believes that he is serving the future of Gaelic Ireland by turning into a consistently heroic, nationalist fable the life of the rebel Earl, Hugh O'Neill, which was in actuality (as the audience saw in Act One) interestingly inconsistent. The exiled O'Neill, ending his days in Rome as a pauper client of the Pope, watches aghast as the great book on the lectern which dominates the stage in Act Two fills up with a story hardly recognisable as his own. Inconvenient details such as his English upbringing at the court of Queen Elizabeth and his linguistic flexibility (amusingly conveyed in Field Day's production by Stephen Rea's switches to Belfast intonations) are relegated to near oblivion. The historian prefers not to see the cultural possibilities in the tricky but loving and creative relationship between Irish O'Neill and his downright English wife, with her Staffordshire accent. 'Mabel will have her place' is Lombard's bland, unyielding response to O'Neill's plea to make her as 'central' in the history as she was in his life.

Peter Lombard tells someone else's story, Gar O'Donnell his own, acting it out in little episodes which rerun the past under the sardonic eye of Private Gar (who shares in the act of narration with the more conformist and reserved Public Gar). Friel rings a remarkable variety of changes on these basic patterns. In *Dancing at Lughnasa* (1990) the story-teller is both outside and inside the story he narrates. As the adult Michael, he tells the story of his mother, her four sisters and his Uncle Jack from a sad distance, but he is located within it too, as his seven-year-old self, visible only to those on stage, not to the audience. It is the narrator's business to give the child life, which he does in abundance, speaking his lines for him and arranging the narrative so that the boy is seen to be a focal point of the sisters' cramped existence. In *Faith Healer* (1979) the story is everything. Outside becomes inside – or vice versa – as the audience receives the story of an equivocal, awesome power in the three versions offered by the monologues of Frank Hardy, his wife/mistress, Grace, and his manager, Teddy. Their stories touch and take cognisance of one another; the story-tellers, never. Another narrator, the 'Sir' of *Living Quarters* (1977), claims to be nothing but a recording force brought into being by the desperate need of the actors in the story to tell it over and over again, to record 'what was said, what was not said, what was done, what was not done, what might have been said, what might have been done' (*SP* 177).

Story-telling, then, is the mode in which Friel's characters have their being. Stories continually thrust their way into the dialogue; form, dissolve, re-form, hover on the edge of myth, compete with one another, struggle for fixity, are ironically undermined or endorsed, often sadly. The phenomenon is not exactly new in Irish theatre. Persuasive story-tellers have dominated it, from Boucicault's shaughrauns and Synge's playboys, with their 'gallous' stories, to Beckett's blind Hamm, busy, as Clov says, with the story 'you've been telling yourself all your . . . days'.[3] Tom Murphy's bedridden old woman in *Bailegangaire*, unable to finish her story because it is too painfully rooted in her life, is a female virtuoso in this same tradition. But Friel's achievement is a kind all his own. It illustrates what Lady Gregory called 'our incorrigible Irish genius for myth-making'; but it is myth-making conducted within a frame which forces questioning and analysis. The story-tellers have become more highly conscious than they used to be, more taken up with 'what might have been done'. They are as much on trial as Lombard is in *Making History*.

Friel's story-tellers follow in the footsteps of an author who began his career as a writer of short stories. He gave up this form of writing, he said, at the point where he recognised how difficult it was;[4] an explanation that hardly explains (some have thought his short stories more accomplished than his early plays). What did the theatre offer the born story-teller to tempt him from a craft that came so naturally? Most obviously, and importantly, a live audience; heterogeneous, unpredictable, a crowd of individuals, feeling themselves a community while the play lasts. The need for each other of story-tellers and audience is at the core of Friel's drama.

The focus in this essay is on the astonishing diversity of Friel's methods for exploring that relationship. From one play to another he finds new ways to bring us to the same place; a region of huge importance to him (and, it is implied, to us) where life and stories, story-tellers and audiences are made to scrutinise their strange, often dangerous intimacy. It is a place where contradictions are brought into the light, alternatives juxtaposed, stories tested for their truth to life. What is history but telling stories, says Lombard. The sense of history as a giant story hanging over all of us is one of Friel's most remarkable and distinctive effects.

In aid of achieving that effect he manipulates the stage illusion so as to bring the audience in the auditorium closer to the story-tellers. Sir, in *Living Quarters*, sits downstage on a stool and links audience and actors by addressing both directly. A variation in *Dancing at Lughnasa* and *Faith Healer* has the story-tellers address the audience and no one else in the play. Michael stands downstage 'in a pool of light' and Frank Hardy ends his first monologue by coming downstage *'walking very slowly, until he is as close as he can be to the audience'* (*SP* 340). It is an unnerving confrontation. He looks at us *'for about three seconds'*, but is he really seeing those other audiences, whose coming to him, 'a mountebank', was 'a measure of their despair'? (*SP* 341, 336). Sometimes they seemed to him, so he tells us, only the outpost of an anonymous host, *'legati*, chosen because of their audacity.' Behind us too, then, may there be those others, 'poised, mute, waiting in the half-light'? (*SP* 337). A disturbing thought, the kind Friel likes to provoke.

Another favourite technique, the acting out of an event alongside the narrative about it, is part of a provocative system of oppositions in Friel's theatre which can be seen as reflecting creative contradictions in the playwright himself. One such is a tension between private and public experience. Friel is on the face of it the most public-minded of playwrights. He commonly takes his subjects from history and focuses on big public events: the Land Survey of 1833 in *Translations* (1980), the Flight of the Earls in *Making History*, the banned Civil Rights march in Derry in *The Freedom of the City* (1973). Yet he has said that a playwright should be concerned with 'the dark and private places of the soul' and with those traumatic experiences which are 'sly and dark and devious and generally slip into the unconscious through an unlocked window'.[5] How to translate these elusive experiences into true histories, open to others, is a question that runs through the plays.

Closely connected with this is a contradiction that has puzzled some critics, between the tragic thrust in his plays and the optimism implied in his position as the founder, with Stephen Rea, of the Field Day Theatre Company, an organisation dedicated to the possibility of hopeful change. By taking new plays to remote parts of Northern Ireland and the Republic, where live theatre is seldom seen, they hope to disseminate ideas, and, in Stephen Rea's phrase, help people to 'choose the history that is enabling to you rather than one that holds you back'.[6]

Tragedy certainly threatens on Friel's stage. Often stories are told under the shadow of approaching death, as in *Volunteers* (1975) and – most traumatically – *The Freedom of the City* (1975) where the audience see the corpses of the three civil rights marchers laid out, front stage, pathetic objects to be categorised and disposed of, before they come alive to re-enact their story. Painful or violent events loom large and there is a strong sense of doom, making it very understandable that Ulf Dantanus should consider Friel's a 'tragic sensibility'.[7] Mutability is a constant theme. Friel's delicate adaptation of *Three Sisters* (and Turgenev's *Fathers and Sons*), along with his own versions of the 'temps perdu' theme in plays like *Aristocrats* (1979), have caused him to be seen as the Irish Chekhovian *par excellence*.

Yet it was Friel who set Field Day on its course. Can these contradictions be resolved? The story-telling techniques provide an answer. They are ingeniously designed to make the audience scrutinise the tragic stories they are offered, whether presented as history, myth or 'reportage'. To induce a fuller understanding is the overriding aim.

Rethinking the story, remaking the history; these revisionist emphases draw Friel's audience along a somewhat Brechtian line but not by an overtly Brechtian method. Friel's way is more oblique: doubts and questions are subtly insinuated into the gaps between one story or another or between story and live event. Unusually, in *The Loves of Cass McGuire* (1966), the eponymous heroine attempts to involve the audience more directly in her story, looking out to the auditorium and invoking her 'folks'. She does not draw them into argument, however, or even sustain the relationship; in the end she can no longer see them, and is unsure even of her memory: 'I could ov sworn there were folks out there'.

The truth of the stories is a key issue, though not a criterion accepted by all the story-tellers. For Lombard it is not 'a primary ingredient': the historian's task, he says, is to select from many accounts 'the best possible narrative'.[8] But Friel usually deploys the theatrical illusion so as to convince us that there is a truth, however hidden; a 'real' life against which the narratives must be measured. It is this life we feel in the wonderful moments when the characters move into another, freer dimension of the imagination and we go with them; as in the transcendent Irish/English love scenes in *Translations*. And there are the very different moments when a repressed or obscure truth forces its way out through stories about some other.

The 'other' in *Volunteers* is one of Friel's most haunting and poignant stage images; the Viking skeleton, with a mysterious hole in its skull, unearthed in the archaeological excavation. Before the IRA prisoners return to prison (and a violent death at the hands of their fellows, 'punishment' for volunteering for the dig), they find a way to express themselves by inventing stories about the unknown Leif. 'You tell us his story', Keeney demands, and Pyne responds with a revealing fiction, imagining Leif returning to Ireland to meet a grim fate. 'Why did he come back?' 'Sure he had to come back with his mate, hadn'd he'. He becomes confused, agitated: we see why Keeney warned him, 'Once upon a time – keep up the protection of the myth'.[9] But the true stories push through the fiction. When Butt, the prisoner with the 'Celtic head' claims, 'I know his story', Keeney joins him, with passion and bitterness, in clothing the ancient bones with a history only too painfully their own. Was Leif a victim of murder or a ritual sacrifice? 'Maybe the poor hoor considered it an honour to die', says Keeney, 'maybe he volunteered'.[10] A dark community asserts itself, across the centuries.

A closer look at a few plays may show how Friel varies his technique for alerting the audience to the complex relationships that can exist between life and the stories made about it. Right at the start, in *Philadelphia Here I Come*, he laid out a technique on which many changes were to be rung. A frame of commentary by the two Gars is placed round the re-enacted memories and the interwoven scenes of present time, providing the audience with an unusually full means of checking Gar's narrative of feeling. His version of events is sometimes endorsed from outside. Even sensible Madge is irritated by S.B. O'Donnell's routines (which so infuriate his son), notably his graceless habit of taking his false teeth out every night, to read the paper in comfort: 'If you had any decency in you at all, you would keep them plates in while there's a lady in your presence!' (*SP* 68). Gar's resentment of old Screwballs' predictability seems less of an adolescent exaggeration when shared in this way.

Other 'real' scenes, on the other hand, show up limitations in his narrative. He tests his emotional relationship with his father by inviting him to share a childhood memory – of a happy occasion fishing together. The audience knows he has built up this memory into an intense, probably exclusive experience. We have heard him 'telling' it to himself in classic style (and to the music of Mendelssohn): 'once upon a time a boy and his father sat in a blue boat on a lake . . . ' The beauty of the moment, he says, 'has haunted the boy ever since' (*SP* 89). Poor old S.B. cannot rise to these heights. His effort to enter in is touching: there was a brown boat, he thinks, or 'a wee flat-bottom – but it was green – or was it white?' But it falls too far short of the fairy story for Gar to sympathise. 'So now you know', Private Gar tells his other half bitterly: 'It never happened' (*SP* 95). A chance of communion has been lost; the narrative impaired. The irony deepens when S.B., alone with Madge, recalls his own fond memory of his son in his 'wee sailor suit', only to have it shot down: 'He never had a sailor suit' (*SP* 96). Is everything illusion, can the audience resist the play's pervasive melancholy? Friel provides encouragement to do just this in the knockabout turns of Private and Public which bring a robust self-criticism and sense of fun into the narrative. These lively 'shows' and self-mocking Walter Mitty fantasies ('The orchestra is conducted by Gareth O'Donnell and the soloist is the Ballybeg half-back, Gareth O'Donnell' [*SP* 36]) are played out for a stage audience of one. But they reflect Gar's need to find an audience – to see himself from without as well as within – which can be felt as a kind of transforming yeast at work in his dangerously nostalgic story of himself.

The huge, deadly gap between an event and the story made about it is the painful theme of *The Freedom of the City*. Even as the audience observes the innocent entry of Lily and the rest into the Guildhall ('Whose house is this?' says Lily [*SP* 113]), they are bombarded with noisy stories on loud hailer, field telephone, television screen. British Army Brigadier, priest, balladeer, spread their versions of the event, all far distant from the quiet reality in front of us: the three victims amazedly exploring the Mayor's parlour, confiding their humble life stories in each other and risking daring pleasures like tasting the Mayor's port wine. The scenic arrangement keeps us continually aware of how totally the truth is sealed off from the overbearing story-tellers. Yet we have to listen to their 'unconfirmed reports' ('about fifty armed gunmen have taken possession of the Guildhall') or hear overblown tributes at the funeral, as the myth of the 'terrorists' becomes the myth of the willing 'martyrs' (*SP* 117).

It is a tense, uneasy situation, a prison for the audience almost as the Guildhall is for the victims. Every little playful or casual comment from the three in the room highlights the awful wrongness of the stories. The irony is painful, heavy, unchanging. Friel himself became uneasy about the 'reportage' aspects of the play. Looking back later, he reflected that he had written too close to the event: 'the experience of Bloody Sunday wasn't adequately distilled in me'.[11]

Perhaps he felt, as some critics have done, that the inner story suffers from the deliberate imbalance which forces us to see everything from a public angle. It is probably only Lily who achieves full individuality. She creates an island of deeper realism around her with her salty jokes, the lively snapshots she offers of life with her 'Chairman' and their eleven children and her final revelation that the child 'not as forward as the others' is in fact 'a mongol': 'And it's for him I go on all the civil rights marches' (*SP* 155). Though perhaps a rather too neat illustration of Skinner's claim that the marches show 'the poor – the majority – stirring in our sleep' (Friel saw it as a 'play about poverty'), the moment is poignant (*SP* 154). But the hidden places of the mind are not really on show here.

Stories of private life have more tenacity in two plays about a family reunion, *Living Quarters* and *Aristocrats*. Story-telling is a communal process here, conducted within the family, though as always, the larger stories of history press upon it. From different points in the history of Ballybeg, the Butlers and O'Donnells review their past, desperately searching out its significance. The characters in *Living Quarters* are oppressed by a predetermined scenario (a fatalistic impression pointed up by the play's reference to a bleak Greek tragedy in its sub-title, 'After Hippolytus'). At the other extreme, in *Aristocrats*, the O'Donnells suffer from the sense of no longer having a story they can call their own. The Big House of the scattered Catholic family has become a 'decaying hall' where the once powerful father has been reduced to a voice heard at intervals through the 'baby-alarm', the bedridden man's only remaining means of direct communication with the outside world.

Friel adapts his narrative techniques subtly to these different situations. The narrative frame round the action in *Living Quarters* imprisons it. The characters may have invented 'Sir' and the 'ledger' which contains their account of 'what happened' but they seemingly have no choice but to follow his direction. The story must run its course to the dreaded moment when Frank Butler learns that his young second wife has betrayed him with his son, and shoots himself.

In Act One there are attempts to change the way the story is told. Helen questions the surface pleasantness of one early scene ('It's distorted – inaccurate' [*SP* 188]): Father Tom tries to resist the ineffectual role as priest and family friend imposed on him by the ledger, the 'corrupt ledger', he calls it. But Sir upholds its authority: 'Believe me, it's exactly right'. How can the role of 'final adjudicator' they have conferred on him be reconciled with the attempts to circumvent him? 'Curious, isn't it?' (*SP* 178), he says.

Curious but not absurd. Sir himself provides a rational motive; the hope of finding 'the key to an understanding of *all* that happened' (*SP* 177). Understanding involves revision and each intervention, even when overruled, keeps the feasibility of revision in mind. So does the extraordinary change of mood after the suicide. The actors relax, light cigarettes, are soothed by their director: 'That wasn't too bad, was it?' (*SP* 242). The re-enactment has brought relief, perhaps by penetrating further into the psychic depths, distributing the moral responsibility. A whole world of painfully knotted feeling is revealed when Frank Butler reacts to Anna's confession by talking not of her but of his first wife; dwelling with an agony seeming still fresh, on the pain she suffered in her long illness.

Finally, we learn from the closing sequence between Sir and Anna that the ledger, if not 'corrupt', is incomplete: it has blank pages, still to be filled in. There is room for change, perhaps the more hopeful kind made possible by deeper understanding. The scene *'must not be played in a sad nostalgic mood'*, says Friel (*SP* 242); a telling and characteristic comment.

In *Aristocrats* the O'Donnells have no Sir to push their memories and family anecdotes in a purposeful direction. Chekhov's displaced aristocrats seem very close in this play (Friel's version of *Three Sisters* was seen on stage in 1981). The unsuitable wedding for which they are gathered is one of the many events they cannot assimilate into a family history such as they would like, one with coherence and dignity.

Friel highlights the failure by including in the *dramatis personae* an American researcher who hopes to find rich material – 'Family lore, family reminiscences' (*SP* 265) – in this particular specimen of the Irish Catholic ruling class (O'Donnell was a District Justice). His surname, Hoffnung, means 'hope'; an ironic touch, for his note-taking among the O'Donnells yields nothing he can generalise as part of a meaningful history. The gentle, eccentric only son of the house, Casimir, excites him with tales of John McCormack and a host of celebrities, visiting at Ballybeg House ('precisely the material . . . ' [*SP* 261]). They are 'false', as the audience must guess (well before the researcher does) from the amusing moments at the start when Casimir invests each commonplace object in the room with a grand story; the George Moore candlestick, the Yeats cushion. 'Haven't I told you that story?' (*SP* 306), he says when Tom picks up a stray remark about Grandfather O'Donnell hearing Chopin play. The dates are all wrong, as usual. Other versions of the family history, such as the bitterly critical 'gothic novel' offered by Eamon who married into the big house from the peasantry, prove equally imperfect. Tom leaves the play, as a reviewer observed of a London revival in 1988, 'without having obtained one verifiable fact beyond the desperate, absurd scenes he observes with his own eyes'.[12]

It is in these scenes, however, that the true history lies, if only they could be read properly. We see this clearly from time to time, when, for instance, Casimir reacts like a terrified boy to his father's disembodied voice, eerily restored to stentorian vigour, booming commands through the baby-alarm. This is what lies behind his tall tales: like his sister's obsessive playing of Chopin on the off-stage piano, it is a desperate attempt to construct an alternative history to live in. The play ends, after an all-changing event, the father's death, with a sense of utter relaxation: the characters sing lazily, the afternoon, 'relaxed, relaxing', seems as if it 'may go on indefinitely'. It is one of Friel's most open endings; the O'Donnell story is changing again, perhaps into a last phase of enervation – or, as Alice says 'Perhaps maybe a new start' (*SP* 324).

The truth of the story becomes a matter for complex imagining in one of Friel's greatest plays, *Faith Healer*. The audience are drawn into a spell-binding narrative from the moment the voice of the faith healer is heard, coming out of the dark, mesmerically chanting the Celtic place names that chart his imagination (Aberarder, Aberayron, Llangranog, Llangurig . . .). When the lights go up, what we see is the quintessential story-teller, alone on stage, with his props and three rows of empty chairs to stand in for his audience. By the power of the narrative, the empty chairs will fill up with those invisible audiences: the ten afflicted souls at 'Llanb[l]ethian in Glamorganshire in Wales', all cured in one night, or the 'wedding guests', sitting in the convivial circle which turns into a killing ground.

All the contradictions and oppositions of Friel's theatre are confronted and transcended in this play. It is at once most private and most public. We never see the three narrators except as performers, addressing us from a stage that bears dynamic traces of past performances: the poster announcing 'The Fantastic Frank Hardy', the theme tune, 'The Way You Look Tonight' coming, naturalistically and eerily, out of the 'abused' record we hear so much about in the stories (*SP* 354).

Yet this most open, public experience is our way in to the furthest reaches of three individual minds, those 'sly and dark and devious' places which Friel sees as the theatre's proper subject.[13] Deviousness is the keynote here. We cannot rationalise what happens when the crooked finger is straightened in the Ballybeg pub, nor gain full entry to the slippery mental processes of the man who straightens it. What is the nature of the 'unique and awesome gift' (*SP* 333) that torments him with its fugitiveness? It is one of the unanswerable questions he is wrestling with at the start of the play – and is left open, as it has to be, at the end.

Our role as audience is to enter the experience by way of a narrative which reflects it exactly. The four-part story is full of contradictions and omissions. As Grace replaces Frank on stage and Teddy, Grace, we begin to notice discrepancies, wait for the next account to throw light, as in a detective story. Some points are fixed. A similar formulaic wording is used in all the narratives to describe sites of trauma. Kinlochbervie, where Grace's stillborn baby was buried, is, for each speaker, 'about as far north as you can go in Scotland, and looking across to the Isle of Lewis in the Outer Hebrides' (*SP* 362). Elsewhere the stories diverge disconcertingly. Frank makes no reference to the stillborn child, seems indeed to obliterate it in his final monologue: 'I would have liked to have had a child. But she was barren' (*SP* 372).

Is this an example of the 'twisted' mind which the others ascribe to him, along with his 'magnificence'? Or does it express a profounder knowledge? Do we take Teddy's point of view: 'But for Christ's sake to walk away deliberately when your wife's going to have your baby in the middle of bloody nowhere . . . that's some kind of bloody-mindedness, isn't it?' (*SP* 363). If so, we have to re-think, along with him, when he speculates that perhaps Frank was present in his own way, that he knew Grace's suffering, 'down to the last detail'. Gradually we understand that each presents the story as he/she must. Teddy, with his passion for Grace, cannot but see himself at the centre of the consoling rituals following the stillbirth. While in her story it must be Frank who 'made a wooden cross to mark the grave and painted it white and wrote across it *Infant Child of Francis and Grace Hardy*' (*SP* 344). She only feels herself alive in the story he creates for her; when he dies, her story must end too.

The audience are engaged in the same building work as the story-tellers. We piece together the separate narratives, shape them into a meaningful whole, struggle to get at the truth by attending to the fine points, 'the last detail'. Our reward is to 'see' – with the inner eye which allows the faith healer to look into the minds of others (he cures Teddy of his tormenting passion in a look). Finally, as he goes to meet McGarvey, knowing there will be no cure and the 'bloody savages' will destroy him, he is able to assimilate even his own death into his story; a remarkable form of resurrection.

The audience may well feel by then that they have performed an act of faith which is somehow, mysteriously, connected with healing. We have not come to the theatre to be confirmed in our despair, like the audiences Frank imagines, the legati of the hopeless. In its strange, dark way, *Faith Healer* carries the Field Day message: 'an inner drama of possibility', in Seamus Heaney's phrase, has been opened up.[14]

Friel's founding of Field Day in 1980 followed naturally on his vision of the itinerant showman, taking his 'gift' to remote audiences in the 'dying Welsh villages' (*SP* 332) and mythical Ballybeg. In the first play written for Field Day, *Translations* (performed, with great irony, in the Derry Guildhall), a literal translation rather than a story is central, but a crucial issue is the effect of the translations on the stories, the mental landscape. As Owen and Yolland chart the country round Baile Beag (so soon to become Ballybeg), ironically it is the Irishman who regrets the changes least. If a more descriptive name like 'Crossroads' were substituted for the cryptic Tobair Vree, he says, what would be lost but a 'trivial little story' about disfigured Brian and his well, which in any case no one in the parish remembers. 'Except you' (*SP* 420), Yolland replies. He chooses to retain the old name in this instance, a gesture of regret that 'something is being eroded' (*SP* 420) (though he is as committed to the change as the insensitive Captain Lancey).

Other, more powerful stories are told in the hedge-school. Jimmy Jack, who speaks Greek and Latin but no English, starts the play off with an exuberant extract from the *Odyssey* and the hedge-school master closes it with a loaded, melancholy one from the *Aeneid*. The goddess cannot prevent the fate in store for her cherished city: 'a race was springing from Trojan blood to overthrow some day these Tyrian towers' (*SP* 446–7). Hugh stumbles in his reading – 'What the hell's wrong with me? Sure I know it backwards' (*SP* 447) – and repeats the lines; an effective way of highlighting the mood of elegiac sadness.

Is this the dominant mood of the play? Some have thought so and that Friel over-idealises the hedge-school culture by linking its stories with those of classical antiquity, creating the illusion of heroic continuity which charms Yolland: 'Jimmy Jack and your father swapping stories about Apollo and Cuchulainn and Paris and Ferdia – as if they lived down the road' (*SP* 416). Friel said the play was offered 'pieties' not intended by him.[15] Is he 'refurbishing an old myth', as Edna Longley suggests (one that looks backward too much)?[16]

The answer must be sought, as so often in Friel's theatre, in the space between narrative and live event. In Donald McWhinnie's production the love scene in Act Two when Maire and Yolland run in, fresh from the dance, and exchange vows in words neither understands, created an extraordinary sense of freedom, stronger by far than the sense of displacement which is also there.[17] We experienced a strange illusion, recognised 'Irish' when English was spoken, felt free of both languages. In the future the lovers dream of, might not such freedom spread, open up for others, as for them, an 'inner drama of possibility'? That question, prompted by the scene, retains its force, despite Yolland's disappearance, linked to the sinister Donnelly twins and other black notes. Maire will learn English – 'I must learn it I need to learn it' (*SP* 446) – and Hugh will teach her, a decision that marks a difficult but not despairing acceptance of change. The elegiac strain at the close is subtly modified by these grace notes. They lure the audience in to an expansive view, offering the 'perceptions of new adjustments and new arrangements' which Friel sees as the purpose of art.[18]

In *Making History* a more schematic arrangement of 'life' and story removes Mabel and her sister at half time; a sad loss, theatrically. The audiences who saw the play on its Field Day tour in Northern Ireland and the Republic, however, certainly took the point which the relative thinnness of the second act reinforced: that Lombard's history diminished O'Neill's life – and impoverished posterity – by editing out the robust and promising 'marriage outside the tribe'. In one interview recorded by Radio Telefeis Eirann for the television programme, *Making History* (BBC Television, 16 December 1988), a young member of the audience at Armagh announced that his view of history had been 'totally' changed: it was not the story taught at school, the heroes had become human. Perhaps, suggested a commentator, the symbolism of the happy marriage between O'Neill and Mabel, with her English yeoman virtues, would prompt beneficent new thought about what the Protestant community in the North could bring to Ireland. The sombre history was effectively invested with a new, hopeful meaning.

The relationship of story-teller and story is different again, more subtle and delicate, in *Dancing at Lughnasa*. As the lights slowly come up on the characters frozen in the postures of life, Michael presents them to us from his youthful self's puzzled viewpoint. He recalls the sisters, 'those kind sensible women' turned to 'shrieking strangers' in their wild dance, sees the forlorn figure of Uncle Jack 'shuffling from room to room as if he were searching for something but couldn't remember what'. Anxiety is the dominant impression: things were changing too quickly, 'becoming what they ought not to be'.[19] Later, he recounts, with unsparing exactitude, the squalid end of Agnes and Rose.

Much of what we see on the stage endorses the sombre view. In the Abbey Theatre's production in London (National Theatre, 15 October 1990) Alec McOwen's Uncle Jack was all the more alarming for being so cosily matter-of-fact as he wandered in his limbo between cultures, having to be restrained by Aunt Kate from beating out an African rhythm for a dance ritual with sticks from the boy's kite: 'They aren't ours. They belong to the child' (*DL* 42). The sisters' 'dervish' dance to the Irish ceili music had the hint of parody – music too loud, movements somewhat caricatured – which Friel required (one reviewer thought it celebrated the unattainable 'with a smile of hardened irony').[20] Like the expression on Maggie's face, the dance could be seen as only 'a crude mask of happiness' (*DL* 21).

But running strongly against the currents of irony and anxiety was another, more powerful impression of immense inner resilience and vitality. A rare warmth of feeling spread through the theatre, a response to the humour and bravery of the sisters, their gift for enlarging their pinched lives with joyful excitement: a few Wild Woodbines could do it, or a child's kite. The dance to the old Irish music may have been only a shadow of a folk rite, but it came over as something thrilling and necessary. The audience rejoiced, with sporadic ripples of applause, when decorous Kate threw away restraint and joined the bacchanal, dancing by herself, *totally concentrated, totally private* (*DL* 22). We should all have liked to join in when Stephen Dillane's debonair Gerry took his Chris (and then, touchingly, Agnes) dancing a foxtrot round the garden to beguiling thirties tunes from the old radio. Foot-tapping began in the auditorium and currents of sympathy flowed toward the scapegrace. Against the brilliant scenic image of the glowing, golden cornfield which comes right down to the house, the rites of Lughnasa were properly celebrated.

It is the golden view that prevails. Despite the dark shadows cast by unnerving cultural change, adult Michael's closing memory of 'that time' is of the so alluring and so mesmeric music on which 'everybody seems to be floating'. It is a memory that 'owes nothing to fact' (*DL* 71), he says. Perhaps, rather, it transcends fact. It is an 'enabling' memory, in Stephen Rea's phrase; not one that will 'hold you back'. It seems an appropriate note on which to end a discussion of Friel's tragic and richly 'enabling' drama.

Notes

1. For a complete list of Friel's plays to 1988, see *Contemporary Dramatists*, ed. D.L. Kirkpatrick (London: St James Press, 1988). Since 1988, Friel has published *Making History* (1989) and *Dancing at Lughnasa* (1990).

2. *Philadelphia, Here I Come*, in Brian Friel, *Selected Plays* (London: Faber & Faber, 1984) p. 88. All quotations from *Selected Plays* are from this edition; hereafter, page numbers will be given in the text, preceded by *SP*.

3. *Endgame*, in Samuel Beckett, *The Complete Dramatic Works* (London: Faber & Faber, 1986) p. 121.

4. Brian Friel, interviewed by Fintan O'Toole, 'The Man from God Knows Where', *In Dublin*, 165 (28 October 1982) 21.

5. Brian Friel, 'Extracts from a Sporadic Diary', in *Ireland and the Arts*, ed. Tim Pat Coogan (London: Quartet Books, n.d.) p. 58.

6. Stephen Rea, interviewed by Michael Billington, BBC Radio 3, 8 April 1991.

7. Ulf Dantanus, *Brian Friel: a Study* (London/Boston: Faber & Faber, 1988).

8. Brian Friel, *Making History* (London: Faber & Faber, 1989) p. 8.

9. Brian Friel, *Volunteers* (Lougheven: Gallery Press, 1979) p. 62.

10. *Volunteers*, p. 28.

11. 'The Man from God Knows Where', p. 22.

12. Michael Ratcliffe, *Observer*, 5 June 1988.

13. 'Extracts from a Sporadic Diary', p. 58.

14. Seamus Heaney in television programme, *Making History* (BBC 2, 16 December 1988).

15. 'The Man from God Knows Where', p. 21.

16. Edna Longley, *Poetry in the Wars* (Newcastle: Bloodaxe Books, 1986) pp. 190–3.

17. Donald McWhinnie's production was first at the Hampstead Theatre (12 May 1981).

18. Brian Friel, 'Extracts from a Sporadic Diary', in *The Writers*, ed. Andrew Carpenter and Peter Fallon (Dublin: O'Brien Press, 1980) p. 43.

19. *Dancing at Lughnasa* (London: Faber & Faber, 1990) p. 2. All quotations are from this edition; hereafter, page numbers will be given in the text, preceded by *DL*.

20. John Peter, *Sunday Times*, 21 October 1990.

7

Tom Murphy: Acts of Faith in a Godless World

Richard Allen Cave

It is not easy to characterise Tom Murphy's style of drama in a few terse epithets. Murphy is a searcher, intellectually, aesthetically, morally, emotionally.[1] The searching has taken him quickly beyond the confines of traditional Irish drama in terms of form and subject. It is possible to trace a pedigree behind some of Murphy's earliest works: his history play, *Famine*, and his exposure of the patriarch and the mother-figure as monsters, and of the claustrophobic pettiness of small-town life in plays like *A Whistle in the Dark* and *A Crucial Week in the Life of a Grocer's Assistant* have their obvious precedents, though this does not rob Murphy's treatment of vitality and original insight.

But Murphy comes into his own when he actually makes the idea of a search the subject of a play and particularly when the search is for grounds on which to bring one or more of his characters to make an act of faith. This is not to imply that Murphy's is a religious drama in the conventional meaning of the phrase, nor that his plays are in any way doctrinaire.[2] Most of his characters feel themselves situated in a godless or godforsaken world; yet what is often profoundly moving in Murphy's plays is his conviction that even in a godless world humanity retains some religious instinct which compels them for good or ill to shape their own strange rituals of belief behind which one can still sense as it were a palimpsest of Western traditions of faith and practice.

To some degree this places Murphy outside the tenets and stage-craft of postmodernist theatre: he is not flamboyantly theatrical for its own sake; he may challenge but will not offend an audience in the manner of Handke and his disciples; he shapes plays towards 'meanings', though the approach to significance may be enigmatic, startling, indirect and purposefully illogical. His adherence is still to the conventions of stage realism, though his searching may push those conventions beyond their customary spheres of reference (he rarely lets an audience feel safe within the bounds of the comfortably predictable).[3] Murphy is a contemporary rather than a postmodern dramatist, conscious of a cultural inheritance which he treats with enlightened scepticism rather than with modish disdain; his is not a nihilistic art of total subversion. Though he is fascinated by the arts of performance, and in two of his finest plays actually makes the constituent arts of theatre the subject of his enquiry, the investigation of performance is preoccupied with more than technique and accomplishment: performance must for Murphy be to some purpose.

What makes Murphy something of an original in the context of modern European drama is his increasingly confident depiction of that purpose as metaphysical. His most recent work, *Too Late for Logic*, is in fact a ghost play, a dreaming-back through a mind's experience from the standpoint of an after-life by a character who commits suicide in the opening seconds of the play. The dramatic technique involves a series of fractured scenes, each conforming in style to the realist manner, but the overarching impetus to the action is the portrayal of how a mind seduced by philosophical abstractions steadily abstracts itself from the very impulse to live by shaping its uniquely personal hell. It is one of several plays by Murphy in which the death of the heart is shown as bringing inevitably in its wake a death of the spirit. (*Conversations on a Homecoming* is another).[4]

His finer and more courageous plays in the wider context of theatre in the seventies and eighties are those which explore the possibilities of spiritual regeneration. These are plays where the sense of a search is strongest, even to a compulsive degree, but where a fearless and determined quest is ultimately liberating. Technically in each case Murphy extends a meticulously observed realism into a surprising but credible poetic dimension.

Murphy's first success with this style of theatre was *The Sanctuary Lamp*, where the thematic intent of the piece is perhaps too immediately made apparent by the setting, which must suggest the dark vastness of a church interior out of which only three objects – the lamp of the title, a pulpit and a confessional – emerge with any distinctness. The three main characters are all metaphorically on the run from lives that have become wounded and desolate; none has religious faith, though each seeks sanctuary beneath the lamp. Their night of refuge is an unconscious vigil in which individually they review their past lives by telling stories about themselves. A mundane, routine existence was relieved for each of them, it transpires, only by the sense of possessing a special gift. Harry has formidable strength; Francisco can juggle; and Maudie confesses to a penchant for climbing, acrobatics and self-display. She is little more than a child; the men were one-time performers in a circus. All have had a capacity to go beyond themselves in feats of daring, yet all presently feel guilt-ridden, at odds with themselves, devoid of a proper dignity; their daring is now only a subject for talk.

Harry and Maudie's tales are hushed, confidential intimacies; Francisco's is assertive, commanding attention. Each, however, does find occasion to tell that tale to the others, and the action hovers between confessional and pulpit in more than a literal sense. Formerly they found ways of channelling their misery into their 'art' when they escaped briefly from the thinking being, which seemed to immobilise them, into the body where they found a more rewarding means of expression. The characters seem benighted, given up to death in life, an idea that takes on tangible form when Harry uses his strength to upend the confessional and lay it on its back with the intention that they sleep in its three compartments. As they climb into position, the image is of a medieval tomb where in canopied niches the deceased lie in resignation or repose. A change in the lighting-state suggests a passage of time: Maudie now sleeps; Francisco is sitting in his 'coffin', smoking; Harry, at first meditatively apart, replenishes the guttering candle in the lamp. The men talk quietly together, almost unconsciously renewing the easygoing friendship that we have several times been informed they once shared; gone now are the (at times) near-murderous animosities that have fuelled their relationship through the play on account of their rivalry over Harry's wife. Maudie stirs awake to announce her decision to return on the morrow to her grandparents; she mutters sleepily of forgiveness. A calm has settled over the scene and the characters; when Francisco refers to the 'talking' he and Harry used to do in the past, Harry gently corrects him: 'Discussing, actually'.[5] As the lights fade for the end of the play, the renewed sanctuary lamp gleams in the darkness.

Telling a tale about one's past is to accept it as over and finished, as dead experience. Telling that tale with the proper decorum that allows a sensitive listener fully to hear and register the cry of pain that provides its focus and motivation can bring a sense of release from any further obligation to that past. The sacrament of confession ideally effects such a movement of consciousness towards freedom. Here there is no practising cleric to guide the process. Yet in the course of the night's action, pain is assuaged; the characters enact a process of dying; but with a brief alteration in the lighting-state the image of death is transformed into one of resurrection and renewal: perverse, sacrilegious perhaps, but all three gain a will to go on. They will return to their former patterns of living, but there is no sense that return is futile: the pattern has been viewed and interrogated from a benighted perspective, and a process of reorientation results. The choice to return is not defeatist but a necessary part of the process of renewal.[6] The characters have each risen above the guilts that afflicted them, the sense of having in some way debased themselves, betrayed their humanity. The sanctuary lamp does not here represent orthodox Catholic belief so much as a humanist conviction in the power of the mind to create its own mysterious rituals through which to heal its torn condition.

If one has a criticism of *The Sanctuary Lamp*, it is that the actual moment of transformation is perhaps too hurried in terms of stage time compared with the detailed examination of the characters' descent to an emotional nadir. This is not a criticism one could level against *The Gigli Concert* where the pacing of the psychological developments is meticulously judged. From the first our attention is fixed on the minutiae of the processes involved, so that no nuance in their development is missed. We are in the world of psychotherapy; and are immediately gripped by a sense of the dangers inherent in intruding into the privacies of another person's psyche (for one thing, the client here spends a large part of the play clutching in his pocket an object that looks suspiciously like a gun).

The client (referred to throughout anonymously as The Man) is a self-made businessman of considerable prosperity who has all the material satisfactions that a hard-working life can afford by way of reward. He is married, has fathered a son, lives in respectable decency and knows the business world as thoroughly as he needs to. Yet periodically the instinct for the search still surfaces in him; he has, we learn, been possessed by sudden enthusiasms that approach being obsessional. He has one such now: he longs to sing like Gigli.

Psychiatrists and psychologists he dismisses as quacks, yet he knows he needs help; on impulse he visits a practitioner of a new 'cult', an American-inspired, alternative therapy: dynamatology. He suspects the practitioner, J.P.W. King, may be a phoney; and King, dishevelled and down on his luck, more than suspects as much himself. There is little that is dynamic about King at first until the Man's evident pain galvanises him into action. The Man *chooses* to remain anonymous; asked for biographical details, he conflates some few facts about his actual life with a great many concerning Gigli's. He has lost any sure sense of identity; he talks of Gigli with some degree of awe as 'the devil', and yet it is difficult to know whether he is possessed or play-acting; everything about the Man is vague, indeterminate, shifting, except for his manifest longing. It takes a great deal of careful handling of the situation before King earns the Man's trust sufficiently to be confided in.

Oddly enough, the confidences are forthcoming when King is being flippant, having grown tired of the Man's evasions; losing patience, he suddenly turns on the Man and bids him 'snap out of it', but in doing so he addresses his client as Benimillo (an affectionate derivative of Gigli's actual name). The tone changes instantly: the Man growls with outrage at the insensitivity implicit in the phrase 'snap out'. He feels demeaned and is goaded for the first time to explain:

> D'yeh think I'd be this way if I could help it? When I listen to him – I-can't-stop-listening-to-him! Fills me. The – things, the – things – inside. Tense, everything more intense. And I listen carefully. And it's beautiful – But it's screaming! – And it's longing. Longing for what? I don't know whether it's keeping me sane or driving me crazy . . . [7]

The confessions come thick and fast: how he longs to take his young son aside and confide how he feels 'it would be better if I disappeared'; how his wife interrupted his listening to a recording of Gigli, caressed him, urged him to try and talk to her, spoke of her love for him and how all he could do was stand and roar obscenities at her. The story is the more disturbing for the controlled quietness of the delivery. King hears the pain, but its magnitude leaves him feeling utterly inadequate; he is totally out of his depth.

What follows is a wonderful evocation of a growing friendship. The Man is convinced King is 'the right man for the job' and King begins to engage imaginatively with the Man's nature; the Man's search for the source of his pain becomes for King too a process of learning and discovery. Again we touch on the idea of the search: much of Murphy's drama is about learning how to follow the processes of the mind. However static the drama may be in a superficial sense (and much of *The Gigli Concert* focuses on two men talking together or listening to Gigli singing on records), it is full of the restless energy of psychological movement, as is implicit in the idea of a process. The process is not the objective of the search, but it can lead to a greater intuition of the nature of that objective when, as here, it is rooted in impulse rather than reasoned decisions. King begins to abandon all the other ties in his life and his imaginative identification with the Man verges on a fixation; he too is willingly allowing himself to become possessed; the crucial factor is that he is possessed less by the Man than by his condition. The Man's need has become his own, especially when he voices a desperate appeal: 'Don't try to take him [*Gigli*] away from me, Mr King' (42). They argue, they drink together, they demolish each other's illusions; but they continue to share the search with a gathering, at times frenetic, excitement.

The search takes a more explicitly metaphysical turn when the Man arrives with a recording of Gigli singing as Mephistophele and King becomes fascinated with exploring ideas about the imagination and creativity, and about how they have the potential to realise a spiritual dimension within mundane life:

> We understand our existential guilt, our definition of ourselves is right from the start – I am who may be – and, meanwhile, our paradoxical key, despair, is rising, rising in our pool to total despair. That state achieved, two choices. One, okay, I give in, I wait for the next world. Two, what have I to lose and I take the leap, the plunge into the abyss of darkness to achieve that state of primordial being, not in any muddled theocentric sense, but as the point of origin in the *here-and-now* where anything becomes possible. (52)

He is elated at the prospect of finding a way of endlessly transcending the self within conventional time; that is the temptation that Gigli's singing held out to the Man and which he tried desperately to articulate when he first approached King. It is a hunger for reliable spiritual satisfaction in a man who can admit to being beholden to no conventional creed.

When the Man next appears he has reached a nadir of despair

like that which King previously theorised about. His wife and child
have left him; he recalls in his misery a moment when in his youth
he tried to transcend an emotional barrier that existed between
himself and his brother and was crassly repulsed in a way that
has left a life-long wound. Noticeably the Man is talking about his
own family now, not Gigli's. It is a powerful scene because the two
men begin to exchange intimacies about injuries to their self-esteem
in a way that conventionally men very rarely confess to each other,
fearing such admissions of sensitivity might unman them, except
perhaps in the company of the very closest of friends. But there is
no reservation here, no holding back, no dread of being adversely
judged. Perversely King has a sudden lapse of concentration and
resorts to one of his flippant strategies, suggesting that he 'sum up'
what has just elapsed. The Man mutters dangerously that he does
not feel inclined to forgive anyone, but King leaves him to make
tea; the Man is beside himself, roars 'Sum up!', starts to voice his
absolute hate, but collapses into tears. At first 'a few whimpers
escape' him, then 'savage, inarticulate roars of impotent hatred'
which soon develop into unstoppable sobs: *'Terrible dry sobbing, and
rhythmic, as if from the bowels of the earth'* (58). Even as in the Man's
tale of his relations with his brother, a confidence was seemingly
won only to be immediately lost; the volume of grief and its raw
expression is overwhelming. Exhausted, the Man falls asleep.

    Ironically, it transpires that King's flippancy has effected the
necessary cure. Noticeably when the Man first ever tried to express
what listening to Gigli meant to him, his words struggled beyond
the superficial cliché, 'beautiful', to terms that were altogether
more inward, more personal and unexpectedly paradoxical: 'But
it's screaming! – And it's longing'. King has unconsciously created
the means and the mood by and in which the Man could give voice
to his own primal scream. It is a kind of rebirth, a ritual purging of
the psyche. When we next see the Man, he is confidently at ease
again with himself, his wife, family and friends and is no longer
haunted by the shadow of despair. He has transferred that burden to
King. If the Man pursued the first of the two modes of dealing with
metaphysical grief envisaged by King and found temporary peace
with himself and with society, that leaves King himself with the
second option: to travel through and beyond what is conventionally
understood to be the nature of despair to a point where anything
becomes possible. Frantic, torn between doubt and daring, King
takes alcohol and an overdose of drugs; strange wailing sounds

begin to well out of the depths of his being too, the mouth shapes itself for foreign vowels, the lungs take galvanic breaths; forced to his feet, King cues in an imaginary orchestra and sings with all of Gigli's full-throated rapture 'Tu Che A Dio Spiegasti L'Ali' through to a *'triumphant, emotional ending'*. As he sings the stage fills with an intense red glow, but in the silence ensuing after the aria's ending this radiance is displaced by the cold, clear light of the dawn. Have we witnessed a drug-induced fantasy, a pact with the Devil, or another self-generated ritual of release? With the onset of morning, King is ebullient, purposeful (if a shade unsteady on his feet); he packs and departs to a new life.

We are left to interpret as we will, aware only that both characters leave the play totally transformed from the men we encountered at the start. Wholly non-religious men, they have yet found different ways of satisfying their inner yearning for spiritual release: the Man turned the focus of his consciousness inward and discovered how to acknowledge and voice his pain at its most intense; King opened himself to his consciousness and let it realise the impossible through him. Whether we believe in his transformation or not depends on how closely we identify with the action on stage as more than theatrical trickery or illusion; to believe would require of us an act of faith, that theatre is on some level *real*. And that is the challenge that the play leaves us with.

The more important point is that we have accompanied both men on their search and have watched the two distinct processes of purging that their minds undergo. What Murphy has done is confront us with the issue of what catharsis in the experience of tragedy might mean. Does the art of theatre provide us with a temporary outlet for a primal scream at the uncertainties of existence, which allows us to live again for a while at peace within the constrictions of conventional society? As King observes of the Man at their last encounter, when he gleams with good health and bonhomie: 'You have taken yourself captive again. But dread still lies nesting, Benimillo' (73). He goes on to thank the Man for what the Man has given him: 'I longed to take myself captive too and root myself, but you came in that door, with the audacity of despair, wild with the idea of wanting to soar, and I was the most pitiful of spiritless things' (73). The Man does not understand the nature of this gratitude: that he has given King the gift of hope. That hope, when the Man has gone, propels King into his last experiment with consciousness. For the climax of the play to work, director and

actor must excite an audience willingly to suspend their *disbelief*. If
they succeed, then we as audience too have known a transcendent
experience: we have been privileged through theatre to share a
vision. Few modern plays have so confidently invited audiences
to celebrate the extraordinary metaphysical potential of the art of
theatre in performance.

The art of the theatre came relatively late to Ireland compared
with most of Europe. The more traditional art was that of the
shanachie, the dramatic storyteller, gifted with the ability to capture
the imagination of listeners by playing in her or his own person all
the characters within the tale. If *The Gigli Concert* carries its search
to the heart of the experience we call theatre, Murphy's next play,
Bailegangaire, subjects the art of the storyteller to a similar, intensive
scrutiny. Throughout the play, Mommo, an ancient woman, wan-
dering somewhat in her wits, concentrates her attention on telling a
story for the benefit of an imagined audience of children. She offers
it as a moral tale and throughout she endeavours to preserve the
seeming detachment of the omniscient author. She does have an
actual as distinct from an imagined on-stage audience in her two
granddaughters: Mary, whose life is devoted to Mommo's care (not
that Mommo chooses to recognise her attentions or be grateful for
them); and Dolly, who works to achieve a modest income for
them and her family (her husband works away in England) by
prostitution.

Both have clearly heard the tale endless times before; indeed, they
know it by heart, and can prompt the old woman with her lines
when she loses her way. Telling her tale has become compulsive
for Mommo and the girls are inclined to dismiss her efforts as
just a manifestation of senility. We, of course, are hearing the
story for the first time; and so, as with all well-told tales, we
are all attention. The many disruptions and divergencies from
the main narrative serve merely to augment our curiosity as to
the outcome. But our concentration on Mommo, our longing for
her to get on with the story about a village whose inhabitants lost
the gift of laughter, makes us conscious of the granddaughters'
very different response, their weariness, nervy tension, desperation.
The pathetically inadequate household, the anxiety over even basic
provisions, the run-down look of the younger women, begin to
make storytelling seem something of a luxury: quaint, charming
even, but patently useless. In such circumstances it hardly seems
worthy of the designation, 'art'.

The story is about a journey to market by a couple referred to as the strangers; they fail to sell their goods and find the return journey difficult in the inclement weather since their cart has trouble negotiating hills; they pursue a roundabout way and find themselves at an inn where the stranger-husband gets drawn into a laughing match with the local clown; the prize will go to whoever outlaughs the other. The stranger-wife spurs her husband on to the contest. The tales to provoke laughter get wilder and more grotesque; no subject, not even death, is safe from ridicule. The whole company at the inn are helpless with laughter to the point where the laughter becomes mechanical, utterly compulsive, whatever is uttered by either of the contestants. Like many a good Irish yarn, the tale vacillates in its moods from the mysterious to the risible; from the farcical to the eerie. For a long while Mommo is alone in the house with Mary while Dolly is visiting a client and Mary seems determined to stop the story in its tracks by a variety of ruses; but none succeeds. She determines to pack and leave Dolly to supervise Mommo, but she lacks the strength of will to do more than fetch a suitcase and add to the litter on stage with her piles of clothes. Everything seems in a state of deadlock or limbo; and Mary, overwhelmed by it all, suddenly just gives up. She collapses into a chair at the table and sinks into a posture of complete listlessness.

In that state a different part of her consciousness starts to listen to Mommo, registers the urgency behind the constant telling of the tale, senses a motive in the obsession. Till now we have heard the tale only on a superficial level, relishing the narrative for its own sake largely, and occasionally admiring the expertise of the narrator. Mary's newly-alert interest prompts us to engage with the tale at a different imaginative level. She ponders whether she is in the wrong for harassing Mommo in an attempt to get her to stop, and whether Mommo is perhaps endeavouring to tell the tale completely once and for all and herself make a definite end of it. She has engaged now not with the story but the teller, and the idea of the obsessional relentlessness of the activity stimulates her pity. Tonight, she decides, Mommo must get to the end and she will not let anything prevent that; if Mommo must snatch a minute or two of sleep then she, Mary, will continue the story till Mommo wakes and takes up the thread. Dolly when she returns ridicules the idea and settles to sleep, musing over the imminence of a baby conceived out of wedlock and the likely violence of her husband when he discovers the situation. She has asked Mary to take the child into her home along with Mommo, but Mary has refused, resisting the possibility of further drudgery and obligations. Mommo alone occupies her thoughts; and Mary's singleminded concentration on the narrative renews and deepens our engagement with it.

The tale changes its tone again, telling how the stranger-contestant would end the match seeing his opponent near-prostrate with exhaustion, and how his wife insisted he continue to decide the winner properly and not lose the match by stopping when he was so close to victory; and how the village clown was struck down with apoplexy and died, and how the villagers turned against the strangers and tried to kill them; how they got away and returned home, where they found their three orphan grandchildren, left in their care but forgotten overnight in the heat of the contest, 'wor safe an' sound fast asleep on the settle'.[8] Mommo gently bids her imagined audience say their prayers and go to sleep; her tale is done. During the final stages Mary has undressed and got into bed alongside Mommo; taking Mommo's hands in her own, she begins the narrative again, shifting the perspective and putting a different ending to it all. She tells how the three grandchildren waited through the night for their guardians' return, excited at the prospect of receiving gifts for Christmas; how they let the fire burn low, and how the youngster of the family, Tom, tried to rekindle the blaze by pouring paraffin on the embers; how he had been severely burned and how he and the grandfather had both died shortly afterwards. The laughing match had ended in a tragedy costing three lives, and all because the stranger-wife had refused to let her husband withdraw from the contest. As the tale nears its end, Mary and Mommo frequently stumble over the words and 'grandad' keeps slipping in where previously 'stranger' had referred to the husband; at the last Mary names the two surviving grandchildren as herself and Dolly.

The tale is Mommo's autobiography, despite her efforts at omniscience, and it is Mary and Dolly's tale too: the story of how they came by their joyless condition. Mary's retelling of the ending ensures Mommo accepts the full implications of the tragedy as in part her responsibility. A calm descends on Mommo who herself begins to pray for the departed and for the three of them left 'mourning and weeping in this valley of tears' (76). Her prayers finished, she addresses Mary by her own name for the first time in the play and sees them as united and contented: ' . . . and haven't we everything we need here, the two of us' (76). Mary agrees fervently and tears of gratitude well up in her eyes; cries pitched between anguish and the laughter of relief escape her as she decides to add a postscript to the story by way of a conclusion that glances towards the future:

> . . . To conclude. It's a strange old place alright, in whatever wisdom He has to have made it this way. But in whatever wisdom there is, in the year 1984, it was decided to give that – fambly . . . of strangers another chance, and a brand new baby to gladden their home. (76)

Mary will foster Dolly's child as her own; together, she and Mommo have found a way to redeem the past and have been rewarded with the sense of a future.

In most of Murphy's plays silence prevails in performance for considerable stretches of stage-time towards the close. It is not the uneasy silence of Pinter's drama in which the characters nurse their wounds and calculate their next strategies against their antagonists, nor the silence textured with anxiety of Beckett's plays, where the characters dread any hint of the cessation of being and fear silence as self-extinction. Silence in Murphy's work tends to be replete less with a sense of finality than of achievement, an intimation that the search has found an objective; such silence is like balm. Silence in *Bailegangaire* marks Mary's firm telling of the proper end of Mommo's story as tragedy and that silence prompts Mommo to pray; and it is out of silence that Mary, named and accepted into Mommo's affections, finds the strength to speak her final affirmation. This process of two minds working in total accord, scrupulously sensitive to each other's needs, is a beautiful, unforced expression of love.[9]

The play is again a ritual of purgation, but one which the characters must shape and direct for themselves. Though Mary's final words hint at a belief in God, such a statement has not been possible until she has found the way to free herself and Mommo from the burden of the past. Mary found that way when she began truly to *listen* and, listening, to imagine. Murphy, through Mary, shows an audience how to distinguish degrees and levels of response.

At first Mommo's tale is delightful entertainment, but Mary's renewed interest in its development carries our response to a deeper level of engagement; with no loss of involvement in the narrative, we listen now to what the artistry intimates through complexities of tone is lying behind the words of the story, to the theme, and behind that theme to the motive spurring the teller to seek an audience, even if only an imagined one. We are being shown how there are many kinds of reception to arts of performance, how engagement at its most profound is a sharing in the act of creation, which is an act of love. Mommo's storytelling demands great courage because it is at root a revelation of her past and continuing vulnerability and guilt; Mary's listening and understanding ultimately restore to Mommo her dignity, because through sharing the telling she gives her the confidence to admit her identity, her *place* in the tale, to show that the story is much more than idle fancy.

Like *The Gigli Concert, Bailegangaire* is a magnificent defence of the art of performance; but the later play shifts the focus significantly to examine the phenomenon of audience reception. Both plays end with the characters recovering a proper human dignity: the Man and King are energised, their senses and sensitivity acutely alert; Mary and Mommo find a complete repose through their recovery of an inner joy. The rituals of purgation that make up the fabric of these plays restore to the characters a poignant kind of innocence, because such processes of the mind enable them to travel to the further reaches of pain and despair. Murphy's achievement in these two plays is his frank interrogation of the art that we know as theatre; he deconstructs that art from a variety of standpoints the better to convince us of its absolute necessity as a means of monitoring the health of the human spirit. Murphy shows theatre to be at its finest a spiritual art for a non-religious age. As King says while he listens again to the great tenor's voice as the curtain falls at the end of *The Gigli Concert*:

> Do not mind the pig-sty, Benimillo . . . mankind still has a delicate ear . . . that's it . . . that's it . . . sing on forever . . . that's it. (75)

Murphy's theatre continually fine-tunes an audience's perception of that remarkable delicacy.

Notes

1. For a complete list of Tom Murphy's plays to 1988, see *Contemporary Dramatists*, ed. D.L. Kirkpatrick (London: St James Press, 1988). Since 1988, Murphy has published *Too Late for Logic* (1990). It would be very confusing with Murphy to give dates after the first mention of play titles in the text; he has the habit of rewriting as a consequence of performances. Printed texts of his plays often appear some time after initial productions and then again some years later in revised form. To give dates of first performances would give no real idea of his actual chronological development, and neither would dates of publication.

2. Murphy's only play that deals directly with an avowedly Christian society is *Famine*, and there John Connor's personal act of faith continually exposes the lack of genuine Christian principles in the English, the Irish landlords and their agents. A whole religious culture and its attendant political morality are being put to the test and found wanting, and that leaves John as the victim of the devastating hypocrisy of his age, which in practice is seen to be devoid of the one quality enshrined in the Christian creed: charity. In most of Murphy's other plays the act of faith is in support of no traditional creed but rather an assertion of the most primal value of all: the dignity of the individual human being.

3. The definition of postmodernism that is implicit behind my argument here is drawn from the writings of Patrice Pavis and especially his recent publication, *Theatre at the Crossroads*, trans. Loren Kruger (London/New York: Routledge, 1992).

4. This play depicts a collection of sour middle-aged individuals descending into drunkenness to stave off their pressing sense of having failed their grand sixties idealism. The bitterest of the men is Tom, a schoolteacher, who continually vents his spleen against his fiancée, Peggy. She is required to play Ophelia to his lacklustre but all-too-moody Prince. (Tom's pretentiousness and cruelty are defined deftly by his endless quoting from *Hamlet*; he has clearly used and abused Peggy for years as a shoulder to cry on and as a whipping post to flail with his sarcasm when he feels 'judged' by her enduring trust). Marriage seems a bleak prospect: like Ophelia, she is compelled to a life of enforced celibacy and is endlessly repulsed when she tries with quiet reasoning to resist being marginalised in this way. And yet Peggy is the one character who finally can make an act of faith, which she does by singing unaccompanied and with increasing confidence a song that once meant much to the whole group. Singing it is Peggy's way of being true to the past and values that once motivated them all, which the rest have betrayed. The song comes like a benediction to the turbulent souls in the bar, relieving them at least momentarily of some of the pressure of guilt.

5. Thomas Murphy, *The Sanctuary Lamp*, rev. ed. (Dublin: The Gallery Press, 1984) p. 52.

6. This is the theme too of Murphy's play, *A Crucial Week in the Life*

of a Grocer's Assistant (originally entitled *The Fooleen*). The action of the play shifts between the daily social life and the nightly dream-life of John Joe Moran. The choices before him seem to be simple: either to stay in the small town where he was born and be a put-upon non-entity or to emigrate to England or the States. His dreams show him the choice is not quite so simple: what he yearns for is independence from his parents and from the pettiness that afflicts his friends and neighbours; and in a nightmare he appreciates that leaving will not necessarily affect his ambition, if he leaves his 'soul' behind in Ireland and becomes, when abroad, guilt- ridden and prone to nostalgia and sentimentality. He achieves independence ultimately by freeing himself from all his ties and commitments within the town in a way that allows him the freedom to *choose* to remain there if he wishes on his own terms and as his own master. This is another play which makes highly inventive use of the arts of the theatre, and especially the technique of the actors who are required to act according to the tenets of realism in the daytime scenes and as bizarre caricatures of these roles in the dream sequences. The juxtaposition of these two styles of acting makes for some choice comedy.

7.   Thomas Murphy, *The Gigli Concert* (Dublin: The Gallery Press, 1984) p. 28. All quotations are from this edition; hereafter, page numbers will be given in the text.
8.   Thomas Murphy, *Bailegangaire* (Dublin: The Gallery Press, 1986) p. 74. All quotations are from this edition; hereafter, page numbers will be given in the text.
9.   Though the technique and style are wholly different, the tone and the situation here are powerfully reminiscent of Beckett's *Footfalls*, where telling a shared narrative also becomes an expression of profound love between two women, a mother and daughter. For a fuller account of this play, see my publication *New British Drama in Performance on the London Stage: 1970–85* (Gerrards Cross: Colin Smythe, 1987) pp. 122–7.

8

Edward Bond: A Political Education

Anthony Jenkins

Looking back at his youthful self, twenty years later, Edward Bond saw a political naïf: 'I had grown up in a war situation. . . . I tried . . . to put down what it was really like, to describe the problem'.[1] He could not then *analyse* the problem. Nor, for that matter, could the English Stage Company (ESC) at the Royal Court Theatre where Bond's instincts drew him in 1958. John Osborne's *Look Back in Anger* (1956), which did articulate the frustration of the young, had given the Court an aura of controversy, but neither the directorship nor the audiences on whom the company depended wanted revolution. At the time of Suez, Hungary, and the CND (Campaign for Nuclear Disarmament), Osborne's Jimmy Porter angrily denounced the Establishment, yet his nostalgia for the values and grace of the past was equally a symptom of the times. So the ESC was saved from financial collapse both by Osborne's play and a star-laden revival of *The Country Wife*, which transferred to the West End. To survive, the ESC had to be eclectic.

Fortuitously, George Devine, the artistic director, had wide-ranging tastes and, crucially, a 'passionate concern for certain people and what they were doing';[2] thus the Court embraced writers, directors, designers from a variety of political and cultural schools. An amalgam of kitchen-sink reality, absurdism, star attractions and revivals kept the ESC afloat while its Sunday night 'productions with decor' gave new talents a practical apprenticeship. In particular, the Writers' Group under the director, Bill Gaskill, and the Court's playreader, Keith Johnstone, focused on the way 'things should be shown happening in the theatre, not analysed and talked about'.[3] That emphasis on images and action influenced Bond profoundly:

103

'The Group was always run by directors . . . it made the members aware of the plastic, visual nature of theatre'.[4] The Court's tight budgets and relative intimacy encouraged an expressive simplicity which clarified the text, and Bond responded to that philosophy, discovering a theatrical rather than a polemic language with which to show the effect of a diseased culture on his characters' behaviour.

The Pope's Wedding, his first staged play (directed by Johnstone as a Sunday production in 1962), begins with a social happening.[5] It's the night before payday. Young farm-workers cadge cigarettes from each other, kick a stone about, try to raise money for a beer: in seven hours they'll all be back at work. On a bare stage, with only a railing to lean against, Bond conveys a rhythm whose meaning grows plainer in scene two. An apple stands surrealistically on stage as the lads, at lunch-break, scythe a cricket-pitch for Saturday's match. Bill's boss is determined to win that contest and invents a way to keep him out of the game; all Bill can do is threaten to 'poison 'is bloody cow' or 'thread 'is missis'.[6] Without explicit comment, the scene shifts to a shabby figure who stands rigidly by the door in a corrugated iron wall, listening, then darts about with sheets of newspaper. Alien, frightened, he adds to the stack of papers on which he stands, listening. A bang at the door: the figure sighs: black-out. That mime encapsulates and heightens the hostile world in which the characters act out their frustrations; it then collides with an almost wordless scene in which everything becomes magically free. Until then, Scopey had been one in a crowd, twelfth man on his team. In cricket whites, he dashes from his crease, ignoring his partner's caution, to scatter fours and sixes. His world is gloriously at one. Such synchronised energy should impress an audience; it certainly dazzles Pat who can't forget how he looked 'beautiful all in white' (250). Bond's direct presentation of sequential images conveys a world which the characters themselves cannot articulate; they have no ideas beyond their present needs. Like Alen in his peculiar hermitage, they don't see their imprisonment. Pat's glimpse-beyond fades once she marries Scopey and is again circumscribed by cigarettes, sex, food, pay-packets. Semi-consciously, though, Scopey wants more. A postcard from a girl who married a Yank from the airbase prompts him to complain that the view is too clean, its sky too blue; it doesn't show enough: 'Where's the people an' the corners?' (264). But he would like a room entirely papered with postcards, and he is drawn magnetically to Alen, whose ways are apparently different.

Bond wanted audiences to stare warped lives in the face, and his bare stage, made strange by an isolated railing or one apple, gives the action a poetry which lifts beyond realism's slice of life. Poetry conveys the inexpressible. Bond's characters don't have the words anyway. Seeking answers, Scopey envies Alen's individualism only to discover him peeking at the world beyond his iron wall from a pile of old news. The hermit who seemed to shun society was himself abandoned. He has forgotten what he is there for and so surrounds himself with canned food, photos bought in junk shops, meaningless hymns; there is nothing in the sewn-up pockets of the greatcoat he gives Scopey. We experience the angry pain of that disappointment, but not the ultimate violence of Scopey's search for something as impossible as a Pope's wedding. At play's end, he sits in a daze, surrounded by five hundred cans of food, and stares at a bundle (Alen's corpse) on the floor: 'I took one 'and on 'is throat an one 'eld 'im up be the 'air' (307). That blank statement and Pat's panicked "Elp!' create a chill which resolves nothing.

How the frustration of the dispossessed could be resolved remains an unasked question, though Bond's next play, *Saved* (1965), shows with devastating clarity how public injustice warps private lives. Fred, for instance, enters the play (sc. 2) as a joker, product of a society whose values have little or no meaning to the working class. As he helps Pam out of a boat, one sees his automatic response, 'Very nice . . . Very 'ow's yer father',[7] and how his by-play reduces her to a thing: a means to assert himself. His mates in the park (sc. 3) have the same attitude. The more unfeeling they are about other people, women and children in particular, the tougher and grander they are to their pals. So Fred's time in prison makes him a hero, and in the café, after his release (sc. 10), his contempt for Pam and the food his mates buy him ('I couldn't eat in this bloody place if they served it through a rubber tube' [116]) shows how his punishment (for stoning the baby) has simply made him harder: living proof to his mates that he's beaten the system. Len's comment at the end of the scene underlines the authorities' futility; 'They ain' done 'im no good. 'E's gone back like a kid' (116). Though the play centres on private worlds, the characters' relation to the Establishment has become more explicit. Each episode demonstrates behaviour's social causes, and the linear action creates a *pictorial* analysis of institutions (schools, work-places, law-courts) that have failed.

The play's structure is Brechtian, though its effect is emotional. Gaskill, who directed *Saved*, has described the impact of Brecht's Berliner Ensemble when they first came to London in 1956: 'Serious theatre, a large scale company, subsidised theatre and a group of people working as a permanent ensemble – that image of what theatre could and should be dominated many of our lives for a long time'.[8] Their technique, rather than their politics, inspired the directors at the new ESC: the economic realism that soon characterised their productions and the work of the Writers' Group was not simply the result of budgetary and spatial restrictions. But without a state-subsidised ensemble the ESC had to address middle-class patrons, and *Saved* teaches through visceral images rather than dialectic argument. Brecht's alienation-effect which temporarily distances a spectator's empathy, creating time to think, becomes Bond's aggro-effect, aimed at the sensitivities of bourgeois audiences. The murder of Pam's baby (sc. 6) is horrifying because Bond implants it within the characters' motiveless apathy. The scene begins wistfully as Fred and Len sit together, fishing-rods *'out over the stalls'* (57). Fred joins the lads, and their listless boredom leads to a game of push and shove. The pram becomes part of that, and the baby, drugged to insensibility by Pam, is also a thing to be spat on, punched, stoned: 'What a giggle!' While 'it' seems a non-person to the group, 'no feelin's . . . Like animals' (77), the audience sits physically trapped (by the theatre's etiquette) in speechless outrage. The scene ends gently as Pam returns for the pram and, mouthing baby-talk ('to herself' [82]), wheels it off without noticing what's happened. Here the ironies strike at the spectators' minds. Bond's modulated rhythms attack bourgeois certitudes, a strategy which depends as much on lyric imagery as on aggressive shock-tactics. At the end of *Saved*, Len and Harry reach out to each other. Len lies on the floor with a knife in his hand; Harry appears in white combinations and a bandaged head: a corpse meets a ghost in a house of angry recrimination. There's a logic behind this picture, but its estranging features elicit a compassion for Harry's inadequacy or Len's confusion as he tries to understand how Harry can endure and worries about Fred's damaged character: 'E'll finished up like some ol' lag or an ol' soak' (126). The residual pathos of these fumblings carries over into the final scene, an almost silent picture of the way Len, with instinctive kindness, tries to mend a chair. Stylised illustration, which precludes resolution, ought to linger hauntingly as audiences return to their insulated lives.

The way *Saved* is shaped and presented on stage controls its effect yet, responding to the written text, the Lord Chamberlain's office refused to licence its performance unless the stoning episode and a suggestive encounter between Len and Mary (sc. 9) were removed: Bond refused. Gaskill (as the ESC's new artistic director) supported him by resorting to the age-old dodge of restricting performances to 'members only'. After one of the officers who policed the production was not required to show his membership card, the ESC was prosecuted. The magistrate upheld the law with a token fine which underlined its stupidity and so accelerated the campaign to end it. Two years later (1968), *Early Morning* was banned entirely and, since censorship was soon to be abolished, the ESC presented one Sunday performance and, under pressure from the Court's licensee, 'a critics' dress rehearsal' matinée. Censorship ended that September and, early in 1969, the ESC staged a season of Bond's plays, uncut and in public. That support showed The Royal Court was indeed a writers' theatre, and the fracas made Bond more conscious politically. His preface to *Saved* (published 1966) turns the conventional reaction to its urban wasteland upside-down by calling the play 'irresponsibly optimistic', and he now appeals for social change: 'this means teaching morality to children in a way that they find convincing' (311).

The end of censorship was but one of the events which revolutionised theatre in 1968. Disillusioned by the Viet Nam war and by the consumerism of Western society, the counter-culture of the sixties had come to regard established politics as an insane con-game. In *John D. Muggins is Dead* (1965), London's first alternative theatre group, CAST (Cartoon Archetypical Slogan Theatre), showed how Muggins had been sold the idea of freedom by official American pop-culture and so died in Viet Nam. In *Mr Oligarchy's Circus* (1966), Britain under Harold Wilson's socialist government was 'a circus, the ruling class was the circus master and the Labour Party was its bedfellow'.[9] The same feelings were voiced by students who, in May 1968, brought Paris to a standstill by demanding a culture that would enrich rather than stupefy, and the defeat of that Movement fuelled the energies of those for whom official culture no longer made sense. Bond himself has said that 1968, and the proliferation of political theatre groups thereafter, clarified his attitude and gave him a 'conceptual language with which to enlighten myself or others'.[10] This is especially true of the prefaces he attached to his published work from *Lear* (first published 1972) onwards, which set out a provocative idea of culture in an idiosyncratic, though ultimately Marxist way.

But the 'language' of the plays themselves was already tuned to the mood of the time and did not alter fundamentally until the mid-seventies. *Early Morning* had mocked imperial history by picturing Queen Victoria's court as a madhouse whose inmates scrambled for power with farcical abandon. The way this dog-eat-dog metaphor turns literal amongst the lower class, who dismember a man who jumped the queue outside Kilburn State Cinema and then eat him, echoes the political absurdism which shaped CAST's plays and the French Situationists' philosophy. Queen Victoria's hilarious pronouncements – 'Put him on oath, but don't let him touch the Bible. King James would turn in his grave'[11] – have the cartoon mechanics of agitprop, yet, in the tenderness of Prince Albert's last meeting with Florence (sc. 20), Bond hints at a human solution.[12] *Early Morning* combined cynical iconoclasm and reformist ideals, whereas the troupes that emerged on 'The Fringe' tended to move in one or other of those directions. Bond's staged pictures already had the accents of fringe theatre, but their syntax, poised ambiguously between horror and pathos, was designed to worry mainstream audiences: 'I don't believe in reducing characters to caricatures of their class role or function. That can only confirm audiences in what they already know . . . But learning is a more subtle experience'.[13]

As 'a theatre in which the best new plays could be done as well as possible', The Court was seen by fringe groups as part of the Establishment and, though he found this 'disturbing', Gaskill tried to bridge that divide: 'The founding of the Theatre Upstairs in 1969 was an acknowledgement of something that had already happened that we had to take cognisance of. But it wasn't something that I'd really activated and I think alternative theatre has produced a split in the theatre'.[14] The ESC had already welcomed American alternatives, the Open Theatre and Paperbag Players (1967); in 1970, the British fringe arrived with their multi-media, agitprop festival: *Come Together*. By then the upstairs theatre played host to fringe companies, and writers associated with those groups were presented on both the main and upstairs stages. In the opposite direction, Bond wrote *Black Mass* for the Anti-Apartheid Movement (Lyceum, 1970) and *Passion* for the CND (staged by The Court at Alexandra Palace Racecourse, 1971); those darkly funny cartoons affirmed, in a deliberately one-sided way, their particular audiences' convictions.

His playlets satirise the ruling class and the dehumanising effects of the military (which had disgusted him during his own years of National Service and which he would develop gruesomely in *Lear*). Yet the thoughts of the Dead Soldier at the end of *Passion* insist on a natural humanity that could assuage tyrannical madness: 'Madmen, peace! / You who bend iron but are afraid of grass / Peace!'[15]

That appeal to humanist values grows increasingly louder in the major plays that Bond came to see as a series culminating in *The Sea* (1973). Scopey's freedom on the cricket pitch, Len and Pam's stunted dreams of future happiness and his attempts to make her love her baby hint at a restorative union between man and Nature or between fellow beings. That possibility glows dimly behind the mad puppets of *Early Morning*: a dawn which is neither glorious nor certain. Prince Arthur rises from his coffin into the sky, unnoticed by the cannibal court. The Last Supper and Resurrection are parodied to show the ineffectiveness of Christian icons and the way authority absorbs them, since Victoria has persuaded the masses Arthur died to let them feed in peace. Arthur had tried to explain that earthly souls die young, living on as ghosts to haunt each other. Florence didn't understand that, yet she sits apart from the others: 'There's something in [her] eye', an irritant which might make her see Victoria's 'law and order, consent and co-operation' (223) differently.

A similar ambiguity surrounds the final moments of *Narrow Road to the Deep North* (1968). As Kiro disembowels himself, a man emerges from the river behind him. Complaining he could have drowned, he turns away to dry himself as Kiro topples into death. This conjunction of images dramatises Kiro's despair and the man's insularity, but it could also suggest renewal: a man rises naked and unformed from the water.

Bond had no utopian solution but he does show how the powerful and their victims, at their most inhuman, grope bewilderedly for something better. Bond detests Samuel Beckett's negativity: 'I believe in the survival of mankind. I don't believe in an *Endgame* or *Waiting for Godot*'.[16] So Lear, defeated and blinded, begins to see that 'decent, honest men devour the earth' and tears at the power-structure (the wall) which the 'decent' have built against social 'chaos'.[17] Images of farcical horror and strange lyricism activate the viewer's sensibilities but avoid the sort of programmatic message which, as Bond says in *Lear*'s preface, tends 'to coerce people to fit into it. We do not need a plan of the future, we need a *method* of change' (11). Even *The Sea*, which proclaims a future, is open-ended. Evens sees himself as 'a wise fool' who can never know enough. He does believe in the rat and the rat-catcher, a combination of growth and destruction which, like the sea itself, ensures a living universe, but he doesn't know how to stay human within that flux. Everyone must find his own solution, but the truth waits patiently for those who refuse to despair. 'You must still change the world', he urges. How Willy and Rose will do that, as they journey together, is as enigmatic as Willy's unfinished sentence which concludes the play.

Bond recognised 'the dishonesty and irresponsibility that's involved in almost all public use of ideas, especially by politicians and academics'.[18] As his own ideas grew more political, he probed deeper into the *artist's* social responsibilities. In *Narrow Road* Basho's art was an absorbing mystique; from those heights he dismissed suffering as man's fated lot, welcomed the barbarians (obviously inferior) and so became their creature. In *Bingo* (1973) Shakespeare is just as much the product of his society's values, but Bond lays the blame for that on the artist whose creative imagination ought to make him live compassionately. Instead, Shakespeare sides with the rich against the weak, unlike his Lear, and withdraws from his wife and daughter. Both he and John Clare, in *The Fool* (1975), retreat to private worlds and are destroyed by that. As one of the poor, John could write about his friends' misery, but those with the money to buy his poems hate any 'smack of radicalism'.[19] Frustrated by that, he turns inward, obsessed by self-pity and escapist dreams, whereas he should have taught 'men how to eat' (148). The artist's private vision has become a trap. As Bond announced in his preface (1976), 'To say "X" is wrong . . . isn't enough. The right course or emphasis must be illustrated . . . We can't function efficiently as ant-like units in an organization, because each of us carries the whole community in himself' (76–7).

In the mid-seventies many left-wing theatre workers deliberated the course their art should take. By 1974 Gaskill had left the ESC to found Joint Stock with Max Stafford-Clark (from Edinburgh's Traverse) and the writer, David Hare. With no theatre-building to maintain, they could concentrate their resources on each new production and, with their actors, had time to explore a play's politics: 'we were constantly examining ourselves as political, social and economic beings. I think the process was strong and fertile and had a tremendous effect on the finished product'.[20] One of their venues was The Court's Theatre Upstairs whose own productions, bound by the ESC's economics, could not be developed in that concentrated, political way. Howard Brenton, during his tenure as The Court's resident dramatist in 1973, determined to 'get my plays on as big a stage as I could'; so when The National offered a commission, he insisted on their largest theatre. Impatient with the fringe's dream of slow but inevitable reform, he would confront the system head on: 'If you're going to change the world, well, there's only one set of tools, and they're bloody and stained but realistic. I mean communist tools.'[21]

Bond's Marxism led in the same direction. His libretto, *We Come to the River* (1974), for Hans Werner Henze, premièred at Covent Garden (1976). The opera's blind General is as articulate as Lear, but his example points the right course to the collective good more assertively. Bond began to urge his actors away from individual pathos. For *The Swing* (Inter-Action, 1976) he wanted the flurry over a supposed rape to end in farce. Stylised speech and gesture would show how the mechanical reactions of decent folk escalate into sadistic vengeance: 'we won't help anyone to understand how they could do it by trying to give their lives the dignity of tragedy' (Author's Note).[22] Bond was also committed to the collective force of playwrights and, from 1976 on, took an active part in the Theatre Writers' Union. The changed emphasis of Bond's politics shaped *The Woman* (written for The National, 1975–7). In Part One, Hecuba's misery makes her a hapless pawn of the Trojan War; in Part Two, she and the miner rise above their pitiful weakness to determine events. As individuals they struggle 'to take decisions . . . that is the only way in which they can represent large forces working through centuries: they are ordinary people who change the world'.[23]

The Bundle (Royal Shakespeare, 1978) exemplifies the 'rational' theatre Bond had arrived at. Reworking *Narrow Road*, he abandons ambiguity and humanism. The fisherman who ignores economic reality by rescuing a deserted baby brings greater poverty and ill-health upon his wife and himself. Their years of sacrifice persuade the child to offer himself to servitude in order to save them from the flooded river. But Wang learns from that and, freed from Basho's service, hurls a second orphan into the river in order to stay free. He sees that the river controls the peasants' lives and fights so they can master it. Whereas the warring factions in *Narrow Road* reacted violently through fear, Wang's battle against the landlords, at whatever cost to himself and his parents, will ensure the peasants 'food and clothes and knowledge'.[24] As a materialistic parable, *The*

Bundle's clear, logical structure is forceful, yet the new order Wang fights for is depressingly soul-less. In demanding we learn from the past, Bond's rational fable slants the history of present-day China to its own political ends.

The manipulative nature of these new poetics is even more apparent in *The Worlds* (1979), first performed by students in Newcastle while Bond was a Northern Arts Literary Fellow. Working with those actors and, later, with the Activists Youth Theatre at The Court, he urged them to interpret each character's social function. The play's 'two worlds' are both public: the 'real world', where money shapes 'our lives, our minds, what we are, the way we see'; and the 'apparent world' of humanitarian concern in which we think we live (78). Like Timon of Athens, Trench is surrounded by sycophants; but whereas Shakespeare's parable, distanced from the present, established itself as a Morality through pageant-like action and allegorical speeches, Bond's realistic account of capitalist greed presupposes shades of character. Denied those, the technocrats represent the world of appearances while politically-conscious workers and terrorists live in and for a 'real world'. The strings that pull these puppets show badly when businessmen mouth opportune platitudes and revolutionaries mouth dogma: 'We cannot patiently wait for society to fall apart. Reaction armed with modern technology could make the end of this century a graveyard . . . Therefore we fight' (26–7). Such was the lesson of the seventies when Labour governments seemed as enamoured of affluence and armaments as the Conservatives who, under Mrs Thatcher, took power in 1979. Whereas that history made it 'hard' for Marxist dramatists like David Hare 'to believe in the historical inevitability of something which has so frequently not happened',[25] Bond reacted with uncompromising urgency. 'Human history has reached a critical and probably decisive point', he warned in a book that celebrated twenty-five years at the Royal Court; 'it requires (as it did in the past) a reinterpretation of what it means to be human . . . It seems to me that you cannot any longer create art without socialism and that therefore it is not only nonsense to ask an actor to act in Beckett one night and in Brenton the next – it is also nonsense to expect the audience to enjoy one and then the other'.[26]

The ESC had not become the theatre he wanted: 'I think of Joint Stock as in some ways being the Royal Court in exile'.[27] Impossible though it was to alter course, even when Stafford-Clark had become the ESC's new artistic director, the company would launch the most dynamic version of Bond's rational style. In *Stone* (Gay Sweatshop, 1976), *Grandma Faust* (Inter-Action, 1976), and *The Cat* (libretto for Henze, 1979), he had allowed the cardboard figures of Morality, Cartoon, or animal fable to step out from their *play* into occasional songs which crystallise their situation while serving the conventions that define them. In *Restoration* (ESC, 1981), a comedy of manners, these songs give the characters an historical awareness; they can look back at the passive roles that imprison them and forward to their present-day relevance. This playfulness is signalled by Lord Are (the royal We) whose self-regarding stance as Restoration fop permits *asides* which criticise his world; then Bond extends that licence to the servants whose songs voice a power their masters keep from them. Their words are amplified electrically as a rock-band on a metal bridge above rolls downstage to enclose them in a new framework, and they sing of factories, rockets, gas chambers as products of their servile past: 'For fifty thousand years I was governed by men of wealth / Now I have learned to make the laws I need for myself' (20). When they step back in time, only Frank and Rose perceive their chains, but he disintegrates in powerless rage while she must 'stay quiet an' wait for the chance: it'll come' (38). As a West Indian black, she knows what slaves are, but her English husband, Bob, thinks he'll survive if he learns his employers' ways: London's 'churches an' palaces an' docks an' markets' impress him' (13). Condemned to die for a murder Are committed, he does odd jobs for the hangman and, spelling out his letters, *Man is what he knows*, lets the Parson instruct him. The fetters on his leg have no lock, yet he can't be the 'giant' Rose says he is. Society has shaped the way he sees, and his mother, another illiterate, burns the pardon Rose fought for. At the end, Rose looks from the bridge at a Blakean vision of grime and servitude. Determined to learn from Bob's death, she will be as hard as iron and as flexible as steel: 'I cross the bridge and go into the streets' (100).

Both levels of action allow audiences to see for themselves how knowledge is power and, through those insights, to participate in that power. But in *Summer* (National, 1982) the characters are prejudged by Bond's ideology. How they lived during the German occupation brands them for ever as pro- or anti-Fascist; there can be no middle ground. So history becomes an indictment instead of a way to learn and change. The play's realism, which invites one to assess nuances of behaviour, underscores its doctrinaire rigidity. Bond is essentially a fabulist and visionary. Shaped to that stance, *Human Cannon* (1985) effectively presents a family's journey to political consciousness during the Spanish Civil War, in the manner of Brecht's *Senora Carrar's Rifles*. But Bond finds no way to relate that story to the economics of Spain after Franco or, by implication, to Common Market affluence. So this play, too, seems locked in the past. However, the Falklands War and the ensuing jingoism that led to Mrs Thatcher's re-election, roused Bond to envision an apocalyptic future. *The War Plays* (Royal Shakespeare, 1985) moved beyond narrow politics. War turns men to beasts and the earth to ashes; worse still, the few survivors begin to repeat old patterns of fear and aggression. The impact of that trilogy and the RSC's revivals of *Lear* (1985) and *Restoration* (1988) confirmed Bond's status as a modern classic. Yet his failure to confront the collapse of Eastern Europe makes him an increasingly marginal figure in the nineties when hardline monetarists *and* Marxists can both be called right-wing.

To evade that accusation, 'A Short Book for Troubled Times' (1987) anatomises, with matter-of-fact simplicity, the inequities of Thatcherism;[28] yet, after *perestroika*, Bond cannot specify a communist alternative. In 'Notes on Post-Modernism' (1990), he wraps his theories of culture in the terminology of contemporary aesthetics. 'A Socialist Rhapsody' (1980) had begun by insisting that 'all explanations (even in the time of Derrida) rely on a theory of the working of cause-and-effect'. Bond's 'Notes' deconstruct that to stress the lateral 'relationship between people, technology and authority' (213)[29] and call the politics of staged action a 'meta-text' that would free theatre 'from the illusions of Ibsen's determinism, the nihilism of absurdity, and the enervating sensitivity of Beckett' (244). Of the plays which reflect those poetics, *Jackets* (Lancaster University, 1989) does present a new configuration of history. Part Two, in which a soldier kills himself for betraying his class, does not erase the fable of Part One, in which a Japanese schoolboy sacrifices himself for his Emperor. Both past and present are just as meaningful: Derrida's both/and replaces the traditional either/or.

In the Company of Men (1990), however, is a rambling, self-indulgent account of post-modernist society where man's *needs* become the *wants* of consumerism. That play is unproducible, while the gnomic style of the 'Notes' is difficult to penetrate. Bond has lost touch with his audience. Whereas *Derek* (RSC Youth Festival, 1982) gave a clear and painfully comic lesson on the way money controls thought, *September* (Canterbury Cathedral, 1989), written for the World Wildlife Fund, turns the murder of Chico Mendes and the destruction of Brazil's rainforest into a surreal and private vision of greed.

The writer who stood with the vanguard in 1968 now seems to have lost his way, like his own John Clare, who 'wandered round an' round'. As a school drop-out, unencumbered by established views, Bond knew injustice. Stage pictures gave him ways to show it, and the theatre caught up with him when it became politicised. British society gradually shaped his ideology and taught him words. Abandoning humanism for collectivism in the mid-seventies, his plays grew increasingly polemic. By the late eighties, as Marxism lost ground in Europe, his rational analysis of socio-economics turned esoteric, on stage and off. As Clare said in his isolation, 'We should hev come t'gither'.

Notes

1. Edward Bond, interviewed by Catherine Itzin for *Stages in the Revolution: Political Theatre in Britain Since 1968* (London: Methuen, 1980) p. 80.
2. John Osborne, 'On the Writer's Side', in *At The Royal Court*, ed. Richard Findlater (New York: Grove Press, 1981) p. 22.
3. Ann Jellicoe, 'The Writers' Group', in Findlater, p. 54.
4. Malcolm Hay and Philip Roberts, *Edward Bond: a Companion to the Plays* (London: TQ Publications, 1978) p. 8.
5. For a complete list to 1988 of the plays of Edward Bond (b. 1934), see *Contemporary Dramatists*, ed. D.L. Kirkpatrick (London: St James Press, 1988). Since 1988, Bond has published *Two Post-Modern Plays* (1990).
6. *The Pope's Wedding*, in Edward Bond, *Plays: One* (London: Methuen, 1977) p. 243. All quotations are from this edition; hereafter, page numbers will be given in the text. The three volumes of the Methuen series contain all Bond's plays from *The Pope's Wedding* to *The Woman*. Separate editions of his other works are also published by Methuen.
7. *Saved*, in Edward Bond, *Plays: One* (London: Methuen, 1977) p. 36. All quotations are from this edition; hereafter, page numbers will be given in the text.
8. Itzin, p. 222.
9. Ibid., p. 15.
10. Ibid., p. 79. For an overview of the *événements* in Paris and their impact on The Fringe, see John Bull, *New British Political Dramatists* (London: Macmillan, 1984) pp. 1–27.
11. *Early Morning*, in Edward Bond, *Plays: One* (London: Methuen, 1977)

p. 148. All quotations are from this edition; hereafter, page numbers will be given in the text.

12. Agitprop is deliberately one-sided since, as propaganda, it agitates support for a particular agenda. Brief and simplistic, such plays are designed for the streets and workers' assemblies.

13. Hay and Roberts, p. 67.

14. Itzin, pp. 226–7.

15. *Passion*, in Edward Bond, *Plays: Two* (London: Methuen, 1978) p. 252. All quotations are from this edition; hereafter, page numbers will be given in the text.

16. Hay and Roberts, p. 26.

17. *Lear*, in Edward Bond, *Plays: Two* (London: Methuen, 1978) p. 93. All quotations are from this edition; hereafter, page numbers will be given in the text.

18. Hay and Roberts, p. 45.

19. *The Fool*, in Edward Bond, *Plays: Three* (London: Methuen, 1978) p. 124. All quotations are from this edition; hereafter, page numbers will be given in the text.

20. Bill Gaskill, quoted by Itzin, p. 222.

21. Howard Brenton, quoted by Itzin, pp. 187–8.

22. Edward Bond, *The Swing*, in *A-A-America! and Stone* (London: Methuen, 1976) p. [34].

23. Edward Bond, *A Socialist Rhapsody*, in *Plays: Three* (London: Methuen, 1978) p. 270.

24. Edward Bond, *The Bundle* (London: Methuen, 1978) p. 46.

25. David Hare, 'A Lecture Given at King's College, Cambridge, March 1978', in *Licking Hitler* (London: Faber and Faber, 1978) p. 62.

26. Edward Bond, 'The Theatre I Want', in Findlater, pp. 121–3.

27. Ibid., p. 123.

28. Introduction to *Plays: Three* (London: Methuen, 1987).

29. In *Two Post-Modern Plays* (London: Methuen, 1990).

9

Stoppard's Theatre of Unknowing

Mary A. Doll

It should come as no surprise, given his background, that Tom Stoppard should be a playwright of paradox. His personal as well as professional life speak of a penchant for double, not stable, coding. Born in Zlin, Czechoslovakia, 3 July 1937, Tom Straussler became a child without a country, fleeing the effects of World War II by living with his family in Singapore, then in India, and finally in England – all before the age of nine. When his mother remarried after his father was killed, his name changed to Stoppard and his life changed from that of an immigrant – he called himself a 'bounced Czech' – to that of a privileged student in English preparatory schools.[1] Stoppard began his career as a journalist and theatre reviewer, although his real interest was in creating, not critiquing, plays. When at the age of twenty-nine he achieved world fame with his first play, *Rosencrantz and Guildenstern are Dead*, he became known as a university wit – without yet having attended university.

Such contradictions in Stoppard's personal life helped shape his multifaceted career. Unlike most of his artistic contemporaries, Stoppard has produced work in all media and in all genres, including critical articles in journals and newspapers; short stories; one novel; radio, television, and film scripts; and, of course, stage plays (twenty-four: sixteen original, eight adaptations) for which he is best known.[2] True to his sensibility Stoppard demonstrates that any attempt to name, point, place, picture or record any event as fact is completely ironic – irony being his chosen mode since it puts the point beside the point. Stoppard presents serious issues – like war, death, love, art, deceit, and treachery – with a light touch. His intention is to divest us of certainty, which he sees as an

117

arrogant attitude inherited from the postures of logical positivism and classical science.

The nearest attempt to categorise Stoppard has been made by Martin Esslin, who places the playwright beyond the Absurd in what he calls the post-Absurdist tradition.[3] Post-Absurdists go even farther than Absurdists in dispensing with unities of plot, character, and action, together with the illusion of certainty such unities assume. Esslin's word replacing 'unity' is 'mystery' or 'mystification' – the latter a word Stoppard uses.[4] Another word for Absurdism, 'paradox', Stoppard also employs to suggest the doubling quality inside his drama. 'Paradox and tautology', he once said. 'They don't have to mean anything, lead anywhere, be part of anything else. I just like them'.[5] In a Stoppard play doubling is a recognisable feature, including motifs of doubletiming, coincidence, and doublecrossing. There are – and this is a Stoppard hallmark – plays-within-plays; characters who are twins; characters who are different characters with the same names; and characters who are at the same time spies and counter-spies.

A second post-Absurdist trait of Stoppard's work is ambiguity. 'My plays', he has said, 'are a lot to do with the fact that I JUST DON'T KNOW'; such not-knowing he calls the '"definite maybe"'.[6] He often features a detective, a philosopher, a sleuth or a spy who, in the spirit of Isaac Newton or Sherlock Holmes, applies cause-and-effect logic to any problem at hand. Newton's postulate – from same beginnings will follow same ends – is ludicrously explored by Stoppard's detectives. Instead of a Newtonian universe, where problems can be solved, Stoppard ascribes to what post-modern science calls 'chaos theory'. Gaps, punctures and breaks in sequence sabotage every logical attempt to formulate a hypothesis. Indeed, Stoppard's greatest contribution to theatre may be his concept of the indeterminacies of what it is 'to know' as a hired professional, a spectator, or even as an ordinary human being.

A third quality of Absurdist drama is its plumbing of comedy for the presentation of serious themes. Where Stoppard clearly departs from the Absurdist tradition is in tone. Stoppard's tone is paradoxically both lighter – 'English high comedy' as Esslin puts it – and weightier.[7] Important issues are presented elegantly, often in the guise of gaming, including everything from bridge and billiards to ping pong, charades and cricket. But these games are really stylised rituals, meant to be seen as the games people play against two parts of themselves, against others, or against some higher ethical code.

Stoppard's first play, *Rosencrantz and Guildenstern are Dead* (1967) earned him deserved world-wide recognition. A comic-tragedy, it proposes a theme that runs through all his work – that what we witness is unrelated to reality or truth – and sets forth his post-Absurdist use of doubling, ambiguity, and elegant play. Doublecoded here, of course, is Shakespeare's *Hamlet*, which, like Stoppard's later *Dogg's Hamlet, Cahoot's Macbeth* (1979), places traditional theatre with its expectations of top-down authority and elevated blank verse alongside post-Absurdist theatre with its confusion in rank ordering and idiomatic speech. Stoppard thus deconstructs Shakespeare. 'Ros' and 'Guil' – mere functionaries in Shakespeare's world – enter Stoppard's world centre stage. It is they, not Hamlet, who ponder the serious issues of death, probability, relationship. It is they, not Hamlet, who emphasise the metaphor of theatre as a place where one can 'come to know' – but only in play time; for while Ros and Guil play-act their Shakespeare lines, we watch them watch the king watch the Players play the role of Hamlet's father ghosting the play. No one 'comes to know' with an assured Aristotelian sense.

Stoppard's second play, *Enter a Free Man* (1968), takes the existential themes of being and the impossibility of knowing into a new situation. The essence of being, Stoppard suggests, consists in playing ourselves as different people when we enter different situations. We are never 'free' since within our seemingly stable orders lie strange attractors luring us into other trajectories. The play concerns the underhanded schemes of George (he would like to escape his average home life) and daughter Linda (she would like to marry her motorcycle boyfriend), both of whom seek adventure outside the realm of the wife-mother Persephone (whose real home, we know from myth, is in the underworld, the realm of the hidden other self). To have an identity that stays the same in all situations is to engage in myth; but myth, Stoppard suggests, is a reality of sorts.

In *The Real Inspector Hound* (1968) Stoppard again takes up the issue of reality, this time inside the context of the whodunnit. What better character type to illustrate the indeterminacies of problem solving than an inspector and a spectator? The play is ostensibly about two drama critics reviewing a production, but the play-within-a-play motif provides a frame for Stoppard's borrowings from chaos theory. Indeed, as the philosopher of science Steven Toulmin comments, Stoppard has put to death the whole notion of what it is to be a spectator, since would-be spectators are transformed into agents, making us all agents in what we observe.[8] Stoppard plays with the idea of 'the death of the spectator' on two levels, both in terms of plot (one of the drama critic spectators, drawn into the living room whodunnit, gets murdered) and in terms of the spectator's role. The play is not about drama critics but about perception. If classical theatre, like classical science, depended on a stable order, then the study of chaos, like a Stoppard play, depends on dynamic orders. Perception shifts, disequilibrium ensues, and the part-whole relationship of observer to thing-observed – once considered fixed – erupts. Chaos theorists call the eruption of these new patterns 'fractals' or structures which are self-similar at different levels. Fractal patterns arise spontaneously and engage in activity that doubles, echoes, and mirrors – producing thereby an irregular order that does not depend on individual components. Stoppard spectators similarly must relinquish their role, classically defined as objective observers.

Part of the erupting order in this play is Stoppard's parodies of criticisms levelled at his work. The two critics, Moon and Birdboot, comment on the play they are viewing, which concerns a drawing room murder at Muldoon Manor. The play, they say, is a trifle; the characters are ciphers; the second act fails to fulfil the promise of the first act; there is hardly a whiff of social realism. More to Stoppard's point, however, is his fascination with the possibilities afforded art by non-linear dynamics. At issue is a storm, a house party, an intruder, a murder. A cosy order is disrupted by a murdered body. The statement about killing Simon Gascoyne seems to be a clue to the murder but is attributed to every suspect, making conclusion impossible. This particle of information loops and repeats, embedding layers of complexity. Like the manor house set apart in the storm with no roads leading to it, the observed problem cannot be 'gotten at' by traditional channels of thinking. We spectators are in the midst of a chaotic situation, adrift from tradition.

After Magritte (1971) contains a similar comment on methods of logical deduction leading to smug conclusions – falsely, of course. Matters which appear to the senses defy eye witness accounts and 'private eye' ratiocinations. Not only is Stoppard critiquing again the spectator theory of knowledge – where what one sees is what one knows – but he is also presenting issues concerning non-mimetic art, which in *Travesties* (1975) and *Artist Descending a Staircase* (1973, 1989) become central foci.

René Magritte (1898–1967) is a natural model for Stoppard since, like Stoppard's, Magritte's work multiplies ambiguities. In what Michel Foucault describes as a 'calligram', Magritte's painting 'aspires playfully to efface the oldest oppositions of our alphabetical civilisation: to show and to name; to shape and to say; to reproduce and to articulate; to imitate and to signify; to look and to read'.[9] Art's role is *not* to name, signify, shape, or show; it is to be insouciant, to celebrate difference. Magritte names his paintings wrongly in order to focus attention upon the very act of naming. But, as Foucault observes, 'in this split and drifting space, strange bonds are knit'.[10] Just as Foucault's writing about Magritte is a cornucopia of wisecracks meant to draw attention to absurdities, so too are Stoppard's plays.

Overlaps with Stoppard and Magritte are instructive. In *After Magritte* the stereotype detective Foot (flat-footed, literal) and police constable Holmes (after Sherlock) formulate a false hypothesis based on simple sensory data and mere shreds of evidence. Stoppard employs the metaphor of a light bulb – there are numerous references to Thomas Edison, inventor of electricity – to indicate ironically that with such reliance on ratiocination there can be no light, no sudden inspiration, and certainly no real seeing. 'Eye' witness accounts all prove wrong, and details which 'speak volumes to an experienced detective' speak the wrong volumes loudly. The situation in this play is of witnessing a bizarre spectacle – Mother lying on her back on an ironing board – presuming she is dead; witnessing the strange behaviour of Harris and Thelma – Harris dressed in thigh-length waders, Thelma dressed for ballroom dancing – and presuming there has been a crime. The absurdity of the situation might seem merely derivative of Magritte were it not for the fact that a similar incident actually occurred in the United States, when a museum guard observed through a museum window a grey-haired woman seated in a chair, not breathing; he called the fire department, which rushed to the rescue – of an art exhibit of a woman in a chair.[11]

Ambiguities of naming and knowing are centrally shown in *Jumpers* (1972), which features a professor/ philosopher, George Moore, named after George Edward Moore (1873–1958). The real George Moore's preoccupation, expressed in *Principia Ethica* (1903), had to do with questions of ethical theory (the meaning of 'good', 'right', and 'duty'), the theory of knowledge, and the nature of philosophical analysis. Of Stoppardian interest is Moore's obsession with the verb 'to know': how the act of 'knowing' relates to observation, to perception, and to expression. In the tradition of logical positivism, Moore attempted to define 'to know', endowing knowledge with qualities of certainty above and beyond what can be discovered through the five senses or articulated through imprecise language. George Edward Moore's leaps of logic become the ironic metaphor of *Jumpers*, where eight amateur acrobats form the backdrop against the speechifying character George Moore.

George is attempting to pinpoint the existence of God by examining data, looking for logical inferences, putting two and two together, and coming up with God. His mental gymnastics – spoofed by the somersaultings of gymnasts – only prove that 'the point' will not stand its ground. The positions of the acrobats shift – we learn they are trying to hide a corpse. So too does the position of George shift as he tries to hide his logic behind such philosophical corpses as those of Plato, Newton, and Russell. His jargon recalls the speech of Lucky, a slave to a tyrannical master in Samuel Beckett's *Waiting for Godot*, where phrases like 'established beyond all doubt' are positioned against phrases like 'for reasons unknown'. Dorothy, George's wife, is 'dotty': she sings stereotypical moon songs and needs therapy because her fantasies about the moon, thus about love, have been invaded either by technological moon landings or by her husband's excessive rationalism. While Stoppard's satire is clever, if overworked, a more serious theme runs through the play: the yearning for carnal knowing and for another kind of mind-knowing.

Stoppard continues to raise issues inside high comedy with *Travesties* (1975). The play takes its energy from a little-known event in literary history – a travesty of seriousness – and Oscar Wilde's *The Importance of Being Earnest* – a travesty of earnestness, the first event intersecting with the second. Amused by the anti-art Dada movement, Stoppard cheerfully seeks to dislocate his audience. Henry Carr, for instance, is the improbable fringe catalyst of chaos who remembers his time in war chiefly through recollecting what he wore (war/wore) – twill jodhphurs, silk cravats – war a metaphor for fashion. The first act introduces historical and fictional characters, who play with issues of art (Tristan Tzara, the Dadaist, is a character), history (Karl Marx is a character), and literature (James Joyce is a character). The first act, however, is parodied by the second act when a pretty girl delivers heavy speeches on Marxism and the theory of value – undercutting, thereby, the clever speeches of the fashionable first-act men.

Travesties shares many of the same concerns as the radio play *Artist Descending a Staircase* (1973), later turned into a stage play (1989). In both, art – not history or philosophy – conveys insight (to those who are not blindsighted), since the necessary 'fall' artists must make from the literal staircase of rationalism opens up the province of imagination. Tristan Tzara becomes perhaps the first Stoppard mouthpiece to articulate a clear position on the seriousness of play. Not only does he insist on the right of the artist to delude audience expectation but he insists on the ethical function of such denunciation, noting that wars are really fought for words like 'oil' and 'coal', not for words like 'freedom' and 'patriotism'. Dada art, like post-Absurdism, is thus committed to the serious enterprise of exposing the sophistry within every rational argument.

Stoppard has been criticised for trivialising serious issues or for being too neutral in the exposition of political ideas. Such indeterminancy, the critics argue, reduces the author's intent. Rather than answering his critics, Stoppard utilises their thinking to his own post-Absurdist effect. Switzerland, a neutral ground with its reassuring air of permanence, becomes in *Travesties* the centre of flux; a little-known event becomes the raw material from which the story draws its energy; uncertainty and confusion are like the cuckoos of Swiss clocks. It is not that chaos is chaotic, but that order has a false sense of security dressed in fancy clothes (tra-vesties).

Dirty Linen, and New-Found-Land (1976), a 'knickers farce', were reviewed negatively as 'undergraduate satire' or as 'altogether intolerable'.[12] While Stoppard's post-Absurdism here leans toward panache, it nevertheless reflects a serious Orwellian point about politics and the English language that the critics seemed to have missed. Spoofed in *Dirty Linen* is Parliamentary procedure, insti-tuted to safeguard government from corruption, but in fact safe-guarding government from the people's right to know. Similar to other social rituals, government committee proceedings pro-vide gaming situations where politicians can 'score' with Maddie Gotobed (an unsubtle name), and journalists covering committee deliberations can 'win' readers. 'Public trust', which must 'air its dirty linen', becomes just a meaningless phrase like *che sara sara*, *c'est la vie*, or *quel dommage*. Stoppard suggests that the devaluing of democratic principles is as universally accepted as the degen-eration of plain talk. This concern about democracy and language is mirrored in the second play, where America, the supposed new-found-land, is exposed as merely a trite idea propped up by stereotypes. The character Arthur takes us on a Whitmanesque celebration of 'America' coast to coast. But poetry dies inside bombast, as does meaning inside politics. Doublespeak leads to adultery in the private sphere and disinformation in the public sphere, and what mediates the lie in each is the noble-sounding word.

Every Good Boy Deserves Favour: a Piece for Actors and Orchestra (1977) – André Previn conducting – places Stoppard's comedy squarely inside a post-Absurdist framework, where the really serious issues of our time can no longer be discussed seriously (we have lost the capacity to hear) and so a new strategy must be found. One of Stoppard's new strategies is music, which speaks to the soul, not the mind. The setting, a mental institution inside a Soviet totalitarian regime, offers Stoppard yet another occasion to critique the logics that uphold institutions, be these 'democratic' or 'communist', and to show these logics as false. But with music as a background to the grim themes of torture, political prisoners, repressive regimes and mental illness, Stoppard softens his attack; and by exposing interrogation methods as bizarre, he shows the craziness of logic.

Recognisably Stoppardian is the situation of two men with the same name, Alexander Ivanov, one 'sane', the other 'insane'. Both characters rebel against the norm, but for different reasons. The case of the 'insane' Alexander reveals the validity of Greek culture, which saw a harmony between music and math. Deluded by the notion that his body contains an orchestra, Ivanov the lunatic brings back the wisdom of the Greeks, which in Euclidean geometry proclaimed two fascinating axioms: first, everyone is equal to the triangle; second, a point has position but no dimension. The first axiom warns against dichotomous, either/or rigidities. Accordingly, the lunatic plays a triangle, an instrument he uses to sabotage rigid regimes; he 'plays' against two-sided oppositional thinking with the triangle. His delusion, therefore, is ludic, a gaming protection against absolutes. The second axiom applies to the other Ivanov, the political prisoner, whose protest against totalitarianism has given him his public 'point' but has denied him his private 'dimension' with his son, Sacha. This character is thus a prisoner inside a belief system that excludes the middle: life lived among and between other people, like sons. That he is imprisoned by a totalitarian regime is symbolic of a frozen relationship with his son, a touching sub-theme.

In *Night and Day* (1978) the focus is again on language and politics and the war between the two. Set in a fictional black African country, Kambawe, the play concerns a nation faced with an internal revolution caused by conflicting economic and political systems. But of greater interest than the revolution is the attitude of the two journalists covering the war, their at-war viewpoints about reporting and factuality. Milne and Wagner are like night and day: the former a cynic, a self-seeking capitalist and a scab; the latter an idealist who believes that his profession is the Fourth Estate, capable of correcting the lies of politicians.

The play is also about colonisation: how not just countries or journalists but ordinary people like Ruth Carson can be occupied by foreign forces. Ruth engages inner speech, delivered outwardly, to suggest her contrast to the doubletalk of politicians; hers is the speaking back and forth from one 'country' of the self to another, in clear recognition that she has been colonised. In a particularly dramatic moment Ruth rails against the cant for which people die. Speaking between her two selves, she comes to see that winning wars is not for the liberation of Kambawe but for the ownership of Kambawe's resources: *King Solomon's Mines* played for 'reel'.

Stoppard continues language considerations in *Dogg's Hamlet, Cahoot's Macbeth* (1979), where in the preface he suggests that the play is an answer to Ludwig Wittgenstein's philosophical investigation proposing that different words describe different shapes and sizes. Ever fascinated with systems of thought, Stoppard exposes the assumption within the assumption, playfully and hilariously. In *Dogg's Hamlet* the language system to be learned is Dogg talk. Professor Dogg, to whom the play is dedicated, has his own set of words which Abel, Baker, and Charlie, in fine military fashion, understand. These three schoolboys are erecting a stage for a performance, but to put all the planks in place they need to know the lingo. The audience watches as they place planks on cue by a single command, much as dogs perform for masters. Spectators, not understanding the language, must themselves become doglike, trying to master tricks. The first thirty pages of playtext are, subsequently, Dogg talk, followed by the last fourteen pages, which derive from Shakespeare's *Hamlet*, including Hamlet's loaded line, 'Words, words, words', and Polonius' response, 'Though this be madness, yet there is method in it'.

Doublecoded within this situation is another situation, that of another Shakespeare play, *Macbeth*, dedicated to the Czechoslovakian playwright Pavel Kohout. Stoppard has instructed his audience sufficiently in the first part of his production so that when Easy enters, speaking only Dogg language, he becomes easily understood. The point of the nonsense seems to be this: plays within plays illustrate political situations; the Czech revolution, with its accompanying censorship of artists like Pavel Kohout, 'ghost' every attempt by Tom Stoppard, born in Czechoslovakia, to write in the free world. Both Macbeth and Hamlet have at their dramatic centres a ghost; so does Stoppard have at his centre a ghost – his own dead father and the censored artist from his fatherland. While British audiences are well schooled in understanding such rituals as parlor games and tea, these same audiences have no way of dealing with the black holes of totalitarianism. Stoppard brings forth spectres of his 'checkered' past (re-presented through Shakespeare) so that British ears may acquire new hearing, British eyes deeper seeing.

With *The Real Thing* (1982) Stoppard further engages serious themes. Like his first play, it won a Tony Award, deservedly so; it is a gem of a play, raising all of Stoppard's issues of the sixties and seventies with a new eighties elegance. The problem of language, the question of art's role in politics, the question of reality: these comprise the concerns which have almost become Stoppard hallmarks. Less familiar is Stoppard's treatment of 'knowing' as a carnal, not just an intellectual concern. *Knowing* – the yearning *to be known* without the mask – becomes a powerful theme because an impossible reality.

Two members of the writing profession, Brodie and Henry, are professional antagonists with different ideas of their trade. Brodie, committed to politics, believes that art should make a point about public policy; his language is unequivocal but trite. Henry believes that art is not 'about' anything: it is the thing itself. His play *House of Cards* is a metaphor for his theory of aesthetics as a house decked to fall. The spectator must acquire the skill to see that false claims or noble words are flimsy frames for truth. With its emphasis on the title word 'real', this play addresses the impossibility of knowing – in relationships, particularly – when truth is obscured by language.

Of central interest is Henry's desire to find for himself the undealt card of carnal knowledge. Knowing the flesh *in extremis* is stripping off the public mask, becoming finally naked to one's lover, one's self. But carnal knowing offers no guarantee of fidelity. In this play everyone carnally loves everyone else's spouse. Stoppard once again double codes Shakespeare – this time *Othello* – to show the tragic ends to which logical proofs can lead. A mere handkerchief 'stands' for more than it can define – betrayal – a reality which can never be defined to satisfy the condition of pain. *The Real Thing* is central to Stoppard's aesthetic intention. Through a mix of doubling, ambiguity, and playfully elegant wit, Stoppard makes his post-Absurdist point. Not only is it impossible to equate the thing 'named' or shown to the thing 'experienced', it is wrong, ethically and morally, so to do. In an impassioned speech for the function of paradox in language, Henry (speaking for Stoppard), says this:

> Words don't deserve . . . malarkey. They're innocent, neutral, precise, standing for this, describing that, meaning the other, so if you look after them you can build bridges across incomprehension and chaos. But when they get their corners knocked off, they're no good any more. . . . [13]

Words have corners, just as truth does: shades of meaning, opposite definitions, different parts of speech. The terrible irony is that words standing for 'this' while describing 'that' invite lying, publicly as well as privately. The solution is not to make ever more precise the terms of our knowing; the solution is to open up our ability to see the dead ends to which big words can lead when their corners get knocked off.

Hapgood (1988) is the most recent of Stoppard's work to advance the post-Absurdist motifs of mystification, ambiguity, and playfulness – this time with overt reference to spectator notions borrowed from scientific chaos theory. According to David Bohm, no continuous motion such as that presupposed by Newtonian cause-and-effect logic actually exists in nature. Instead, an examination of the dual role of both matter and energy reveals that things can be connected any distance away without any apparent force to carry that connection.[14] Rather than parts organising wholes – deduction's code of reasoning – it seems that parts *are* wholes. It seems, too, that discrete individual units (called 'the quantum' in science, 'the spectator' in theatre) are constantly attracted by turbulence and self-contradiction. How we know is a mystery based on an overall interrelatedness of things – a statement which chaos theorists readily accept. An interesting irony here is that Stoppard may ultimately appeal more to scientists schooled in chaos theory than to literary critics schooled in Aristotle.

Hapgood is a play about a character who is unable to pinpoint the truth she is seeking, either in her professional life as chief intelligence officer (called Mother) or in her private life as a single parent (also called Mother). No matter how Elizabeth Hapgood figures it, her seeing always eludes reality. The pivotal character is a Russian physicist, Joseph Kerner, who, like Barley Blair of the Stoppard-scripted movie, *The Russia House* (1990), has defected to the West to continue his research but who feeds back to the Soviet Union information that will mislead the Soviet scientists. That Kerner, Hapgood's lover, has a twin complicates the problem Hapgood has in trying to 'see' who he is (she, however, also plays at twinning). This doubled situation demonstrates the scientific property of electrons, which in quantum mechanics can be in two places at the same time.

While something subversive pervades Stoppard's post-Absurdist perspective, it is also curiously liberating. Stoppard shows us that every ordered system has rituals, which he delights in stylising so that we can see their mannered form. To consider any code as single-layered is totally to misrepresent reality. Reality seen through a Stoppard lens is always ambiguous; but its pain, though real, is not tragic. Stoppard's sharp wit cuts through the nonsense, giving us the grace to accept unknowing when confronted with such axioms as these: I am not who you think I am; the games we play are more serious than we think they are; the wars we fight are not for the causes they tell us they are.

Notes

1.   Stoppard attended a preparatory school in Nottinghamshire and a boarding grammar school in Yorkshire. (See Kenneth Tynan, 'Withdrawing with Style from the Chaos', *The New Yorker*, 19 December 1977, 41).

2.   For a list of Tom Stoppard's plays to 1988, see *Contemporary Dramatists*, ed. D.L. Kirkpatrick (London: St. James Press, 1988). Since 1988 Stoppard has rewritten one of his radio plays, *Artist Descending a Staircase*, for the stage (1973, 1989), and has also written a play entitled *In the Native State* (1991).

3.   Martin Esslin, *The Theatre of the Absurd* (1961; rpt. New York: Penguin Books, 1980). Victor Cahn also categorises Stoppard as a post-Absurdist in his *Beyond Absurdity: the Plays of Tom Stoppard* (Cranbury, N.J.: Associated University Presses, 1979).

4.   For discussion of the term 'mystery', see Esslin, pp. 413, 417, and

425; for 'mystification', see Esslin, p. 21. For Stoppard's use of the term 'mystification', see Stephen Schiff, 'Full Stoppard', *Vanity Fair* (May 1989) 215. Richard Corballis uses the former term in *Stoppard: the Mystery and the Clockwork* (New York: Methuen, 1984).

5. Schiff, op. cit., p. 215.
6. Tom Stoppard, 'The Definite Maybe', *Author* 78 (Spring 1967) 24.
7. Esslin, p. 434.
8. Steven Toulmin, *The Return to Cosmology: Postmodern Science and the Theology of Nature* (Berkeley: University of California Press, 1982) p. 238. That scientific post-modern chaos theories, articulated in the eighties, became metaphors for Stoppard's themes of mystification and ambiguity as early as the sixties suggests that Stoppard's post-Absurdism foreshadowed post-modernism (see note 14).
9. Michel Foucault, *This is Not a Pipe*, trans. and ed. James Harkness (Los Angeles: University of California Press, 1982) p. 12.
10. Ibid., p. 36.
11. 'Statue Brings Rescue to Standstill', *The Times-Picayune* (New Orleans), 4 January 1991, 2.
12. See Thomas R. Whitaker, *Tom Stoppard* (New York: Grove Press, 1983) p. 130.
13. Tom Stoppard, *The Real Thing* (London/Boston: Faber & Faber, 1983) p. 54.
14. See *The Reenchantment of Science*, ed. David Ray Griffin (Albany: State University of New York Press, 1988). See also Paul Davies, *The Cosmic Blueprint* (New York: Simon and Schuster, 1986); and James Gleick, *Chaos: Making a New Science* (New York: Viking, 1987).

10

Making History: the Plays of Howard Brenton

Hersh Zeifman

Since the performance of his first play, *Ladder of Fools*, at Cambridge University in 1965, Howard Brenton has written more than fifty dramatic works – a truly prodigious output for someone his age.[1] Like most major contemporary British dramatists, Brenton began his theatrical life in the 'fringe', with such shoestring companies as Brighton Combination and Portable Theatre. His career, then, is very much a post-1960 phenomenon; it could not really have existed (not, at any rate, in the form it has taken) before the proliferation in England of fringe theatre in the sixties. Brenton's approach to drama was simply too far removed from that of 'traditional' West End theatre; only in the fringe could he find the sort of 'laboratory' in which to explore new concepts of theatrical writing: socially and politically active, aggressively experimental. The fringe thus provided Brenton with a 'poor' theatre that was for him paradoxically rich, a theatre whose very poverty nurtured him. His early play *Gum and Goo* (1969), for example, was created 'with what was to hand – three actors, a few days, a budget of thirty shillings for a ball and three bicycle lamps'.[2] Eventually, however, the confines of the fringe proved more constraining than liberating: while he has never completely abandoned his dramatic roots, his work since the mid-seventies has been written progressively for large mainstream theatres like the National and the Royal Shakespeare Company. This attempt to infiltrate the mainstream with values developed in the fringe was regarded by Brenton as a kind of guerilla action, an 'armoured charabanc . . . parked' within the very heart of the Establishment.[3] 'I'd rather have my plays presented to 900 people who may hate what I'm saying', he commented in 1979, 'than to fifty of the converted'.[4]

The constant oscillation between fringe and mainstream reflects both the restless energy of Brenton's writing and its enormously wide range. Thus, some of his plays are small and intimate, written for just two or three actors, while others are huge-cast 'epics' (though epics 'which [have] nothing to do with Brecht. . . . I'm an anti-Brechtian, a Left anti-Brechtian').[5] Their performance venues have run the gamut from totally makeshift theatre spaces ('Portable plays weren't plays for stages')[6] to deliberately non-theatrical site-specific locations (*Wesley* [1970] was performed in a Methodist church; *Scott of the Antarctic* [1971] in an ice rink!) to the most technologically sophisticated stages in the nation. The bulk of Brenton's drama consists of original plays of which he is the sole author, but he has also written many adaptations and translations, as well as frequently collaborating with other dramatists (most often, and most notably, with David Hare) and occasionally creating plays collectively with particular theatre companies. Further, in addition to many poems and one novel (*Diving for Pearls* [1989]), Brenton's oeuvre encompasses all the performance media: stage, film, television and radio.

Analysing the central characters of some of his early fringe drama, Brenton once commented:

> I'm very interested in people who could be called saints, perverse saints, who try to drive a straight line through very complex situations, and usually become honed down to the point of death.[7]

Specifically, Brenton had in mind such 'perverse saints' in his plays as Christie, the notorious mass-murderer of *Christie in Love* (1969); the eponymous 'heroes' of *Wesley* and *Scott of the Antarctic*; and Violette Szabo, the World War Two British secret agent in *Hitler Dances* (1972). What is interesting about all of the above characters is not simply their shared fanaticism, however, but their grounding in history: each of them is a genuine historical figure.

Brenton's fascination with figures from history is a major thread running through his entire dramatic career[8] – not because he is fixated on the past *per se*, but because an examination of the past can most clearly illuminate the present. '[I]f you don't understand the past, you'll never understand the present, let alone the future', Brenton has stated, adding that he views his drama as '"history plays for now"'.'[9] This compulsion to discover the roots of the present in the past is the engine driving all of his plays: for Brenton, the malignant values of a capitalist cancer are rapidly spreading throughout present-day Britain, and he is desperate to know its origins so as to help provide a 'cure'.

Brenton's politics are thus, inevitably, an integral part of his drama. 'My political views', he has written, 'are . . . naturally and passionately expressed in my plays':

> It is glaringly obvious to [me] that the western world is in thrall to a system that respects nothing but money and power, . . . that our liberation lies in democratic and socialist movements, and if we are to survive and have a common destiny it will be communist.[10]

'I want a socialist government in this country', he has further declared. 'I think it's down to "red" writers to hammer plays with socialist concerns into the centre of the theatre'.[11] Brenton is far too subtle a writer, however, to use a hammer (let alone a hammer and sickle) when a less blunt object can do the job so much more elegantly and efficiently. His weapon of choice is more a rapier, designed to burst the bubble of a pervasive and pernicious comic-book view of history which mythologises historical figures into cartoon 'heroes'. It is this gross distortion of the past, Brenton's plays suggest, that has led to a grossly – and dangerously – distorted present, and thus to a future teetering on the brink of annihilation.

One of the central concerns, then, of Brenton's drama is to demythologise the past by deconstructing representative historical figures. This move on Brenton's part to 'rewrite' history emphasises that history is *written* (or, better, already *re*written), that it is subjectively composed (and therefore ideologically determined) rather than simply a recording of 'objective facts'. As Michael Zelenak has noted: 'The concept that history is a closed system, something "out there", something "objective", an indisputable body of facts, leads to a passive attitude towards the political-economic system'.[12] Brenton's desire to rip open that 'closed system', to reject passivity, was heavily influenced by his reading of 'situationist' political writers in the late sixties:

> The situationists describe our world as 'the society of the spectacle'. There is a screen called public life which is reported on

the telly and in the newspapers. This version of public life is a spectacle, it operates within its own laws. It's a vast, intricate confidence game.[13]

The 'spectacle' of public life is created not only by the mass media but by culture generally – by history books: 'The situationists showed how all of them, the dead greats, are corpses on our backs . . . – how gigantic the fraud is'.[14] In western capitalist societies, history has become like a movie, a 'screen', a series of two-dimensional (and larger-than-life) *images* seemingly impervious to change. It is the 'teflon' view of history: the surface image has become so 'fixed' that nothing potentially subversive can stick to it, can disrupt the spectacle.

Brenton's theatre attempts to expose the 'fraud' of history precisely by disrupting the spectacle. In his play *Magnificence* (1973), the revolutionary Jed recalls once sitting near a drunk in the cinema who became so enraged with a terrible Hollywood film starring Carroll Baker that he chucked his bottle of wine at the screen, 'right through Miss Baker's left tit':

The left tit moved on in an instant, of course. But for the rest of the film, there was that bottle shaped hole. . . . One blemish on the screen. But somehow you couldn't watch the film from then. . . .
The poor bomber. Bomb 'em. Again and again. Right through their silver screen. Disrupt the spectacle.[15]

Brenton's revolution takes a different path from Jed's; instead of hurling a bomb, he disrupts the spectacle by *disrupting speculation*. Brenton's 'attack' is thus mounted primarily against the audiences of his plays, disrupting their speculation in both senses of the word: first *what* they see, and then what they *think* about what they see. The stylistic and dramaturgical disruption of the former, Brenton hopes, will lead to the ideological and political disruption of the latter: audiences will begin to speculate differently about certain historical 'truths'. '[T]here's no dialectic on the stage . . . ', Brenton has stated. 'The true dialectic happens between the audience you address and the play itself'.[16]

The Churchill Play (1974), commissioned by the Nottingham Playhouse to mark the centenary of Churchill's birth, was the first of Brenton's 'epic' plays to deconstruct a historical figure. The play opens in a dim light, revealing four servicemen guarding a flag-draped coffin; we appear to be in Westminster Palace Hall in 1965 (_'a huge stained glass window of medieval knights in prayer'_)[17] where Churchill's body lies in state. This speculation is quickly disrupted, however, by the sound of knocking from within the coffin, followed by a startling 'resurrection':

> CHURCHILL _bursts out of his coffin, swirling the Union Jack. The Churchill actor must assume an exact replica. His face is a mask. He holds an unlit cigar._ (113)

Just as we are trying to make sense of this eerie visitor from beyond the grave, Brenton introduces yet another disruption: neon strip-lights suddenly flicker above the stage, casting an entirely different light on the scene. This is not Westminster, it turns out, but Camp Churchill, an internment camp for social and political dissidents (the twenty-eighth such camp in the British Isles); it is not 1965 but, ominously, 1984; and 'Churchill' and 'the servicemen' are in actuality camp inmates rehearsing a play to be performed in front of a parliamentary inspection committee. The theatrical imagery here – the fact that we begin with a play-within-a-play – immediately establishes the questioning of 'reality' as a central theme in the drama. Everything we have seen so far has been fake; the stained-glass window is only _'a flimsy, paper construction'_ (115), the face of Churchill merely a mask: 'JOBY [the inmate playing Churchill] _pulls off Churchill's face. His own is puckered, shifty, hangdog and sly'_ (115). The man we thought to be Churchill is thus revealed as a specifically dramatic construct; Brenton's point is that the same can be said of the 'real' Churchill. Historical figures are as much a 'construct' as are characters in a play – 'airy nothings' conjured into illusory existence.

Although Churchill was the first historical figure in Brenton's mainstream drama to be 'resurrected' in this manner, his earlier fringe plays provide many similar examples. The title character of _Christie in Love_, for instance, is 'invoked' by two policemen ('Out you come Reg'),[18] rising 'monster-like' from the 'pen' of old newspapers (the prime source of his historical reputation) under which he has been literally buried. Christie's first appearance, Brenton notes, 'is in the Dracula tradition':

> He rises from the grave luridly, in a frightening mask. It looks as

if a juicy evening's underway, all laughs, nice shivers, easy oohs and aahs.

But that's smashed up. The lights are slammed on, and the mask is seen as only a tatty bit of papier mâché. Off it comes, and what's left is a feeble, ordinary man blinking through his pebble glasses.[19]

Those 'constructed' by history as 'monsters' may, in fact, be disconcertingly human. 'Why can't a mass murderer be just a bit diabolical?', one of the cops asks Christie. 'Why can't a pervert like you, already in the annals of nastiness, have fangs or something? Roll your eyes around. Sprout horns' (20). By ripping away the 'mask' history has imposed on Christie, Brenton forces the audience to speculate on the corruption and hypocrisy of the society at large (represented in the play by the policemen as 'moral' arbiters) whose suspect values created that mask in the first place.

Violette Szabo, the 'heroine' of Brenton's *Hitler Dances*, is another historical figure theatrically conjured into being: a 'ghost' invoked by the dead German soldier Hans, himself a 'ghost' whose masked corpse is resurrected from the rubble-heap of history at the start of the play. Hans later offers to tell Linda, one of the children playing on his grave, a 'war story' about a beautiful young woman:

[HANS] *draws his hands down in the air, the figure of a woman.*

Not like the joke, dead serious, putting the grown VIOLETTE *there.*

And before them, a spot comes up, gently, on [VIOLETTE].[20]

Violette is thus 'constructed' almost literally out of thin air; the fact that she is a construct, like all historical figures, is further emphasised by her being played at different times by all three women in the cast. History, generated in this instance by such romantic war films as the ostensibly biographical *Carve Her Name With Pride* (Rank, 1958), informs us that Violette was a courageous British spy, tortured by the Nazis while fighting for freedom and 'civilisation'. The truth, however, unlike the historical myth, is very different, and far more mundane: because of 'administrative confusion' (74), Violette was never in fact tortured by the Gestapo. Her entire mission in occupied France turned out to be utterly worthless.

The Violette of romantic history, the Violette parodied by Brenton, is portrayed throughout the play as if in a film, a figure on a *screen*: her first words are thus spoken in a deliberately exaggerated French accent, while her encounter with the 'brave French officer' with whom she falls in love is presented as self-consciously cinematic (34–5). 'I want to learn to love and kill . . . ', Violette sings towards the end of the play, 'And carve my name in flesh and pride' (53). Her words, however, by echoing the title of the film which falsely glorified her exploits, betray the phoniness of her 'heroism'. Brenton deconstructs the Violette of history because the ideology which created it is an especially dangerous one: the romanticisation of war in general and the 'nobility' of British military strategy in particular. The demythologised Violette Brenton presents us with instead in *Hitler Dances* is the 'heroine' of a specifically 'NASTY story' (62), fighting not to preserve freedom but unconsciously to *subvert* it. As Max Stafford-Clark, the play's original director, commented: 'In order to fight fascism, the country had to become fascist itself. Violette is trained, corrupted, turned into a killer. To fight evil a society often unites and responds in an evil way'.[21]

The figurehead of that fight against evil in a united wartime Britain was, of course, Winston Churchill. Churchill 'saved this country from one thousand years of barbarism', states Colonel Ball, the camp commandant in *The Churchill Play*. 'So no disrespect to the memory of that great man' (119). The question Brenton shockingly poses in the play is whether Churchill indeed prevented 'barbarism' or, rather, *initiated* it:

> The idea that Churchill is universally admired by people who went through the war is not true, but what they always say . . . [is] 'He gave us freedom'. And the question of freedom becomes paramount – you say, 'What freedom? What do we do with that freedom? What have we done with it?' And the answer at the moment is, we are in danger of throwing it away – and also that *it's not freedom*.[22]

The historical myth known as Winston Churchill is systematically deconstructed by Brenton in the inmates' play-within-a-play. Hence their version of the post-war Yalta Conference, for example, staged in a tin bath (symbolising 'Europe, sat upon by 'bums a Super Powers'), with one of the inmates cast as a bar of soap! The soap '[s]tands for historical truth', explains Joby- as-Churchill. 'In all 'er vulnerability . . . , worn away by brutal 'ands. Now a mere slither, a pale thing. . . . Easily lost at bottom a bath' (142). The inmates' play – titled, significantly, '"The Other Second World War", or "You won't believe where I'm going to put my cigar!"' (158) – represents Brenton's attempt to recuperate that 'sliver' of soap. For Brenton has an 'other' history to unfold, one that directly challenges the 'official version'. The Churchill portrayed by the inmates of the camp that bears his name is not at all the great statesman of myth, the Churchill described as looking '[l]ike he'd come down from a cinema screen, out of a film show' (169). In his place, as John Bull suggests, stands 'the archetypal figure of an establishment whose ideology has provided the bricks of the camp'.[23] Churchill's callous and consistent indifference to civil liberties – the subversive reality behind the myth as dramatised repeatedly in the inmates' play – has inexorably led, Brenton argues, to this Orwellian 'English Dachau' (156).

The central character of Brenton's *Weapons of Happiness* (1976), the first new play to be performed at the National Theatre, is likewise a 'resurrected' historical figure: Christie's self-description, 'I pass like a ghost through Society' (23), could just as easily refer to Josef Frank. Frank is a 'ghost' both literally (the historical Josef Frank, we are informed by a note in the text, 'was hanged in Prague on the 3rd of December 1952')[24] and metaphorically – the latter a result of the former. A martyr of the left, the communist Frank was a Czech cabinet minister purged in one of Stalin's notorious show trials. Having bèen 'disinterred' by Brenton and given theatrical 'life' as a labourer in a crisps factory in mid-seventies London, Frank is still 'dead': emotionally, spiritually. 'I'm a . . . Hole in the air', he explains to one of his co-workers, Janice. 'I'm dead to you. You're dead to me. I'm nothing. . . . I'm . . . [a] vacuum' (200). 'Mr Dracula', as Janice calls Frank, '[h]alf in half out [his] grave' (232), has been so traumatised by his experiences under Stalin that he has cut himself off from all feelings and beliefs – especially a belief in socialism. When his young co-workers – all disenfranchised, all 'handicapped' in one way or another – discover that they have been sold out by the capitalist system and decide to stage a 'revolution' by occupying the factory, Frank wants nothing to do with them. History has taught him a painful and bloody lesson: socialist revolution leads only to Stalin and the death camps. Repeatedly muttering to himself the despairing mantra, '[t]oo much lost, too much blood' (206), Frank has chosen as his motto 'I am not involved!' (208).

Frank exists in what he thinks of as a protective cocoon, buried deep among the 'ignorant English, like a warm overcoat' (183). Yet hard as he tries to escape from history, memories of the past keep haunting him – specifically the ghost of Stalin: '*A choir sings. The portrait of* STALIN, *huge, glows through the snow.* STALIN *advances, smiling, smoking a pipe*' (206). By bringing Stalin directly onto the stage, by refusing to temper 'the man of steel' and thus deny or explain away his crimes, Brenton faces head-on the frightening legacy of communism. What Brenton stated about his later drama *Thirteenth Night* (1981), a dystopian 'dream play' modeled on Shakespeare's *Macbeth*, applies equally to *Weapons of Happiness*: 'I get sick of plays about the left, or for the left, which do not mention the basic socialist problem. I mean – the blood in the revolution's cradle. It's about Stalinism'.[25] 'Tyranny is tyranny', Brenton has noted, whether of the right or of the left.[26] Brenton's courage in 'hanging up the left's dirty, indeed bloodstained, linen in public' (especially when that public clothes-line is strung across the stage of the National, the heart of Establishment theatre) is risky but admirable.[27] What gets deconstructed in the play, then, is not so much Stalin himself as the myth of 'Stalinism': the belief that socialist revolt must *inevitably* result in tyranny, in that larger-than-life figure marching ominously through the snow. This, for Brenton, is the truly poisonous legacy of Stalinism: the killing of hope in former (or, more crucially, future) believers, the cynical retreat into apathy.

Unlike Janice, who knows little about history and cares less ('[T]here in't no history. Never happened. And if it did, make it go away' [232]), Frank knows far too much. After Stalin, who can believe in socialism? Frank, however, discovers that he can, and he does so not by turning Janice's blind eye to history but by facing it squarely – the betrayals, the massacres – and *still* affirming his faith. *Weapons* is Brenton's political version of such 'rebirth' tales as Sleeping Beauty, in which Frank finds himself 'awakened' by Janice with a kiss (211), a kiss that symbolically rekindles his socialist faith. Brenton 'resurrects' Frank's 'ghost' in two different senses in the play: recuperating him both from his *literal* death, thus giving him a second life, and from his *spiritual* 'death', thus making that second life meaningful by banishing despair. Boldly deconstructing the historical Josef Frank, Brenton disrupts speculation not about the horror of socialism betrayed (which is dramatised unflinchingly) but about the 'moral' to be drawn from it. For Frank is allowed to recover an important truth:

You do not have the chance for revolt often. And, often, it is
ridiculous. Fleeting. Difficult to think through. But it is rare.
And not to be thrown away. It is the most precious thing on
earth. (244)

This is what Frank and the audience have needed to learn: it is
Stalin's *perversion* of socialist ideals that is tainted and corrupt, not
the ideals themselves.

The Romans in Britain (1980) continues Brenton's deconstruction
of historical figures by focusing, in Part One of the play, on Julius
Caesar and his second invasion of Celtic Britain in 54 B.C. '[T]he
play', Brenton notes, 'takes a rooted, popular myth from the British national consciousness'[28] – that Caesar and his army brought
civilisation and enlightenment to a benighted isle – and turns it on
its head. Our initial introduction to the Roman army occurs in Scene
3, a deceptively innocent one: three Roman soldiers, desperate for
a swim, encounter three young Celtic boys standing between them
and the river. By the time the scene has ended, two of the boys are
dead and the third, Marban, has been violated in a brutally explicit
attempted rape. The attempted rape was designed by Brenton to
be deliberately shocking – partly because of the obscene casualness
of the soldiers;[29] partly because Marban is very young (in his mid
teens), 'sacred' (an apprentice Druid priest) and – most threatening
of all, at least for the men in the audience – a male.[30] As the third
soldier '*cuts* MARBAN *on the buttocks*' before '*attempt[ing] to bugger
him*', the second soldier cheerfully explains his colleague's '[f]unny
little ways' to the stunned Celt: 'My friend has been to the Orient.
Persia? . . . The other side of the world? . . . World? . . . Empire?'[31]
Brenton's point is painfully (and graphically) clear: the Romans in
Britain indeed 'mounted' an 'invasion', an imperialist rape.

That the rape is symbolic of Caesar's assault on Britain is emphasised in Scene 5, the first scene in which Caesar himself literally (and
not just metonymically) appears. The setting is exactly the same as
in Scene 3, the rape scene: the dead bodies of the two Celtic boys
still litter the ground, soon to be joined by the corpses of their foster
parents killed in a concurrent 'little massacre' (51). Accompanied
significantly by his historian, to whom he makes occasional remarks
'for the Official Biography' (46), the vain and treacherous Caesar
we encounter is hardly the great conqueror of historical myth. Too
self-involved to register the carnage that surrounds him, Brenton's
demythologised Caesar is blithely indifferent to the cataclysm that

has just occurred. The invasion for him is simply 'a squalid little raid . . . in a filthy backwater of humanity' (44, 46), its victims dismissed as 'wogs' (47) and 'niggers' (46). When the bound and naked Marban is brought before him, Caesar ruthlessly completes what the third soldier only attempted by tying a pendant of Venus around the young priest's neck: '[T]here are new Gods now. Do you understand? The old Gods are dead' (49) – a spiritual 'rape' far more calculated and ultimately deadly than the attempted rape of Marban's body. This scene is ironically titled by Brenton 'Caesar's Tooth' (also the overall title of Part One); for Caesar, the invasion has been simply a minor irritant, an aching tooth easily yanked out and then thrown away, but for the Celts – and for the audience in the theatre – it has meant the wholesale destruction of an entire 'world'.

The Roman assault is not yet over, however, for in Scene 7, the final scene in Part One, Caesar makes a return appearance. Preceded by the sound of a helicopter and the entrance of his army, now carrying two-way radios and machine guns, Caesar and his staff drive onto the stage in a jeep, 'in the dress of British Army Officers' (57). Encountering the 'enemy' (a lone woman brandishing a stone), the soldiers open fire and blast her away; the epitaph subsequently spoken by one of the soldiers over her corpse is brief and to the point: 'Fucking bogshitting mick! . . . Kick the shit out of your fucking country!' (57). This brilliant disruption of audience speculation – the Romans in Britain suddenly transformed into the British in Ireland – is a stunning *coup de théâtre*, and the true focus of Brenton's concern in the play (particularly in Part Two). The myths of history bleed, metaphorically and often literally, from one century into another; as Richard Boon notes: 'Past and present co-exist in one continuum, constantly making and re-making each other'.[32] Brenton's 'collapsed' time frame in Part One subtly reflects this continuum: the roughly two millennia separating ancient Britain from modern Ireland are bridged in only 24 hours (from the darkness before dawn in Scene 1 to the dawn of the next day in Scene 7). Not even a whole day is required: in a single heart-stopping moment, one Celtic society is instantly conflated with another. And both are shown to be destroyed by the weapons of Empire, among the most potent of which are the mythologised 'constructions' of history.[33]

The myths of history are also the subject of one of Brenton's most recent works, *H.I.D.* (1989), a play 'which attempts to dissect the murky entrails of the "truth" of Rudolf Hess's death in Spandau prison using the unscientific precision of drama. . . . '[34] History informs us that Hess, Hitler's deputy, took his own life; Larry Palmer, an investigative journalist in the play, is not convinced – especially after watching a reconstruction, both on videotape and 'live', of Hess's purported (and clearly unlikely) suicide. (Significantly, Hess himself never appears on stage, not even as a 'ghost'). As the play progresses, Brenton gradually deconstructs that reconstruction, forcing the audience to speculate on the process through which Hess's death has been specifically 'constructed' by history. The historical 'official line'[35] ultimately turns out to be as flimsy a construct as the notional 'room' in which the dramatic action is set, its walls formed by long blue tapestries which sway in response to the slightest movement – unstable, fluid, constantly shifting. H.I.D., according to the play's full title, stands for (Hess Is Dead), but what truths, Brenton wonders, are 'hid' in this abbreviation that seems simply to be stating a historical fact? What truths are 'hid' behind the apparently objective 'facts' of history? Like the aptly named Palmer, Brenton is on a kind of holy 'pilgrimage' in his plays, a quest to discover the historical truths that reside 'in the walls beyond the walls. . . . That you can get to through a little door' (62; my emphasis). All of Brenton's drama is finally an attempt to open that 'little door', to allow an audience a glimpse at the 'uncooked' truths that history has consistently 'hid' and suppressed.[36]

'Who will write the history of the rewriters of history?' (50), asks one of the characters in H.I.D. This is the task Howard Brenton has chosen for his theatre. By deconstructing representative historical figures in his plays, however, Brenton ironically appears to be laying himself open to the charge that he too is 'rewriting' history. The crucial difference is that Brenton never pretends otherwise: what we call history is, he acknowledges, always an ideological 'construct'. In disrupting speculation, Brenton thus hopes to 'shake up' his audiences sufficiently for them to examine the hidden biases that are constantly at work in 'making history' – for them to see that history, like any other 'commodity', is literally *made*. What audiences specifically decide to do with this insight is then up to them. 'You don't write to convert', Brenton has stated. 'More – to stir things up. For people to make what they wish of it. When it comes to agit-prop, I like the agit, the prop I'm very bad at'.[37] Strident propaganda has never been a major weapon in Brenton's theatrical arsenal. A truly subversive playwright like Brenton does not hector his audiences into embracing his beliefs; instead, he encourages them to question their own. As Brenton commented in a haiku written during *The Romans in Britain* controversy:

> Writers understand
> Hate cannot amplify truth
> Contradiction can[38]

What Brenton is ideally aiming to produce in his audiences, then, is 'a sense of moral vertigo',[39] a rethinking of previously unexamined ideological positions. It was this 'vertigo' that first attracted Peter Hall, the former director of the National Theatre, to Brenton's work: 'The Churchill Play . . . is quite magnificent. New writing is the only way one can hear the voice of the present. And with this play I heard it alright. . . . A voice which makes you revalue your own attitudes'.[40] Howard Brenton possesses a brilliantly distinctive and disturbing theatrical 'voice' – funny, seductive, compulsively challenging: one of the finest voices in the entire raucous and powerful choir of contemporary British theatre.

Notes

1. For a complete list to 1988 of the plays of Howard Brenton (b. 1942) see *Contemporary Dramatists*, ed. D.L. Kirkpatrick (London: St James Press, 1988). Since *Contemporary Dramatists* Brenton has published *Greenland* (1988), *H.I.D. (Hess Is Dead)* (1989), *A Sky Blue Life*, *How Beautiful with Badges*, *Measure for Measure* (1989; all three plays predate 1989, but none was previously published), *Iranian Nights* (1989; co-written with Tariq Ali), *The Wall-Dog* (1990; English version of Manfred Karge's *Der Mauerhund*, from a translation by Jane Brenton) and *Moscow Gold* (1990; co-written with Tariq Ali).
2. Howard Brenton, 'Author's Note' for *Gum and Goo*, in *Plays for the Poor Theatre* (London: Methuen, 1980) p. 56. Note Brenton's title for this collection of early fringe plays.
3. Howard Brenton, quoted by Sheridan Morley in 'The Man Behind the Lyttelton's First New Play', *The Times* (London), 10 July 1976, p. 9.
4. Howard Brenton, quoted by Malcolm Hay and Philip Roberts in 'Howard Brenton: an Introduction', *Performing Arts Journal*, 3, 3 (Winter 1979) 133.
5. Howard Brenton, interviewed by Catherine Itzin and Simon Trussler in 'Petrol Bombs Through the Proscenium Arch', *Theatre Quarterly*, 5, 17 (March–May 1975) 14.

6. Ibid., p. 10.

7. Ibid., p. 12.

8. In addition to 'resurrecting' the ghosts of history in his drama, Brenton has also written many plays featuring contemporary public figures – sometimes identified explicitly (Margaret Thatcher, for example [the play in which she appears, *A Short Sharp Shock!* (1980), co-written with Tony Howard, was originally titled *Ditch the Bitch*], or Gorbachev in *Moscow Gold* (1990), co-written with Tariq Ali) but more often alluded to implicitly. Thus critics have found barely disguised portraits of recent public figures in such Brenton works as *Fruit* (1970); *Measure for Measure* (1972); *Pravda* (1985), co-written with David Hare; *Greenland* (1988); and *Iranian Nights* (1989), co-written with Tariq Ali. Brenton has also written a number of plays specifically about famous writers (Gorky in *A Sky Blue Life* [1966; rev. 1971]; Byron and Shelley in *Bloody Poetry* [1984]); for the purposes of this essay, however, I am excluding writers from the category of 'historical figures'.

9. Howard Brenton, in Malcolm Hay and Philip Roberts, 'Interview: Howard Brenton', *Performing Arts Journal*, 3, 3 (Winter 1979) 136, 138.

10. Howard Brenton, 'Preface', *Brenton Plays: One* (London: Methuen, 1986) pp. ix–x.

11. Howard Brenton, interviewed by Tony Mitchell in 'The Red Theatre under the Bed', *New Theatre Quarterly*, 3, 11 (August 1987) 196.

12. Michael X. Zelenak, 'The Politics of History: Howard Brenton's Adaptations', *Theater* (Yale), 18, 1 (Fall/Winter 1986) 55.

13. Howard Brenton, quoted by Peter Ansorge in 'Underground Explorations No.1: Portable Playwrights', *Plays and Players*, 19, 5 (February 1972) 16. The central situationist text is Guy Debord, *La Société du Spectacle* (Paris: Buchet-Chastel, 1967); an English translation, *The Society of the Spectacle*, was published in 1970 by the Black and Red Printing Cooperative, Detroit. For an excellent summary of the situationist position, see Richard Boon, *Brenton the Playwright* (London: Methuen, 1991) pp. 54–5.

14. 'Petrol Bombs', p. 20.

15. *Magnificence*, in *Brenton Plays: One*, pp. 95–6. A similar recipe for 'disrupting the spectacle' is offered by the ghost of Emily Davison, the suffragist who threw herself in front of the King's horse at the 1913 Derby, in *Epsom Downs* (1977): 'England at peace on Derby day. It is just a picture, thin as paint. Slash it. . . . See the dirty wall behind'. *Epsom Downs*, in *Brenton Plays: One*, p. 305.

16. Howard Brenton, quoted by Jonathan Hammond in 'Messages First: an Interview with Howard Brenton', *Gambit*, 6, 23 (1973) 26.

17. *The Churchill Play*, in *Brenton Plays: One*, p. 111. All further page references will be cited in the text.

18. *Christie in Love*, in *Brenton Plays: One*, p. 12. All further page references will be cited in the text.

19. 'Author's Production Note' for *Christie in Love*, p. 2.

20. Howard Brenton, *Hitler Dances* (London: Methuen, 1982) p. 33. All further page references will be cited in the text.
21. Max Stafford-Clark, quoted by Peter Ansorge in 'Underground Explorations No. 4: War Games', *Plays and Players*, 19, 8 (May 1972) 16.
22. 'Petrol Bombs', p. 15; my emphasis.
23. John Bull, *New British Political Dramatists* (London: Macmillan, 1984) p. 58.
24. *Weapons of Happiness*, in *Brenton Plays: One*, p. 180. All further page references will be cited in the text.
25. 'The Red Theatre', p. 200. The ghost of Stalin also makes a brief appearance in *Thirteenth Night* – the answer to, and thus the judgment on, Jack Beaty's attempt to justify his crimes for the sake of a 'larger goal', the establishment of a truly socialist government in England: '"So what does it matter, what does it matter? If good comes of it, the dead are forgotten. A century on and all will be well. All manner of things". *The figure of* STALIN *walks through the shadows'*. *Thirteenth Night*, in *Brenton Plays: Two* (London: Methuen, 1989) p. 157.
26. Howard Brenton, 'Preface', *Brenton Plays: Two*, p. xi.
27. Ibid. Brenton is referring here specifically to *Thirteenth Night*, but again the sentiment applies equally to *Weapons of Happiness*.
28. Ibid., p. vii.
29. See 'The Red Theatre', p. 198.
30. As Philip Roberts notes: 'It would not have worked so powerfully if the object of the rape had been a woman and thus a confirmation for the audience that the received wisdom of how armies act does not need further exploration'. See Roberts' 'Howard Brenton's Romans', *Critical Quarterly*, 23, 3 (Autumn 1981) 17. The rape scene caused an enormous uproar in England. Mary Whitehouse, of the National Viewers' and Listeners' Association, took legal action against the play's director, Michael Bogdanov, under the 1956 Sexual Offences Act: Bogdanov was charged with having procured an act of gross indecency. The case came to trial in March 1982, but after three days in court the prosecution's charge was withdrawn.
31. *The Romans in Britain*, in *Brenton Plays: Two*, pp. 34–5. All further page references will be cited in the text.
32. Boon, p. 208.
33. *The Romans in Britain* was not the first Brenton play to attack imperialism through the deconstruction of historical figures. In *Scott of the Antarctic* (significantly subtitled *or What God Didn't See*) Scott's expedition is 'haunted' by a character who 'slunk through the action, always on the edge of spots . . . , a kind of anti-Scott', thus constantly subverting the myth of Scott's 'heroism' ('Author's Note', *Plays for Public Places* [London: Methuen, 1972] p. 9). 'Scott was not on the ice to get to the pole . . . ', Brenton has commented. 'He was there because of his public school, his C of E religion and the British Empire' ('Underground Explorations No.1: Portable Playwrights', p. 16).

34. Howard Brenton, 'Author's Note', *H.I.D.* (*Hess Is Dead*) (London: Nick Hern, 1989) p. i.
35. *H.I.D.* (*Hess Is Dead*) p. 11. All further page references will be cited in the text.
36. In *H.I.D.*, Nicole, one of the academics/media experts charged with establishing the 'official line' on Hess's death, uses the metaphor of 'cooking' to acknowledge this manipulation and betrayal of history: 'To remove impurities. To add artificial sweeteners. . . . Why was cooking invented? As a measure against the near poison of everything we eat. . . . So cook the news. Reality is salmonella' (51–2).
37. 'Petrol Bombs', p. 20.
38. Howard Brenton, 'Haiku for Margaretta D'Arcy on Her Rubbishing of My Play', *New Statesman*, 14 September 1979; cited in *File on Brenton*, ed. Tony Mitchell (London: Methuen, 1987) p. 38.
39. 'Underground Explorations No.1: Portable Playwrights', p. 16.
40. Sir Peter Hall, *Peter Hall's Diaries: the Story of a Dramatic Battle*, ed. John Goodwin (New York: Harper & Row, 1984) p. 100.

11

Forgiving History and Making New Worlds: Timberlake Wertenbaker's Recent Drama

Ann Wilson

Dispossession is a recurring theme in two of Timberlake Werten-baker's recent plays, *The Grace of Mary Traverse* and *The Love of the Nightingale*.[1] Related to this theme is power. Why has this displacement occurred? Who has authorised it? Her exploration moves beyond suggesting that dispossession is a discrete condition by positioning it within a complex web of ideology which buttresses the power of the ruling elite.[2] In so doing, Wertenbaker critiques the cohesiveness of the ideological apparatus which supports hegemony, implying that the fissures which such a critique exposes might effectively be used as the sites of social change. For her, the nature of social change is problematic. Whereas *The Grace of Mary Traverse*, like her later play, *Our Country's Good*, ends optimistically, *The Love of the Nightingale* suggests that social change is a complex problem: how can we speak of oppression when language is itself shaped by the dominant ideology?[3]

Although conventions of contemporary criticism caution readers about seeing a relation between literary works and the life of the author, the few published facts about Wertenbaker's life tempt a reading of the theme of displacement as autobiographical. In interviews, Wertenbaker is reluctant to discuss personal issues. She told Robert Crew of *The Toronto Star*, 'There are four things I do not talk about: my name, where and when I was born, and what I am working on at present'.[4] Despite her adamant refusal to divulge details about her background, a few facts about her are known: she was born in America; her father was Charles Wertenbaker, a foreign correspondent for *Time* magazine; she was educated in schools in France, returning to the United States to attend St. John's College in Annapolis. Since her graduation from college, she has worked as a journalist in both the States and in England, and taught French for a year in Greece before she began to work full-time as a playwright. As a consequence of having lived in North America and Europe, Wertenbaker eschews identifying herself with a particular nation, saying,

> I feel I am an American but not completely. I grew up in Europe so I am not an expatriate. Really, that's just narrow nationalism and I don't know why people can't accept that you can have several cultures. The whole thing about being a writer is that you can have a floating identity anyway.[5]

Perhaps the idea of 'a floating identity' which can be constructed is most clearly indicated by her name, 'Timberlake', which appears to be assumed: a standard drama/theatre reference cites her given names as 'Lael Louisiana'.[6] The theme of displacement which recurs in Wertenbaker's work seems to echo her life, which is characterised by her movement from milieu to milieu, of being herself displaced and transplanted into new cultures.

Wertenbaker's career as a dramatist has been centred in London, where she has worked with a range of small theatres – most notably the Royal Court Theatre, which produced both *The Love of the Nightingale* (a commission from the Royal Shakespeare Company) and *Our Country's Good*. Her position within theatre is somewhat unique – she is one of the few playwrights who is not only a major force in contemporary British theatre but whose work was virtually unknown in that country a decade ago. The acclaim which her plays have received has been reinforced by the many awards she has received, including the Plays and Players Most Promising Playwright Award in 1985 for *The Grace of Mary Traverse* and the Eileen Anderson Central Television Drama Award in 1989 for *The Love of the Nightingale*. Of her numerous plays (including *The Third, Case to Answer, New Anatomies, Abel's Sister*), only five have been published: the two I consider in this essay, *New Anatomies, Our Country's Good* – perhaps her most popular play – and *Three Birds*

Alighting on a Field.
Common to her work is the theme of dispossession which has been explored in an excellent essay by David Ian Rabey.[7] Dispossession and its related themes of dislocation and loss occur throughout her work. Often the characters experience geographic dislocation – in *New Anatomies, The Love of the Nightingale* and *Our Country's Good,* characters are physically displaced, and the geographic dislocation results in cultural dislocation. In all Wertenbaker's plays, characters move into new worlds and cultures which are unfamiliar.

As if to emphasise the unfamiliarity of the world for the audience, *The Grace of Mary Traverse* is set in the eighteenth century but is not, the playwright cautions, 'a historical play. . . . I found the eighteenth century a valid metaphor, and I was concerned to free the people of the play from contemporary preconceptions'.[8] The play begins with the protagonist, Mary, facing an empty chair to which she makes conversation under the eye of her silent father, Giles. Her means of perfecting conversation is to deliver a monologue, as if her interaction with the other person were irrelevant. Indeed, the ideal of woman critiqued by the play is that she is self-effacing, virtually invisible, weightless. When she walks on the carpet, she leaves no imprint – either on the carpet or on history – because she is removed from society, sequestered in either her father's home (as in Mary's case) or her husband's. She is never allowed to express her own desires but must instead devote herself to facilitating men's expression of theirs; her role is to adore man and to be his adornment. Women's isolation, which results in her having no agency, effectively denies her life. But, as Mrs Temptwell (the Traverses' housekeeper) points out, death is the ultimate realisation of the feminine ideal of passivity:

> She was so quiet, your mother, it took the master a week to notice she was dead. But she looked ever so beautiful in her coffin and he couldn't stop looking at her. Death suits women. You'd look lovely in a coffin, Miss Mary. (5)

Forced into a metaphoric death by her father, but having some awareness of the possibility of life through representations of it, Mary accepts Mrs Temptwell's offer to take her into the streets of London. 'The world out there isn't like the books' (6), the housekeeper promises. When Mary sees the world with its squalor and suffering, she complains, 'I do wish these people weren't so ugly. . . . They ought to go back to the country and be beautiful peasants' (9). Though she is repulsed by what she sees of life, the world, nevertheless, holds a particular fascination for her after Lord Gordon threatens to rape her at knife point. At that moment, a young peasant woman, Sophie, passes. As Lord Gordon reaches out to grab her, Mary escapes and watches in fascination the rape of which she was the intended victim. She comments, 'I couldn't stop looking, but it's not at all as pretty as in the books and I think I'd rather be him than her' (11).

With great economy, Wertenbaker uses this scene to begin to chart the intersection of gender and class. Mary is spared enduring the rape because Sophie stands as her surrogate. She realises that the other woman is being violently abused and that she should intercede, but as a result of her inexperience in the world, she doesn't know what action to take. Mrs Temptwell assures her that Sophie will not mind being raped because 'virtue, like ancestors, is a luxury of the rich' (11). The only context in which Mary understands the rape is literary: 'Will he turn himself into a swan, a bull, a shower of golden rain? Is he a god?' she asks (11). Immediately the limitations of reading the world through this paradigm are obvious: the rape isn't 'as pretty as in the books'. This off-hand comment, which in no way accommodates the pain of the victim, is somewhat startling until we begin to understand that Mary 'reads' the scene from a male perspective. As we have seen in the opening scene, she has learned to converse under the aegis of her father. Her mother seems to have no influence on her life, existing not even as a memory. In this family the father dominates because the mother, epitomising the feminine ideal, is dead. Later in the play Mary comments, 'It's my father who taught me to talk, sir. He didn't suspect he'd also be teaching me to think' (38). Mary thinks like a man but like one who has been emasculated because he does not enjoy access to power. Her identification with Lord Gordon, the rapist, is not surprising because he is such a man.

In his monologue which opens the rape scene (scene 3), Lord Gordon makes it clear that he rapes because he feels powerless. His impotence is not simply sexual but social and, more particularly, linguistic. His satisfaction in attacking Mary, and then Sophie, is the empowerment of making another person feel fear. When the frightened Mary tells him that she wants to go home, he says, 'Not yet. Not until you've been even more frightened. Yes. I'll show you my strength' (10).

Lord Gordon's show of strength through his sexual violation of Sophie begins with his drawing his sword to raise her skirts, and is completed sexually by his penetration of her. Rape, however, is represented as an act of violence articulated through sexuality: his genitals are a weapon used against the victims. The rape occurs within as structure of displacement and substitution: Sophie substitutes for Mary; Lord Gordon's sexual domination of a woman restores his sense of masculinity by allowing him to feel empowered on a number of registers (including the social – he feels equal to his peers – and linguistic: he believes that he, too, is capable of wit).

What is horrifying is not so much the rape, which Mary reports to the audience, but her shifting her initial identification with the woman who is victim to the man who is empowered by this act. This shift occurs because she has been taught to read from a male perspective which sees woman as essentially passive, the supplement to man. Such a perspective cannot adequately represent the experience of a living woman who might have agency. Consequently Sophie, who represents a potential for social change, speaks little in the course of the play. The rape scene ends with Sophie coming towards Mary, '*walking with pain. They look at each other*'. Without uttering a word, Sophie walks away. Mary says simply, 'Blood' (12). It is as if Mary, who looks directly at Sophie, can neither read nor understand the language of the other woman's suffering because masculine idioms cannot express it. From Mary's perspective, if you are going to have life, then it must be as a man.

Acts Two and Three chronicle Mary's exploration of this world of men. In Act Two, Mrs Temptwell procures the services of the male prostitute, Mr Hardlong, who initiates Mary into sex, advising her to forfeit the romantic ideals of love advanced in novels because they 'mask a selfish act with selfless acquiescence' (18). Instead he urges her to use her hands, 'Take what you want, Mary. Take it' (19). She '*stretches out her hand*', commenting: 'At first power. I am the flesh's alchemist. Texture hardens at my touch, subterranean rivers follow my fingers. I pull back the topsoil, skim the nakedness of matter. All grows in my hand' (19). For Mary, like Lord Gordon, sex is access to power; but whereas Lord Gordon achieves his power by employing sex as a weapon of physical aggression, Mary's power comes from buying Mr Hardlong's sexual labour. Part of the economic arrangement between them involves Sophie, who is now Mary's servant, having sex with Mr Hardlong as partial payment for his services to Mary. Sophie is again used by Mary as a surrogate, this time standing as the currency which replaces money in the transaction between the buyer and the seller.

Wertenbaker uses the scene to establish that Mary enters this world by assuming the prerogatives of masculinity. This negotiation of the world as if she were a man is even more pronounced in the next scene where she challenges Mr Hardlong to pit his fighting cock against hers. The double entendre of the scene is realised fully with such exchanges as:

> MARY: . . . My cock's risen and stricken Mr Hardlong's
> . . . .
> MR HARDLONG: My cock's failed me.
> MARY: That happens, Mr Hardlong, even to the best. And
> I triumph again. I keep winning. I keep winning.
>
> (29)

Mary's desire is not satisfied by winning the cock fight. Her initiation into the complex economy of desire onto which power (a male prerogative predicted on a hierarchical structure of the victor and vanquished, of the moneyed and the impoverished) is mapped leaves her feeling dissatisfied because she can never enjoy power as a man. Her access to this male world is only possible through the mediation of surrogates: she has a fighting bird, not a penis. Dissatisfied that her desires are not being met, she turns to Sophie who provides pleasure and satisfaction to men, raises her skirts and urges:

> Look. Surely it's more appealing than their drooping displays? Or do you share their prejudice? . . . Ah, Sophie, how sweet you are, I understand why they love you, but I can love you more than they ever have. (30)

However problematic Wertenbaker's representation of lesbian desire as mimicking a male erotic, the scene suggests that Sophie does not respond, and so Mary returns to her sport with men. 'Mr Manners', she asks, 'shall we race the old ladies?' (30). She bets a huge sum of money that her hag (who is Sophie's aunt) will defeat Mr Manner's; but she loses at this game.

Act Three begins with Mary, pregnant and impoverished, waiting in Vauxhall Gardens to meet her father, who is coming to employ a prostitute. Instead he finds himself facing his daughter whom he repudiates when she reveals her identity to him, exclaiming, 'You're a whore' (39), as if prostitutes are unfathered. Wertenbaker uses the moment to make an ironic comment on the ideal woman as being so passive she may as well be dead. Because her father has earlier allowed Mr Manners to announce that his daughter has died, Mary is able to extort money from him in order that she remains 'dead', thereby ensuring that the terms of her current life remain silent. Yet, despite having some level of financial security restored, Mary does not feel altogether happy. She is 'bored with a boredom that chills the marrow of my bones' (44). She yearns for 'action', but not the 'endless round of puny private vice' (47) which Mrs Temptwell arranges for her. She wonders what men do when they are bored: 'Ah. I know. They make wars, slash at the blinding dullness, cover up the silence with screams. . . . They think about their country and then they rule the country' (47). Even Sophie's boyfriend, a working class man named Jack, has a capacity to dream which seems beyond the women. Mary questions Sophie about her lover's dream, and then decides that it will be hers, that she will proclaim a new world 'ruled by us for our delight. Free' (47–8).

Mary's appropriation of Jack's dream raises the question of whom she includes when she uses 'us' and 'our'. Does this new world empower Sophie? Will she be part of the 'brotherhood of man' proposed by Jack, which Mary envisions resulting in a world which will be 'gentle, wise, free, uncircumscribed'? (50). The answer seems evident in the scene in which Mrs Temptwell and Sophie set out chairs for the midnight meeting at which the plans for revolution are made. It is they, not Mary nor Jack, who ready the room. During the actual meeting when Mrs Temptwell speaks, Mary comments, 'I forgot you, Mrs Temptwell' (53); when Sophie speaks, she shows no intellectual independence but simply supports the position advanced by Mary and the men.

Mary derives enormous satisfaction from organising the working people to petition against the Catholic Repeal Act. Looking out on the crowd, she comments, 'thousands and I've roused them. Oh, this is a delight beyond anything' (58). The protest in the play, based on the Gordon Riots, ends with the crowd rampaging out of control on Holborn, breaking into the distilleries which were set on fire. As the protesters try to get gin, they are set aflame, leaving hundreds dead. Mary, her glorious vision reduced to hundreds of bodies emitting the putrid smell of burnt flesh, pleads with her father,

'It wasn't meant to be like this, please believe me. I had dreams'. 'I know. Your own voices', her father replies (62). Even in political action, Mary has been motivated by her desire to overcome her personal boredom. As if still holding to Mr Hardlong's adage that desire is essentially selfish, Mary's appetite for life is motivated by self-interest and shows little regard for the lives of others, including her daughter. 'I felt a lover's desire for the world', she laments, 'and if I sought to undress it, it was only for a closer embrace. No one told me I'd hug stinking bones, caress putrefaction' (65).

Infected by a deep malaise, Mary proposes to poison her daughter, an act which she perceives as sparing 'the future the danger of her dreams' (65). Sophie vehemently protests telling Mary, 'You think at a distance, you're always ahead, or too far back. If you looked – just looked from near, I know it would be different. Look out of the window. Just look' (67). Sophie's urging Mary to find a new way to think is an appeal to find a new language because thought, the play suggests, is inextricably tied to language. It is significant that Sophie proposes this new way of thinking and, consequently, implies a new language because throughout the play she seems to be paradigmatically feminine. Because of her gender and class, she is mostly silent, defined by her role as a servant who is perceived as having no desires of her own. When she occasionally speaks, as in the scene where the protest is being planned, she parrots the words of men. When Sophie finally speaks in her own words, her appeal is to sensual responses evoked by nature: 'The first light of the morning. . . . The grass is wet and soft. Cold water on the skin' (66). Finally she lifts Mary's child and carries her *'a little away and sings a beautiful song'*. Moved, Mary comments, 'If I were God your song would appease me and I would forgive the world' (68). In contrast to Mrs Temptwell, who is a debased figure of the mother, Sophie evokes through her song the true maternal, so strikingly absent from the play. Wertenbaker suggests that it is difficult, if not virtually impossible, to sustain the maternal in a world which is overdetermined by the patriarchy.

Immediately after singing her song, Sophie is urged by Mrs Temptwell to look out the window at a cart carrying Jack off to his execution. 'See who's in there, Sophie, and then sing to us' (68), she taunts. When Sophie sees Jack, her songs turn to screams. Devastated and embittered that her lover will not speak to her as he goes to his death, she returns the child to Mary:

SOPHIE: You did all this. You should be up there. Go on. Kill your child.
MARY: Oh Sophie, not now. Not from you. Remember what you've said. I know we can find . . . we will.

(69–70)

The scene ends with Mary embracing Sophie, consoling her with the promise that 'we will grieve . . . but we won't despair. Come with me' (70).

The final scene of the play, set in the Potteries – the land which had once belonged to Mrs Temptwell's father – is an image of the restored and renewed family: Mary, Sophie, Giles and Little Mary standing in the gardens. The characters seem to envision their utopia which, significantly, is expressed by Sophie:

I thought it was enough to look, but it isn't. There needs to be much more. I see that now.
MARY: Beauty –
SOPHIE: Not just seen by day. Another beauty underlies it, doesn't disappear at night. Find that too.

(71)

What is particularly striking is that fundamentally, the moment remains incomplete and, hence, unresolved because Sophie can only allude to, but not articulate fully, what constitutes 'beauty'. Partially this incompletion is a consequence of the problematic nature of a utopian vision: once it is spoken, it is within the economies (particularly that of language) of the society which it seeks to reform. In other words, it ceases to be a vision of pure and perfect society because it is now within the determination of social and historical forces. Wertenbaker seems aware of the problem of articulating an utopia because Mary raises the relation between the new world and history: 'And when we know this beauty, Sophie, not just nature's but the beauty recreated by those who have lived in the world, will we learn – not to forget, no – but at least to forgive history?' (71).

The last moments of the play are marked by the failure of the characters to express their vision of the new world. Sophie can only allude to an underlying beauty, but in the previous scene, Mary says, 'I know we can find . . . we will', as if the object of her quest eludes her (70). *The Grace of Mary Traverse* raises a problem: can we imagine a new world within the language of the old? While the speeches in the final two scenes seem to suggest that envisioning an utopia within old idioms is problematic, the stage picture which is created – first of Mary embracing Sophie as if she finally accepts and responds to her needs, and then Mary reconciled to her father, with her child and standing *'side by side'* with Sophie as if they were now equals – seems to suppress the contradictions inherent in imagining a new world. The stage picture is a sentimental one of resolution and reconciliation, of the family on the edge of the new world.

In *The Love of the Nightingale* Wertenbaker returns to the theme of creating a new world but does not resolve the problems of project by covering the contradictions with sentimentality.[9] In her telling of the myth, Tereus, King of Thrace, receives Procne, daughter of the Athenian King Pandion as a reward for having helped to secure Athens' military victory over Sparta. In Thrace, removed from her family, Procne bears Tereus's son, Itys. When the child is five, Procne's loneliness for her family overtakes her and she asks Tereus to go to Athens and bring her sister Philomele to Thrace. Tereus obliges but when he sees his sister-in-law, he falls in love with her. He professes his love for Philomele who resists his advances saying that he cannot love her because he is married to her sister. Tereus then fabricates a story about the death of his wife which removes the prohibition of Philomele becoming involved with him but she does not love him and maintains her resistance. He rapes her. Yet she continues to resist his attempts to restore his sense of masculine prowess by taunting 'that despite my fear, your violence, when I saw your nakedness I couldn't help laughing because you were so shrivelled, so ridiculous. . . . Take the sword out of your hand, you fold into a cloth' (50). She vows, 'Never, as long as I have the words to expose you. The truth, men and women of Thrace, the truth – ' (51). Tereus commits a second act of physical violence: he cuts out her tongue, thereby denying her the capacity to speak, and then, after blaming her for his violence by claiming that she provoked him, says: 'You are more beautiful now in your silence' (52).

Returning to Thrace without his sister-in-law, Tereus explains to his wife that Philomele died at sea during their trip from Athens. Five years later, Procne still grieves for her sister, marking her loss by lighting a candle on the anniversary of the death, after which she goes out and joins the Bacchae. During the rites, she is drawn to a woman who uses enormous puppets to enact the story of her separation from her sister, the double violence of rape and mutilation. Procne recognises the woman as her sister and thus realises what her husband has done. In order to stop this violence, she holds Itys while Philomele kills him.

The thematic parallels between *The Grace of Mary Traverse* and *The Love of the Nightingale* are striking: in both, women are raped by men for whom the violence of the act is empowering and consequently heightens their sense of manliness. Indeed, in both plays, the penis is, in effect, a weapon which is used violently against women. In both, men seem to idealise women who are metaphorically dead, reduced to silence. Men effect the 'deaths' of women by announcing that they have died, thereby removing them from the action; but the women refuse to remain 'dead' and stage their return. In both plays, mothers contemplate killing their own children because this is the only way they can envision that the mistakes of the past will not be repeated. And, in both plays silence – a consequence of the limitations of language – is a major thematic preoccupation. But whereas, in the final scene of *The Grace of Mary Traverse*, despite the speech of the characters being marked by ellipsis and vagueness which amount to a form of silence, Wertenbaker obfuscates the despair which an audience might feel at the impossibility of articulating an utopia by having Mary incapable of actually killing her daughter. Instead the renewed family looks to the future. None of the optimism which characterises the end of *The Grace of Mary Traverse* is evident in the ending of *The Love of the Nightingale*. Procne, after holding her son while her sister kills him with his own sword, explains to the grief-stricken Tereus, 'You bloodied the future. For all of us. We don't want it. . . . The world is bleak. The past a mockery, the future dead. And now I want to die' (64). The implication is clear: in contrast to *The Grace of Mary Traverse*, where Wertenbaker suggests that the maternal, identified with 'natural' unconditional love, can redeem a world ruined by patriarchal values, in *The Love of Nightingale*, there is no such hope because the maternal is a construct within, and hence implicated in the perpetuation of, the patriarchy. The consequence is that, in a society dominated by such values, the maternal is, if not silenced, made virtually inaudible.

In *The Grace of Mary Traverse*, the daughter's value is as her father's child whose acquiescing to his will marks his paternal authority before other men. Similarly, in *The Love of the Nightingale*, Procne, who is schooled in the teaching of the Athenian philosophers (12), is given in marriage to Tereus as his reward for having defeated the Spartan forces which threatened her father's kingdom, thus serving as currency in a transaction between the two men. When the audience first sees Procne in the court of her husband's more barbarous kingdom, Thrace, she is dejected. 'She sits alone, hour after hour, turns her head away and laments', comments one of her Thracian attendants (15). Another comments that once displaced from your home into a new world, 'You will always be a guest there, never call it your own, never rest in the kindness of history' (15). Adds another, 'Your story intermingled with events, no. You will be outside' (15). The terms of Procne's feeling of radical displacement are particularly important. 'Where have the words gone?' she asks. 'There were so many. Everything that was, had a word and every word was something. None of these meanings half in the shade, unclear' (16). Iris, one of the court women, tries to alleviate Procne's despair, reminding her 'We speak the same language' (16). But Procne resists, saying, 'The words are the same, but point to different things. We aspire to clarity in sound, you like the silences between' (16). Language is not simply the words spoken but the silences which inevitably frame the words. The simplicity of the idea makes it easy to overlook its implications: if knowledge is constituted in language, then knowledge of the world is linguistic and is therefore punctuated by silence, which means that the world cannot be perceived fully.

In *The Love of the Nightingale*, silence is not singular but is con- stituted in a variety of ways – perhaps most strikingly in the violent silencing of Philomele when Tereus cuts out her tongue. There are other forms of silence in the play: Philomele is doubly silenced because not only is she deprived of her capacity to speak but she is, in the mind of her sister who believes Tereus, dead. Similarly, Procne is silenced by Tereus, who tells Philomele that her sister has died. There is also the silence of Philomele's attend- ant, Niobe, whose island was conquered by Athens. She believes that silence is the only viable strategy for survival in the face of power. After Philomele has been raped, she counsels, 'Don't be so mighty, Philomele. You're nothing now. Another victim. Grovel. Like the rest of us. . . . Be careful. Worse things can happen. Believe me. . . . Keep silent' (48). The silence of these women is the silence of subjugation. In the face of masculine power, they are either denied speech or feel, like Niobe, that speaking out is not prudent. Like Niobe, the Female Chorus cannot address their concerns about Tereus directly to Procne, which reinforces their earlier comments

on silence as a condition of language. When Tereus fails to return
from Athens, the women of the Thracian court advise Procne to
leave the palace and seek him. But because they use language
differently from Procne, their warnings are not heard by the Queen,
who becomes annoyed with them. 'Enough of your nonsense', she
says. 'Be silent'. Two of the women respond in turn by repeating
her last word, 'Silent' (33). The Male Chorus enacts another kind
of silence. Throughout the trip, they watch as Tereus brutalises
Philomele but refuse to acknowledge that they have been witnesses,
preferring to turn a blind eye to the abuse. When they finally return
home, they remain silent: 'We said nothing./ It was better that way'
(47).

Silence in *The Love of the Nightingale* has several meanings. It can
be the consequence of language which is marked syntactically; of
the exercise of power which forces the victim into silence; and of
the refusal to speak, creating the paradox of inaction, which is
an implicit act of complicity because it allows brutality to persist
unchecked. Wertenbaker is particularly concerned with the first
type of silence. In Scene Eight, the Male Chorus comments, 'What
is a myth? The oblique image of an unwanted truth, reverberating
through time' (31). Tracing the origin of the word (which includes
noting that a myth initially meant 'what is delivered by word of
mouth, a myth is speech, public speech') the Chorus concludes that
a myth now 'is a remote tale' (13). The theatrical presentation of the
myth still carries the archaic sense of myth as public speech but, in
the contemporary context, the notion of what is spoken publicly is
problematic because truth can only be represented obliquely. The
Chorus warns against reading *The Love of the Nightingale* as a myth
'about men and women, . . . a myth for our times' because if you
do, you will be 'beside the myth. If you must think of anything,
think of countries, silence, but we cannot rephrase it for you. If we
could, why would we trouble to show you the myth?' (31). The
implication is that what is being represented on stage is beyond
representation, that it can only be alluded to through the silences
which punctuate the words.

What is being represented in the play if not the story of Tereus,
Procne and Philomele? The answer is given by the Female Chorus
at the beginning of Scene Twenty when they drop their personae as
the women of the Thracian Court and approach the audience:

HERO: Without the words to demand.

ECHO: Or ask. Plead. Beg for. . . .
HELEN: Without even the words to forgive.
ECHO: The words that help to forget.

(62)

Through Iris, the Chorus continues that 'to some questions there
are no answers' and then provides a range of examples of these
sorts of questions, including contemporary examples: 'Why do
countries make war? / Why are races exterminated? / Why do
white people cut off the words of blacks? / Why do people disappear? The ultimate silence. / Not even death recorded' (62). These
horrific examples conclude with questions about why little girls are
raped and murdered and why torture exists. To these questions
– which are difficult even to pose, let alone answer – the Hero
says,

We can ask. Words will grope and probably not find. But if
you silence the question.
    IRIS: Imprison the mind that asks.
    ECHO: Cut out its tongue.
    HERO: You will have this [the killing of Itys].

(62)

The killing of Itys is condemned because 'a child is the future'
(62). And yet what is the answer? How can this violence, which
is legitimised and perpetuated by the patriarchy, be stopped? In
The Love of the Nightingale, Wertenbaker is silent, instead opting to
show the wrong solution, the child being held by his mother as he
is murdered. In some sense, the answer to the difficult questions
regarding the violence which destroys our world are alluded to in
The Grace of Mary Traverse. In that play, Mary's failure to be an
effective agent of social reform is a consequence of her reading the
world in patriarchal language, literally the language of the father.
She enters the world and tries to secure agency in it by living like
a man, a strategy which leads only to destruction and brings her
no nearer to the new world which is locked in silence, rendered
grammatically as ellipsis: 'I know we can find . . . ' (70). What is
implied is that the world needs a new language which creates a
new knowledge of the world, one which potentially would be able
to accommodate the articulation of utopia.
    Wertenbaker's privileging of the child and consequently of the

maternal as representing symbolically this new language is problematic to the degree that it seems not to question the social
production of motherhood as a role which denies the experiences
of women by subsuming women into the singular category of
'woman'. The problem with this perspective is two-fold. First,
it denies the particularity of women's experiences in the world
because the primary component of a woman's identity is biology which is seen as taking precedence over other forces which
shape subjectivity, including class, race and sexuality. Secondly,
'woman', as a universal figure who transcends the determination
of history, is figure of the patriarchy whose primary function is
to define difference: man is different from woman. This structure of differentiation is hierarchical inasmuch as man is the first
element with woman understood only in relation to him. This
way of reading gender difference maintains the authority of the
patriarchy which Wertenbaker seems to want to subvert. Perhaps
a way of re-conceptualising gender is to refuse to consider 'woman'
and instead think of women as having experiences which, when
positioned in relation to men, create an asymmetry which denies
that woman is the complement to man. This asymmetry has the
possibility of creating gaps – linguistically rendered as a radical
silence – and fissures which allow the authority of the patriarchy, no
longer monolithic, to crumble. Given that apparatuses of ideology
are interlocking, a refiguring of gender would necessarily have an
impact on other social relations, thereby allowing us to rethink class,
race and sexuality. Perhaps then, with a new language which allows
us new knowledge, we can begin to make new worlds.[10]

Notes

1. For a complete list to 1988 of the plays of Timberlake Wertenbaker,
    see *Contemporary Dramatists*, ed. D.L. Kirkpatrick (London: St James
    Press, 1988). Since 1988 Wertenbaker has published *Three Birds
    Alighting on a Field* (1991).
2. By 'ideology' I mean the lived relation of people to their world.
    Importantly, this relation involves both our conscious sense of the
    world and our unconscious sense of it. For further explication of this
    use of 'ideology' see Louis Althusser, *For Marx*, trans. Ben Brewster
    (1965; trans. London: Allen Lane [Penguin Press], 1969).
3. For the sake of clarity and convenience I have chosen to focus this
    essay on two of Wertenbaker's plays, *The Grace of Mary Traverse*
    and *The Love of the Nightingale*. Like *The Grace of Mary Traverse*, *Our*

Country's Good ends with sentimental optimism which obfuscates some of the contradictions which are raised by the play's exploration of creating a new world. I explore these contradictions in another essay, '*Our Country's Good*: Theatre, Colony and Nation in Wertenbaker's Adaptation of *The Playmaker*', *Modern Drama*, 34 (March 1991) 23–35.

4. Robert Crew, 'Don't Ask Wertenbaker Why They Named Her Timberlake', *The Toronto Star*, 19 (December 1986) 20.
5. Hilary de Vries, 'Of Convicts, Brutality and the Power of Theater', *New York Times*, 30 September 1990, Section H, p. 34.
6. *Contemporary Dramatists* (see note 1).
7. David Ian Rabey, 'Defining Difference: Timberlake Wertenbaker's Drama of Language, Dispossession and Discovery', *Modern Drama*, 33 (Dec. 1990) 518–29.
8. Timberlake Wertenbaker, *The Grace of Mary Traverse* (London: Faber & Faber, 1985) n.p. All quotations are from this edition; page numbers are given in the text. This play was revised and published with *The Love of the Nightingale* by Faber & Faber in 1989.
9. Timberlake Wertenbaker, *The Love of the Nightingale* (Woodstock, Illinois: The Dramatic Publishing Company, 1990). All quotations are from this edition; page numbers are given in the text.
10. For a further exploration of these ideas see Teresa de Lauretis, 'The Technology of Gender', in *Technologies of Gender* (Bloomington: Indiana UP, 1987) pp. 1–31.

12

Freedom and Form in David Hare's Drama

James Gindin

Assumptions about his political commitments can be derived from David Hare's career, beginning with his own fringe theatre, the 'Portable Theatre Company', in 1968–71, from his collaborations and the settings of his early plays. Yet critics have recognised that explanation in terms of political commitment, both suggested and countered in the plays, only partially and too simply reflects the force and substance of the drama. Venue suggests a focus on political commentary in the early plays: the exclusively social girls' school in *Slag* (1970), the new generation of a Labour M.P. whose politics derive from Aldermaston marches and pot parties rather than from a working-class perspective in *The Great Exhibition* (1972).[1] His collaborations with Howard Brenton, *Brassneck* (1973) and *Pravda: A Fleet Street Comedy* (1985), demonstrate a more committed focus than do most of his others, enough to substantiate Richard Allen Cave's opinion that Brenton's 'anger and moral outrage sustain a powerful satirical vision and a structure that aims frankly at demonstration rather than debate'.[2]

But demonstration is complicated and not amenable to political slogan in Hare's work. His first fully developed play, *Knuckle* (1974), creates a texture that simultaneously invites and counters political interpretation. Here, in a play that is set in the form of American detective films of the 1940s, a young man returns to the town he left years ago to investigate what he thinks is the murder of his sister. He finds numerous political crimes and guilts: property scams, social indifference, and the corruptions of his father's financial dealings. Unlike its detective film models, however, the play grants no thorny social virtue to the investigator, a world-wide arms salesman. In addition, the father may have violated the sister, but is discovered to have released rather than murdered or imprisoned her.

Though political evil is rife in the world of *Knuckle*, no political consequences or solutions are suggested. Similarly, in the most recent collaboration with Brenton, *Pravda*, the politics and violations of 'truth' in the newspaper do not cohere into any statement that might be read as East vs. West or Communism vs. Capitalism. Although an irrelevant old newspaperman prides himself on having predicted the evil of Hitler, changing an early editorial from labelling the leader as 'refreshingly dynamic' to 'unnecessarily dynamic', this has no connection with contemporary corruption and accompanying reportorial dishonesty. Part of the appeal of the play lies in its crowded sets and characters, the jumbled issues of corruption assembled without potential resolution. Hare's visual sense of congested, chaotic social and political worlds is also manifest in some of his film scripts (the greater possibility of noisy, crowded changing venues on screen has helped propel him into frequent work in film as a writer and director).

Another journalistic setting dominates *Dreams of Leaving*, a 1980 film for television, although this centres on a naive young man whose emotional insularity ensures eventual success. A few of Hare's congested, eventful film scripts (like the 1988 *Paris by Night*, about a member of the European Parliament from Birmingham who, losing the sexual and social control over others she had sought, both kills and is killed) descend into melodrama and barely avoid coherent political statement. In these films, as in the plays, although social criticism may be seen from a radical or leftist perspective, no Marxist or other resolution is envisaged, no palliative is offered for contemporary Western chaos and lack of value.

Hare, however, shares the stringencies of most forms of Marxism in his emphasis on socially and psychologically determining backgrounds for his characters. In these, as well as in his more complicated plays, background – both emerging from the plot and done in soliloquy – exerts an inhibiting force on the major characters. The healthy impulse is toward freedom, toward lack of structure; the background and the world impede and restrict, compress into representations of social form. In *Racing Demon* (1990), each of the prelates has a soliloquy on what has formed his life, has determined his subsequent attitudes. The conscience-stricken minister of a slum parish who sees religion as providing social unity begins the play with a soliloquy that asks God to talk to him and recalls his grandfather, the Dean of St. Paul's, who stayed in residence while bombs were falling in 1940. His antagonist, the ambitious young curate, recalls his childhood in the provinces to explain his conviction that 'Christ didn't come to sit on a Committee. He didn't come to do social work. He came to preach repentance.'[3] Other clergymen soliloquise about their own pasts: a socially agreeable one who started as a curate because the parish Gilbert and Sullivan society needed a light tenor, and a now beleaguered homosexual who discussed Teilhard de Chardhin while wondering about the body under his clothes.

In this and many of the other plays set in Britain, the publicly and historically locatable determining past is the Second World War. In *Teeth 'n' Smiles* (1975), for example, about a rock band getting ready for a concert at a Cambridge May Ball in 1969, reference to the Second World War filters through the accounts of drink, drugs, and addiction that are used to explain failure. The chatter, by members of the band, the arrangers and the drunken lead singer, is full of incoherent reference to Marilyn Monroe, Oscar Wilde, and county cricket; but the consecutive, coherent story central to the text is a long account of the 1941 bombing of the Café de Paris, the crucial historical justification for lives of conspicuous waste. Although the final song in the play, in which addiction is never countered and waste never redeemed, is 'Last Orders on the Titanic', the Titanic is used as the decorative genesis for the Café de Paris, the locus of the destruction the play illustrates.

The historical myth of the Second World War receives its most significant dramatisation in *Plenty* (1978), perhaps Hare's best known play. Separate scenes focus on Susan Traherne embedded in history, from her role in France as a member of the Resistance in 1943, through her postwar marriage to a diplomat, and her fury at the public dishonesties and private incapacities of Suez, to her cold disillusion of 1962. 1962 marks both the first and last scenes, the effect visible before Hare probes the cause in the myth of the war as propelling both a dark, secret, valuable sexuality and a sane, temperate public policy of concern for others, as if they could combine in an historical moment of humane significance. Susan is both public conscience and private, honest sexuality, the twin myths that, as Hare dramatises them, represent the English view of themselves during the war that Susan has tried to live since. Various scenes may concentrate on the political or the sexual aspect of Susan's disillusionment, but the sides of the myth of wartime

England interpenetrate. In a preface written for the volume in which *Plenty, Knuckle,* and *Licking Hitler* were published, Hare commented that many in his audience have separated the twin myths, and seen in Susan only sexual self-destruction and objections to any form of society.[4] But he intended Susan to be, like the principal women in *Knuckle* and *Licking Hitler,* a heroine of social conscience as well, unable to tolerate the 'counter-balance' of the play, 'the kind of death so many members of the audience have chosen, a death by compromise and absorption into institutional life', and incessantly struggling against 'a deceitful and emotionally stultified class'.[5] Hare also intended not to concentrate exclusively on the political, citing the skill of the characterisation of Terence Rattigan's Freddy in *The Deep Blue Sea* as one unable to find in peace the sexual roles appropriate for war, without any suggestion of politics or class in the play. The inseparability of the wartime myths operates throughout Hare's history plays, the damage to those characters of conscience who will relinquish neither their fidelity to the social concerns nor the respect for self that they believed had emerged from the war. They live their myths and are not adaptable, unlike the capitalists in *Knuckle* or the accommodating politicians in *Plenty.*

In the mid-1970s, Hare shifted his attention from the world of Britain and Europe to that of Asia, in a conscious attempt to enlarge his social focus. Although he went to Asia, he was conscious that he was a visitor, not a resident, that, as he explained in his preface to the volume entitled *The Asian Plays* (consisting of *Fanshen* [1975], *A Map of the World* [1983], and the film script for *Saigon: Year of the Cat,* shown on television in 1983), he was 'so opposed to the idea that research will of itself validate a work of the imagination' that a 'claim to see the world through Asian eyes is, to me at least, transparently absurd'.[6] In *Fanshen,* he relied on a book by William Hinton, an American tractor technician who went to China to help in the comprehensive land reforms of the late 1940s. The book included politics, medicine, law, military strategy, and agriculture in the village called Long Bow. Hare dramatised the book, using a simple language to record 1946 debates about justice, trials of Japanese collaborators, hearings on agricultural and economic issues, arguments about leadership, and inquiries that demanded self-reformation. Some of the meetings were cast in the form of antiphonal chants; others were insertions of background narration by different characters to illustrate the composition of the community. Values and focus were communal in a play that presented the Chinese attempt to combine land and economic reform with the principles of equality and control over individuals. *Fanshen* does not glorify the Chinese revolution, for the characters recognise that what they have created is far from Utopia, and that their incomplete achievements have been practical rather than abstract triumphs like the creation of justice. The play is scrupulously effective in the bareness and stringency of its focus on humanly intractable problems and the partial, uncertain success of social change, a play of social debates and ideas. The simple language is the transcription of complicated social change into practical forms of language; it has nothing of Brecht's mordantly satiric simplicity or use of political slogan. Without much distinction between characters or any possibility of identification for the audience, the play relies on the scrupulosity and complexity with which it represents what Hare can of a different culture and community.

Despite his interest and sympathy, Hare felt that he could not, by packaged tour in the 1970s, get inside the communal life of Communist Asia. He did, however, spend time in Saigon, still advertised as a locus for tourism, near the end of the American occupation. The dramatic result, the film 'Saigon: Year of the Cat', pointed and effective as it is as both theatre and politics, deals only with those Vietnamese so committed to the Americans that they must be evacuated or betrayed in the rushed and mismanaged exodus of 1975. The principal politics of the script, however, is a probing account of American and British officials in the chaos of departure, their sexuality, guilts, confusions, and identities in a crumbling world. In describing the institutions of the West perched on uncertain Eastern strands, Hare again avoids slogans, easy moral judgments and pretensions to understanding a world he feels he does not know.

A Map of the World is a fully developed treatment of the impositions of organised and well-intentioned Western institutions on the Asian community, specifically a 1978 international conference on poverty held in Bombay. In a noisy, crowded atmosphere, snatches of news contrast the triviality of Western concerns (an American 'genius', at the age of five, is beginning her third novel, this on the life of Mary Tyler Moore) with the poverty and misery of Asian millions. Other issues crowd the text: Zionism, representations of Blacks from America, the legacies of British Colonialism. One of the principal delegates is an Indian novelist who was educated in England, and who has become disillusioned with the empty words, mixed motives, and counter-productive policies of the attempts to alleviate Third World misery. He would scrap the conference, and is publicly to debate a young, socially conscious and concerned Englishman about the conference's value, with the favours of the attractive American actress delegate, once the mistress of the Indian, to be awarded the winner. But the debate, only one of numerous incidents dramatised in a welter of abrupt, film-like scenes, never takes place, and the conference dissolves in the trivia of the resolve to eat only a bowl of rice at the final banquet and talk of valuable antique cars at home. The play's effectiveness, visual and spatial as well as thematic, depends on the speed and variety of its devices: the staged mock films, the quick changes, the overlays of other scenes. Film is constantly connected with fiction, at times both talked of as if they can generate truth, more often discussed as similar lies. The Indian novelist, near the end, talks of both film and fiction occasionally as reinterpretation, but more often as 'betrayal', whatever the intention. Like the social institutions, the forms of our conveyance, our fictions, films, and Hare's self-conscious drama itself, duplicate our persiflage without giving meaning or coherence to our social or communal experience.

As in the early plays, women's sexuality continues to represent valuable individual freedom and instinct. The pains of living with this instinct, with freedom within necessary social and political contexts, are dramatised brilliantly in two short plays, *The Bay at Nice* and *Wrecked Eggs*, both first performed in 1986. The noise, the cover or persiflage, of a work like *A Map of the World* is stripped down to a few characters who convey socially determined forms within which freedom and sexuality are thwarted or destroyed. Women, still, are both instinct and conscience, as in *Wetherby* (1985), perhaps Hare's most effective film, about the numerous ways in which a lonely contemporary woman's attempts at love have been thwarted. *The Bay at Nice*, set in an art museum in Leningrad in 1956, depends primarily on dialogue between a mother who had once studied with Matisse and her schoolteacher daughter. Initially the dialogue is about art, the mother's insistence on the discipline of painting, on rules of representation, the daughter's conviction, as one born after the Soviet Revolution, that painters simply transcribe what they observe (a curator appears to mention a third, more public, alternative that 'all art is loot'). The dialogue expands as the daughter announces her intention to leave her husband (she has two children) to live with a seedy, divorced older man who loves her, citing her need for 'freedom' and appealing for confirmation to her mother's memory of the greater sexual and artistic freedom of student days in Paris just after the First World War. But the mother, as in the discussion of art, is more sceptical about freedom, having chosen to return to a more restrictive and inhibiting Russia, with the daughter as infant, in 1921. Because the child's father was Russian, the conscious choice of constraint was demanded by her own sense of social continuity in raising a child. That the constraints on the daughter, artistically and socially, are narrower and more inhibiting, is 'historical accident', and the mother, with no interest in defending Soviet virtue or policy, thinks the daughter selfish. She cites a story of a rebellious woman friend for whom desire vanished as soon as freedom was possible. Although the mother is willing to help the daughter economically by selling her precious flat, the play ends with the practical issue unresolved, but the mother's voice, like that of Matisse's painting, communicating the human need for restrictive form.

Absence of form is lethally damaging in *Wrecked Eggs*, a play set in the countrified outer suburbs of New York. A married couple has invited many friends to a week-end party to celebrate their split, but only one woman they had not known has arrived. Talk among the three is socially referential and personal, with no line drawn between general observation and private confession. The talk is the texture of contemporary experience: debasements of journalism, social crimes of property developers, quick alliances and equally quick boredom with alliance, fascination with stories like that of a man whose bigamy was discovered only when he was killed in an accident (for Hare, inserted stories comically underline moral themes). Both women at the small party have had affairs and abortions, the numerous and now permanently 'wrecked eggs' of the title. Lacking social or moral form, people institutionalise themselves with ritual, like the two different gourmet meals each member of the dissolving marriage is preparing for guests who never arrive. They envy more meaningful, even if humanly deplorable, rituals, like the family funeral pyres on the Ganges. Life, family, sexuality, and relationship have no form, and eggs are destroyed in a world in which the freedom desired is destructive. The characters envy what, in their impulse toward freedom, they have long ago abandoned: 'Loyalty. Courage. Perseverance. . . . Qualities which aren't just . . . momentary'.[7] They cannot, amidst the proliferating alternatives of contemporary freedom, sustain themselves without the social and personal forms the qualities represent.

Problems of relationship are not resolved in dramatic statement in *Wrecked Eggs*, just as social and political issues are not in other plays. Lack of resolution is conveyed, in all the plays, through the intrusion of trivia, like the elaborate accounts of potential gourmet meals that substitute for meaningful ritual in *Wrecked Eggs*. The depth of human and social pain, combined with the trivia of much of the dialogue, depict human inadequacy, the incapacity to shape a language that reflects and expresses what we feel and fear. At the same time, the trivia of language is also Hare's ingeniously and precisely managed combination of forms of discourse within a compressed setting, his comedy in which intractable problems are presented simultaneously with trivial or preposterous solutions. He has often been praised (deservedly) for his wit, but that praise is vague, for Hare's wit can delay, avoid, underline, palliate, or obscure human attempts to make moral sense of a perplexing social world. Often, humour is satire of the pretentious social proclamation or the offensive anti-social policy; often, the target is human inability to apply relevant or appropriate forms of discourse. *A Map of the World* contains humorous passages that depend on how differently representatives of Third World cultures use the same language; within the same culture, people banter words like 'principle', which might mean 'rationalisation' or 'having something to lose' or 'freedom' or 'bartering', all comically played against each other. Jokes are aggressive assaults, and also 'a product of security', a mode of discourse the rich nations can apply to the poor, who often have not, in English, the skill to reply.[8] One is tempted to conclude from the welter of comedies and satires that Hare is so constantly aware of different patterns of language and politics that one can only accept human complexity. Yet Hare also satirises that idea of complexity. One of the women in *Wrecked Eggs*, in talking of her affair with a young man in revolt against his father, a property developer, says that the old man was loathsome, dishonest, piratical, but was described by journalists as one who gave lots of money to charity. *Fanshen*, another society seen from the outside, is dependent on simple language, flat, not comic, the world seen directly through bags of grain and numbers of animals. But that is a different world. In *Racing Demon*, simple language is used to satirise the stereotypical: the bishop who believes in the ecclesiastical 'team', and whose false dramatisation of any issue is what is coming 'to the crunch'; those devoted to the 'illusion of action'; and the believer in 'community care', which means letting the homeless roam the streets unaided. As one of the characters says, to call all our languages and problems complex is as much a stereotype as any other. Yet, another character responds that the situation *is* complex.

Simplicity of language and social statement are almost impossible to achieve in Hare's dramatic world. At the same time, his humour and acknowledgement of complexity can seem a complacency he never endorses. His characters seek a simplicity they know will distort, as they seek forms, social and personal, that limit and constrain the freedom they desire and are unable to live with. Hare's language itself, its simultaneous use and questioning of complicated comedies, becomes the necessary artistic form through which to create and convey human dilemmas about and requirements of social form.

Freedom is attached to an historical myth that reaches back beyond the Second World War in *The Secret Rapture* (1988), one of Hare's most significant plays. The myth is represented, initially, in the person of a liberal bookseller, humanistic and charitable, at whose funeral the dramatic action of the play begins. He leaves two daughters: Marion, an unsentimental, frighteningly managerial government official, the image of the late 1980s Thatcherite; and Isobel, who runs a small design firm, and who is, at first, represented as continuing the casually humanistic legacy of her father's concerns. Her father has left a more tangible legacy: Katherine, his second wife, a young woman he rescued from the drink, drugs, and amoral irresponsibility of her late 1960s past. The play begins with the question of who is to take care of Katherine, which sister is to absorb Katherine into the structure of her life. Marion asserts that the Conservative Party, with its rules and insistence on profitable achievement, has no room for the Katherines of this world, yet pushes and manipulates the more accommodating, honest, responsible and guilty Isobel into incorporating Katherine into her design studio. Katherine is not just a cipher, not just an irresponsible victim, but, as Irwin (Isobel's lover and partner, who is corrupted by the commercial changes Katherine's presence and Marion's meddling demand) recognises, 'evil' as well. Isobel, the liberal humanist, unable to see 'evil', explaining Katherine as unhappy, maladjusted and self-hating, is destroyed. First her firm collapses, then her love; finally, when a provoked and corrupted Irwin shoots her, her life ends.

The Secret Rapture is only superficially conveyed by the social and political implications of the foregoing paragraph. A theme shaped around the conflict between the uncaring, hypocritical, dishonest efficiencies of Thatcherite capitalism and the irrelevance and naiveté of concerned liberal humanism, even adding Isobel's recognition that her freedom is limited by her need to follow what she thinks her father would have wished, would express only part of the play. The astringent criticism of capitalism is on the surface. The interest of the play, as it progresses, as one sharp vignette fades into the next in a texture of overlapping scenes that suggest the interpenetration of themes, is in probing the social and psychological inadequacies of the tradition of liberal humanism itself, all the 'human stuff' that Marion hates. The central focus is Isobel – not just her humane concern and inappropriate internalisation of her father's form, but the contradictory impulses within her: the self-destruction in her sexuality, the determining pride in punishing herself by absorbing all the world's evil, the consummate guilt, the need to submit. At one point, when Irwin (recognising his own sense of evil and destruction) says he likes guns, and they talk of public assassinations, Isobel says that she likes 'the wound' and that all she remembers of presidential assassination attempts is Alexander Haig running 'through the White House, screaming, "I'm in charge! I'm in charge!", . . . the only time I've ever found a politician sexy'.[9] As the play develops and scenes intersect, Hare uses more references to guns and sudden, explosive violence (Katherine, frustrated in her attempts to sell design through sex and charm, stabs a managing director). The humane liberal form can no longer contain violence, anger, or any deeply held human emotion. Hare uses a quotation from Rebecca West as an epigraph: 'Only half of us is sane: only part of us loves pleasure and the longer day of happiness, wants to live to our nineties and die in peace, in a house that we built, that shall shelter those who come after us. The other half of us is nearly mad. It prefers the disagreeable to the agreeable, loves pain and its darker night despair, and wants to die in a catastrophe that will set back life to its beginnings and leave nothing of our house save its blackened foundations'.[10] The political form of the Thatcherite is empty, false, immoral, and self-deceiving; the old liberalism is more honest and concerned, but no wiser, no better able to accommodate or control the freedom and depths of either others or the self.

In the opening scene, Isobel tells Marion that she has just seen her father's spirit depart from his body, and throughout the play, in increasing desperation, she looks for material form in which her inherited spirit might be expressed. A more successful version of Isobel is in *Strapless*, a film script published in 1989, in which a young doctor, deserted by her entrepreneurial husband, manifests her social concern and her spirit by campaigning against cuts in hospital budgets and supporting her irresponsible and pregnant sister's talent for designing strapless dresses, representative embodiments of their courage and spirit. Isobel, however, faces more difficult problems; her spirit, compounded by her impulse toward self-destruction, has no locus in the contemporary world. Marion has ruthlessly eliminated spirit, turned her generosity into cupidity, and restricted her politics to the mechanical form of attendance at her office every day. Marion's commercially successful husband, Tom, perverts spirit even more ludicrously in his confident claim that Jesus is his friend and helps him conveniently discover material articles like spare parts for his car. Institutional spirituality is also mocked in the irrelevant eulogy delivered at the father's funeral, as if he had been someone else. Any sense of morality or of spirit is, in *The Secret Rapture*, defeated by social and institutional perversions. What had once been a form for spirit, the tradition of humane, liberal, communal concern, was always vulnerable to hypocrisy and complacent confidence in the human being. Now, however, from Hare's perspective, the form of social liberalism has been completely shattered by the evil, violence and self-destruction endemic in the human being. A code created over generations to shape the integrity and identity of the human being has been shattered by its own contradictions.

Hare's growing interest in spirit, in what may not be translatable into material form, leads naturally to his most recent play, *Racing Demon*, which examines the public institution of the spirit, the contemporary clergy. *Racing Demon*'s epigraph is a bold assertion of spirit taken from Walt Whitman: 'Why, who makes much of a miracle? I know of nothing else but miracles'.[11] The clergymen in the play are considerably less certain. The social and ideological conflicts are dramatised within the institution of the church: the bishop, without ideology or social concern, finds unity in the sacraments, the empty 'rules of the club' (2); the liberal clergyman, Lionel, who believes in the Christ who came to help the poor, and whose attempts at social aid and reconstruction in his slum London parish are ineffectual; his adversary and curate, Tony, who wants a more militant church, one that will acquire force by severe insistence on reconstructing its dogmas as the only means to salvation. Tony criticises Lionel's actions and convictions, the ineptitude with which Lionel has tried to help a battered black woman in fear of her husband and the genteel superiority with which Lionel and others evade evangelicals. From Tony's point of view, the tolerant churchman, opposed to the unquestioning intensity of evangelicals or the doctrinally committed, represents English class snobbery: 'Educated clerics don't like evangelicals, because evangelicals drink sweet sherry and keep budgerigars and have ducks in formations on their walls. . . . Yes, and they also have the distressing downmarket habit of trying to get people emotionally involved' (59). Tony's Christ brings not peace but the sword of doctrinal and emotional commitment. New and reasserted intolerance and stringencies have other consequences besides the elimination of Lionel and what he represents. The gentle homosexual clergyman is removed from his parish and shipped to Malta. Tony's former mistress, Frances, articulates the failures in capacity to love and relate in both the increasingly respectable and theologically committed Tony, and the gently feckless, formless Lionel. Tony, although spiteful and aggressive in establishing his judgmental and doctrinally severe role, characterises Lionel with bitter accuracy: 'His forehead is knotted. He gives off one message: "Keep away. I carry the cares of the world." It's true. People don't go near him. He reeks of personal failure. And anguish. Like so much of the Church' (54). Despite Lionel's years of dedication to the parish and his having earned the respect of other clergymen, Tony wins the struggle within the church. As the bishop tells Lionel, in dismissing him,

you are the reason the whole church is dying. Immobile. Wracked. Turned inward. Caught in a cycle of decline. Your personal integrity your only concern. Incapable of reaching out. A great vacillating pea-green half-set jelly . . . people need authority, and every time they come to ask what does the church think? Then they are hit in the face by a spurt of lukewarm water from a rugby bladder. . . . You give an appearance of superiority which is wholly unearned. . . . You parade your so-called humility until it becomes a disgusting kind of pride. (88–9)

Sympathy remains for Lionel's integrity and his lack of the meretricious qualities of the successful clergymen, but he is denied the Pyrrhic victory or consolation of re-establishing meaningful contact with his faithful wife, who has had a stroke. The final lines are given to Frances, who has morality, conscience and no belief at all. She loves the feeling of a plane beginning its climb, but adds that 'vision gets bleary . . . cloud becomes a hard shelf', one sees only 'white and the horizon' and tries to head 'towards the sun' (98).

Although the final metaphor of *Racing Demon* avoids the complete disillusionment of *The Secret Rapture*, the issues of the plays are equally unresolved. Both illustrate a constant conflict between the freedom of human responsiveness and integrity and the restrictive and dishonest forms the human being needs to survive. The conflict is simultaneously personal and public or political, equally insoluble in the mutually dependent spheres. While restrictive form in modern life is often made trivial, and is satirised consistently, Hare suggests or valorises no political alternative. In a social and political context, his moral plays probe experience more deeply than fidelity to political cause or explanation through a dichotomy like Left v .. Right permits.

Notes

1. All dates of plays given in the text are of the first production, rather than the date of first publication. For a complete list to 1988 of the plays of David Hare (b. 1947), see *Contemporary Dramatists*, ed. D.L. Kirkpatrick (London: St James Press, 1988). In 1988 Hare published *The Secret Rapture* and in 1990 *Racing Demon*.
2. Richard Allen Cave, *New British Drama in Performance on the London Stage* (Gerrards Cross, Buckinghamshire: Colin Smythe, 1987) p. 184.
3. David Hare, *Racing Demon* (London/Boston: Faber & Faber, 1990) p. 22.
4. David Hare, *The History Plays* (London: Faber & Faber, 1984); *Licking Hitler* (1978) is a television film set in a country house functioning as a British propaganda unit during the war, in which the young heroine loves and leaves the director as she sees British propaganda efficiently aping the falsity of the German.
5. David Hare, *The History Plays* (London: Faber & Faber, 1984) p. 15.
6. David Hare, *The Asian Plays* (London/Boston: Faber & Faber, 1986) p. vii.
7. David Hare, *Wrecked Eggs*, in *The Bay at Nice* and *Wrecked Eggs* (London/Boston: Faber & Faber, 1986) p. 93.
8. These plays on language are in *The Asian Plays*, pp. 186–93.

9. David Hare, *The Secret Rapture* (London/Boston: Faber & Faber, 1988) p. 21.
10. Ibid., unpaginated.
11. David Hare, *Racing Demon* (London/ Boston: Faber & Faber, 1990), unpaginated. All quotations are from this edition; hereafter, page numbers will be given in the text.

13

Honouring the Audience: the Theatre of Howard Barker

Robert Wilcher

Howard Barker's career as a stage dramatist began with the production of *Cheek* in the Royal Court Theatre Upstairs in September 1970.[1] *Claw* was produced at the Open Space in January 1975 and later that year *Stripwell* opened in the Royal Court Theatre's main auditorium, to be followed by *Fair Slaughter* in 1977.[2] Barker was not destined to become a Royal Court writer, however, although several more of his plays have been seen there. Looking back from the late 1980s, he recognised that what he had always wanted was 'a licence to speculate' and 'the courage to dream', ambitions which could not be comfortably accommodated to the 'documentary' medium favoured by a theatre that was 'resolutely naturalistic' in outlook.[3] His own uncompromisingly *avant garde* stance has meant that some of his plays have remained unperformed for years, and although the Royal Shakespeare Company has mounted a number of productions, they have been confined to its studio spaces (The Warehouse and The Pit). Other plays have been taken up by provincial repertory companies or staged in small experimental theatres. Barker notes ruefully that the National Theatre 'has been offered every play of mine in the last ten years and ignored every one'.[4] It was in response to this situation that in 1988 a group of actors set up The Wrestling School, a company dedicated to performing plays by Howard Barker.

Nicholas Le Prevost, who directed *Golgo* and played the title role in *Seven Lears* in 1989, has testified to the liberating quality of this playwright's texts: 'The potency of Barker's language gives you strength as an actor. It is a joy on both sides of the lights'.[5] Barker himself has always rejoiced in the imaginative freedom and the dynamic nature of theatre, which provides a 'socially abrasive occasion' and encourages people to 'shout and laugh in a public manner'.[6] Never a subscriber to the view that the dramatist is merely a purveyor of 'reconciliation or relief',[7] he has latterly been working towards the creation of 'a new kind of theatre' which seeks to 'locate its creative tension not between characters and arguments on the stage but between the audience and the stage itself'.[8] Such a theatre will honour its audience by offering them the challenge of contradictions rather than the comfort of a spurious clarity:

> An honoured audience will quarrel with what it has seen, it will go home in a state of anger, not because it disapproves, but because it has been taken where it was reluctant to go. Thus morality is created in art, by exposure to pain and the illegitimate thought.[9]

From the beginning, Barker has been preoccupied with the conflict between individual impulse and society's internal and external mechanisms of control. His first stage-play, *Cheek*, explores the Oedipal predicament of a young man who fantasises about a life of sexual gratification and financial success beyond the confines of his parental home and working-class environment. Convinced that 'If you've got the nerve you can do anything', he sneers at his friend's weakening resolve to go after something better than the prospects held out to those who conform:

> They're the failures, not us! They're the berks! They sit in their bloody offices, they stand at their fucking benches, working their lives away. That's not living, is it? Is that what you want?[10]

At the end, he withdraws into the domestic prison, permitting himself to be defined not by his own imagination but by the filial relationships from which he has failed to make his escape.

Barker soon began to feel that he needed to break out of the limits imposed by old-fashioned realism, and that this meant abandoning the domestic interiors which are a powerful emblem of 'the reconciliation that the home enforces'.[11] With hindsight, it appears to be significant that *Claw* (first published in 1977) opens with a mother picking her way through the rubble of her former home on a post-war bombsite. Her son, Noel Biledew, is an early example of the Barker anti-hero, who asserts his identity in action and chooses what he will be. Having absorbed the rudiments of Marxist theory from his idealistic father, he determines to set himself up as a pimp and persuades Nora, a fellow member of the Young Communist League, to sell herself to a policeman on the principle that the guardians of the capitalist system must be subverted by beating them at their own game – 'exchange of goods or services' (141). When the policeman savagely retrieves his pound from the inexperienced pimp after enjoying the 'goods', Noel vows that he will never be struck again: 'I'll tear their skin off first, I'll rip their faces off their skulls, I'll be a great claw ripping them, slitting their bellies like ripe fruits!' (147). Sealing this new version of himself with the name of Claw, he pursues his corrupt trade 'into the exclusive areas where I belong' (162), and by Act Two numbers Clapcott, the Home Secretary, among his customers. Things go wrong for him when he becomes sexually involved with Clapcott's wife, Angie. He soon discovers that, for all his apparent success, he will only be tolerated by those with real power so long as he sticks to his clearly defined role within the system of supply and demand. Dismissed from service first by Clapcott and then by Angie, his threats of public exposure and murder are swept aside by the arrival of a Special Branch Officer. Tension mounts steadily through Act Three, as Claw listens to the chilling reminiscences of two white-coated warders – formerly an I.R.A. killer and an assistant hangman – and makes an impassioned speech about the brotherhood of the common man. Unmoved by his appeal to class solidarity, the state's hired exterminators drown him in a bath, and the play closes with Clapcott's report to Parliament that 'the death of the patient Noel Biledew ... was accidental and in no way reflects upon the capacities or dedication of the staff' (230).

Stripwell (first published in 1977) reverses the perspective of *Claw*, focusing dramatic attention on the attempt of a representative of the privileged establishment – a circuit judge – to cast off a lifetime's public and private dishonesty by resigning from the bench and running away with his much younger mistress. His hopes of escaping from the past and remaking himself are foiled, however, when the girl prefers to throw in her lot with his drug-smuggling son and Cargill, a man he had sent to prison in Scene One for an act of vandalism motivated by 'some ill-defined sense of grievance and social injustice' (9), bursts in and shoots him dead.

Fair Slaughter (published in 1978 and 1984), heralded a sustained examination of the moral decline and political bankruptcy of post-war Britain. It provides an epic survey of the life of a working-class Communist like the elder Biledew, who ended his days in an institution for the aged – from where his ghostly presence exhorted the imprisoned Claw to win over his gaolers: 'Find the eloquence of Lenin, lick their cruelty away' (226). When we first see Gocher, the protagonist of *Fair Slaughter*, he is in the hospital of Wandsworth Prison after killing a fellow-inmate of an old people's home. His history is related in flashback to explain his obsessive attachment to a jar containing a pickled human hand, which came into his possession in Russia in 1920 during his service with the British Expeditionary Force opposing the armies of Bolshevism. The hand belonged to Tovarish, the engine driver of Trotsky's train, who was executed on the orders of Gocher's officer, Staveley; and Gocher has kept it with him for fifty years as a reminder of the ideals that the proletariat had fought and died for. Significant stages in Gocher's life are enacted under the critical gaze of both the audience and Old Gocher, who enters into dialogue with his younger self from time to time. The negotiation of each of his personal and public roles – as music hall entertainer during the Depression, as husband, as Communist Shop Steward during the Second World War, as father – has involved him in compromise and betrayal, and he eventually breaks down with a terrible cry of frustration and despair:

LOOK WHAT THEY HAVE DONE TO ME BECAUSE I WOULD NOT PLAY THE BANJO TO THEIR BLOODY LIES! . . . THE PARASITIC BASTARDS, THEY DRINK OUR BLOOD! I WILL KILL THEM, I WILL KILL THEIR BABIES, IT WILL BE A SLAUGHTER WHEN WE'VE FINISHED, A FAIR BLOODY SLAUGHTER, LET ME, GOD! (1984; 101)

This journey into the past is not only a paradigm of the failed idealism of the Left but also constitutes the education of Leary, a tough prison officer who is moved by Old Gocher's appeal to free himself from the prejudices imposed by his 'sodding uniform': 'Try it. Open yer mind to me!' (64). Unlike Claw's executioners, Leary does respond to his charge's eloquence and helps him to escape from the prison, sustaining the old man's delusion that their journey across southern England is a pilgrimage across Europe to inter Tovarish's severed hand with the rest of his remains in Murmansk.

On the South Downs, they encounter a senile Staveley, who has reappeared as the embodiment of Capitalist evil at various points in Gocher's story. Leary, with the zeal of the new convert, confronts this symbol of exploitation and oppression with the crimes of his class – 'I accuse you and demand the highest penalty!' (103); but Gocher argues for tolerance, since his enemy is now 'an old geezer' and 'barmy', and warns his disciple not to let his idealism destroy his humanity: 'The angrier you feel, the more you have to feed the heart!' (104). The audience has to cope with many contradictory arguments and responses as this complex play approaches its conclusion, with Gocher and Leary struggling over Tovarish's hand. The old man's claim – 'It's mine' – might seem to be justified by a lifetime's devotion to a cause, but it is countered by Leary's astute perception: 'Tov belongs to the people. No one can own Tovarish' (105).

Other Barker plays of the later 1970s explore the failure of social democracy in contemporary Britain from a variety of perspectives. *That Good Between Us* (first staged in July 1977) looks ahead to a time when a Labour Government is dependent upon the power of the army to maintain some semblance of order in a strike-ridden country. Jardine, leader of a Home Office inquiry into the burning down of Middenhurst Prison in *The Hang of the Gaol* (first published in 1982), is a familiar Barker character – a cynical ex-Communist public servant, who despises himself for prospering under a system he knows to be oppressive and corrupt. His unorthodox methods of investigation reveal that the gaol was destroyed by the disillusioned Governor, but Jardine agrees to suppress the truth in his official report, bowing to the argument of Stagg, Labour Home Secretary, that political expediency must sometimes be permitted to override personal moral codes: 'We did not choose the system, but we have got to get the hang of it' (77). *The Loud Boy's Life* (first staged in February 1980) and *Birth on a Hard Shoulder* (first staged in November 1980) form a companion pair to these analyses of the problems of the Left in government, turning the dramatic spotlight onto frightening and farcical manifestations of right-wing discontent among the ruling caste and at the lunatic margins of a decaying parliamentary democracy.

Downchild (first published in October 1985, but written much earlier) brings this cycle of plays to an exuberantly inventive climax, with its exploitation of the properties of a genteel mystery story – a cliff-top wheatfield, a country church, a village pub (the Beggar's

Arms), a feudal manor house, the legend of a local ghost, and a cast that includes a vicar, a mad aristocrat, a Lady Bountiful and a family of colourful yokels. At the explosive centre of this richly traditional mixture is Tom Downchild, who announces himself to a pair of bemused farm labourers as 'novelist, poet, beauty addict, priest of wit and slave to scandal' (57). This 'great big noisy fairground' (77) of a character – one of Barker's most heroically outrageous creations – is better known as Lord Cocky, ageing gossip columnist of the *Daily World*, and has brought his young homosexual lover, Stoat, to recuperate in the idyllic peace of rural England after a spell in prison. His journalistic nose soon sniffs out a story that involves the former Labour Prime Minister, Roy Scadding, and his political secretary and mistress, now Lady Heyday and new owner of the 'big house'. These two, in collusion with the local clergyman, are plotting to murder Lord Dicker, their co-conspirator in financial fraud, whose descent into hereditary homicidal lunacy – he has brained the nanny and taken to biting the heads off peacocks – threatens them with exposure. Stripped naked and humiliated when he falls into the hands of Scadding, the irrepressible Downchild bounces back to preside over a surreal court of justice in the parish church. Enthroned on the altar, he announces **'The Holy Inquisition of Lord Cocky!'** (94) and urges Scadding to a searing self-indictment of his wasted years in office:

I helped old women bleed in gutters. . . .
I stuffed despair through the letter-boxes of the flats. . . .
I kicked hope out the hearts of men I didn't know. . . .
I could have fucked History but I dribbled in my pants. (97)

Three other plays relate to this phase of Barker's work, but in different ways they point beyond the satire on contemporary England that reaches its triumphant culmination in *Downchild* to new developments in the 1980s. The first of Barker's theatre plays to take place entirely outside England, *The Love of a Good Man* (first staged in October 1978, first published in 1980) is also the first of a number of investigations into the aftermath of large-scale historical disaster. Set in 1920 on the site of Passchendaele, it satirises the public and private responses to the horror underlined by Bride, official recorder of the names of the dead, as the War Graves Commission pursues its task of turning the battlefield into 'a Garden of the Fallen' (15): 'I do not want to dramatise, but where we are standing is not ground so much as flesh' (7). While civilian contractors haggle over rates of profit and the Prince of Wales stutters his way through the ceremony of choosing a corpse to fill the public role of the Unknown Warrior, the darkly brooding Riddle nurses a dream of salvation from the hurt of history through orgasm and primitivism in language reminiscent of the later D.H. Lawrence:

> I'm finishing with Europe. I'm finishing with dead continents and dead women. I'm going to a place where there is desire in the hips of the women and a slow look in their eyes, where flesh is flesh and as old as sex itself, where men do not come chattering from books. (41)

Crimes in Hot Countries (first staged in 1983 but written some years earlier) is a satiric fantasia on the British in their imperial role as managers of less developed parts of the globe. Under the influence of Toplis, an army mutineer disguised as a conjuror, sexual and political havoc flourishes briefly in a colonial outpost among a cast of assorted prostitutes, profiteers, senile and incompetent government officials, and common soldiers (including Lawrence of Arabia, incognito as Private Pain), until the experiment in establishing an independent New England is cut short by the arrival of Australian troops. *A Passion in Six Days* (first staged in October 1983) returns to the internal problems of British Socialism, but under the altered conditions created by the Conservative victory at the polls in 1979. It is a powerful dramatisation of the pain of questioning and renewal – in politics and in marriage – among delegates to the annual conference of the Labour Party.

The beginning of the new decade saw Barker undertaking a radical reassessment of the role of the artist in one of his most accessible and eloquent plays, in which the savage mockery and cruel inventiveness of satire give way to the anguish of tragedy.[12] *No End of Blame* (first staged in February 1981 and first published that year) follows the careers of two Hungarian artists from an opening scene set in the Carpathian Mountains in 1918, in which the irreconcilable opposition between an art which seeks to celebrate beauty of form and an art which insists on engaging with the brutal realities of human existence is emblematically established by Bela Veracek's attempt to rape the woman whose naked body his comrade-in-arms, Grigor Gabor, is feverishly sketching. Projected examples of Grigor's idealised nude portraits and Bela's grotesque and politically trenchant drawings provide a visual accompaniment to the ensuing action. A clash with an instructor at the Institute of Fine Art in Budapest in 1921 convinces Bela that he must cut himself free from a society locked into the past – 'Dead place, Grig! Stink of old corpse coming through national flag!' (11); but unlike Riddle among the decaying dead of Flanders, he looks for a new life in the society being strenuously forged in Lenin's Russia, not escape into some haven of unspoiled innocence. The Writers' and Artists' Union soon haul him before a disciplinary committee, however, and by 1936 the growing idolatry of Stalin leads him to migrate to England, where he becomes cartoonist on the *Daily Mirror*. He falls foul of Churchill during the war against Hitler and is eventually dismissed on the orders of the newspaper's proprietor, who finds his grim vision of the post-war world neither funny nor politically congenial. Grigor's dream of escaping from Stalinism by a return to the simple life in the forest – another brand of primitivism – had been scorned by Bela as 'the woods option': 'You don't miss the bullets by shutting your eyes!' (25). When Bela next encounters him, a solitary figure sweeping a path in a London park, Grigor's broken spirit is graphically projected in a *'horribly emaciated female figure in a posture of rejection'* (43), the agonised last fruits of his cult of the human form. Bela himself, sliding into the crazed conviction that he is the sole repository of truth in a world that prefers lies and laughter, fails in a suicide attempt and ends up in the same institution as Grigor. There, he is urged by one of the doctors to refuse society's verdict that his truth is madness. Pointing to the projected drawing of a *'spectacular panorama of Europe in a nuclear fire. Heaped with corpses, and above it a monstrous deformity in mask and goggles'* (45), she accuses him of taking refuge in an egotistical despair, which serves as his own variation of the 'woods option'. If, as he once asserted, the cartoon changes the world while the painting only changes the artist, then he still has an obligation to attack the evil system instead of merely expressing horror at its consequences: 'WHAT ABOUT US? (*She points to the cartoon.*) THAT DON'T 'ELP US! (*Pause.*) Assign the blame' (55). The play ends with one of Barker's most haunting images. The old man staggers from his wheelchair and advances towards the audience with an appeal which insists that they are implicated in his situation: 'Give us a pencil . . . somebody. . . . Give us a pencil . . . give us a pencil' (55). The spectator's role as passive consumer of art is challenged just as Bela's temporary fixation on the pain of his predicament as artist had been challenged by the young doctor's call to action. And in the same gesture, the playwright rejects the role of entertainer and affirms his belief in a dynamic theatre of engagement.

In the year that *No End of Blame* was first performed, Barker was working on *The Poor Man's Friend*, a community play commissioned by the Colway Theatre Trust. Among the things he learnt from dramatising an episode in the history of the town of Bridport was 'the realisation of the utter universality of suffering'.[13] The influence of this may be reflected in the title of *Pity in History* (commissioned by BBC Television in 1982, transmitted in July 1985), and the Bridport venture may also have stimulated him to delve back beyond the twentieth century to find vehicles for his current preoccupations. The television play is set during the Cromwellian period and his next major play for the theatre, *Victory*, in the months following the restoration of Charles II. Barker insists, however, that such works contain 'imagined history' – 'I don't do research, they are an amalgam of intuitions' – and has cited *Victory* as a significant step in his gradual discarding of satire.[14]

The manipulation of power over human bodies for political purposes had been close to the imaginative centre of *The Love of a Good Man*. *Victory* (first staged in February 1983 and published that year) subjects that theme to a much more complex treatment in its story of the Puritan Susan Bradshaw's determination to repossess and bury the scattered remains of her husband, exhumed and dismembered as an exemplary punishment for regicide. Her grim pilgrimage takes her not only to London and into the service of the king's mistress, but also on a more harrowing and heroic journey of self-reconstruction, as she is reduced to begging for her food and is raped by Ball, a Cavalier intent on revenge. With each humiliation, she learns something more about her control over her own body and its resources, and can rejoice at her success in stealing from republican sympathisers who befriend her. When Scrope, her secretary, condemns the callous ingratitude of her deed, she utters the first of many hard moral insights that she will have to learn in order to survive as a body and as a person: 'Do you think I found it easy? It wasn't easy. But that's my triumph. Any fool can rob his enemy. Where's the victory in that?' (27).

The Power of the Dog (first staged in November 1984, first published in 1985) is the bleakest of Barker's evocations of a disordered world. Set in 1945, when Churchill and Stalin meet to divide the spoils of conquest, various 'Moments in History and Anti-History' give substance to the definitions offered by Stalin – 'History? (*Pause*). The incredulous overwhelmed by the incredible' (4) – and by Ilona, a Hungarian fashion model, who has been touring central Europe since 1943 with Victor, a Roumanian photographer, compiling a documentary record of the atrocities of war – 'History is a mad dog' (23). Victor longs to escape to America, but Ilona knows that their fate is bound up with 'this squirming old, dirty old, European place' (17), which Stalin later likens to an 'ant-heap kicked into activity, every road and track jammed with civilians or armies jostling one another as they pass' (28).

Interviewed in 1984, Barker indicated that his next play would explore the twin themes of 'scientific mayhem' and 'sexual love and its redemptive power'. Diagnosing the post-1945 arms race as 'a sickness without parallel in human history', he revealed that his 'pseudo-historical' metaphor for this would be the return of a feudal lord from the crusades, bringing with him 'a technology of repression'.[15] But he added later that the balance of his speculations about 'areas of consciousness that are submerged' was shifting from the political manifestations to the sexual sources of the human will to power.[16] *The Castle* (first staged in October 1985, first published in the same year) pits Skinner, a witch who has infused feminine values into the village community during the seven-year absence of the crusaders – 'Freed the ground, freed religion, freed the body' (6) – against the masculine authority of Stucley, who comes back to find 'minds gone wild through lack of discipline' (4). This contest is initially fought out over the person of Ann, Stucley's wife and Skinner's lover, but is complicated by the presence of Krak, an Arab mathematician brought home by Stucley to plan the building of a new castle. Secure within the abstract rigour of his professional skill, Krak can contemplate its effects with chilling detachment: 'The castle is not a house. . . . It resembles a defence but is really an attack. . . . It makes war necessary. . . . It is the best thing I have ever done' (13–14). Ann's desire for him, however, provokes an uncontrollable surge of answering passion, and he turns in pain and bewilderment to Skinner, prophet of the 'lovely shapelessness' (6) of female sexuality: 'Where's cunt's geometry? The thing has got no angles! And no measure, neither width nor depth, how can you trust what has no measurements?' (37). Ann, pregnant by Krak, kills herself when the horror of the new technology sinks into her imagination; and Krak and Skinner are left to confront the future, the one aware that 'Demolition needs a drawing, too' and the other yearning for an irretrievable innocence – 'There was no government . . . does anyone remember . . . there was none' (43) – while a modern jet streaks low overhead.

Attracted by the 'obsessive linkage between money, power and sex' in Middleton's Jacobean tragedy, Barker continued his exploration of 'the redemptive power of desire'[17] in *Women Beware Women* (published in 1986 and 1989) by fashioning a new resolution of the plot, in which the orthodox poetic justice imposed by the multiple slaughter of the final masque scene was replaced by the more challenging spectacle of Sordido's rape of Bianca on the morning before her marriage to the Duke. Sordido, an embittered malcontent, forms an alliance with Livia to subvert the cynical use of Bianca's sexuality as 'a symbol of the state' (1989; 54): 'I risk death for her privacy. And stealing her toy virginity, all the poor of Florence grab their rights, who had been meant only to swoon with insatiable envy' (53). Livia's passionate involvement with Leantio enacts an existential openness to the transforming power of desire; and Bianca, too, achieves a redemptive insight which foreshadows the extension of Barker's themes and methods in the later 1980s: 'Catastrophe is also birth. Out the ruins crawls the bloody thing, unrecognisable in the ripped rags of former life' (61). In the same year that *Women Beware Women* was produced, the dramatist spoke of a determination 'not to write any more linear-epic plays': 'I'm trying to get an epic quality which is vertical . . . it involves my sense that plays don't need to keep changing location in any practical way, and also a feeling that I want to be much looser in character – for example in the ability of characters to change almost arbitrarily'.[18] His most recent plays are experiments in what he now refers to as the Theatre of Catastrophe.[19]

In an interlude in *The Bite of the Night* (first staged in August 1988, first published in that year), the archaeologist, Schliemann, gives his reason for excavating the site of Troy: 'Because I am a European, and Europe begins in Helen's bed' (64). The play adopts the image of excavation as a model for the vertical odyssey of the last Classics teacher in a ruined university. An antitype of Aeneas, Doctor Savage abandons his wife in the flaming alleys of Troy and rids himself of the impediments of father and son, before plunging into a Faust-like quest for '**Wisdom**, not cleverness, **Knowledge**, not retorts, **Truth**, not wit' (12). Each Troy that he uncovers – Paper Troy, Laughing Troy, Mum's Troy, Fragrant Troy – represents one more attempt to confine or domesticate or extinguish Helen, who embodies instinct's rebellion against all systems of corporate morality or social control. Near the end of his symbolic pursuit of 'Essential Helen' (48) – understanding that each stage of the journey will rip away 'some priceless thing, which feels part of yourself and your identity' (18) and that Helen is 'all that's unforgivable' (20) – Savage embraces the armless and legless trunk of the desired woman, who has been 'pruned' at the prompting of his imagination, with words directed at the audience as well as the figures on the stage: 'I am what you are only in your dreams' (83). Set at a time of crisis for Western civilisation when a Turkish advance was halted at the gates of Vienna in 1683, *The Europeans* (not yet staged) focuses on the traumatic experiences of Katrin, violated and mutilated by the Turks, and the ruthless process of self-invention pursued by Starhemberg, the victorious Imperial General, as vehicles for another celebration of the purposeful achievement of knowledge through suffering. These two characters collude to resist assimilation by the state's ideology and triumph at the end by handing over to the Turks the child, born of Katrin's rape, which the Hapsburg Emperor had named Concilia and tried to hijack as a public symbol.

Early in 1988, Barker declared that his preoccupation with 'class conflict' had been superseded by a view of the world which identified 'ideology as the enemy': 'What engages me today is not so much exposing the pain caused by class in society as speculating about how people frame their lives under oppression'.[20] These speculations are carried forward in two plays which also confirm his move away from linear narratives and consistency of characterisation. The Second Prologue to *The Last Supper* (first published in 1988) accordingly delivers an invitation to the audience 'to hang up the/ Suffocating overcoat of communication' and promises that 'No one will hold your hand tonight/ Nor oil you with humour' (2). Equally uncompromising in its refusal to dispense easy messages or affirm settled assumptions, *The Possibilities* (first staged in February 1988) presents ten self-contained episodes, resonant of middle Europe or the near East during some undefined war or revolution, and involving characters that range from peasants, soldiers and party officials to Tsar Alexander and the Biblical Judith. Each incident hinges on the acceptance or repudiation of some act of violence or betrayal sanctioned by ideology or reason; and each withholds authorial comment on the choice that is made. *The Last Supper* draws upon the Gospels and the iconography of Leonardo's painting and Buñuel's *Viridiana* to examine the process by which a religious myth and a body of doctrine evolve out of the death and sayings of a modern prophet, in spite of his own teaching that 'the very attempt to inflict symmetrical systems is an oppression' (26) and 'only catastrophe can keep us clean' (23). The play is punctuated by 'a cloud of laughter', identified as 'the irrepressible expression of solidarity which has become detached from humanity and drifts over the landscape' (53). Its source is the Public, a deity which intervenes to make demands of the prophet, and by implication of the dramatist: **'Why don't you give us a slogan you snob'** (26).

Barker's next two plays for The Wrestling School develop this device into an unreliable Chorus, which tries to hector the audience into glib responses in defiance of Barker's principle that they should be 'unable to withdraw into the security of known moral postures'.[21] The spectator as individual is thus dared to seek shelter in the 'solidarity' of the audience in both *Seven Lears* and *Golgo* (first staged in October and November 1989). In the first, speculation centres on the reasons for the almost total erasure from the family memory of the mother of Lear's daughters in *King Lear*; in the second, a group of French aristocrats in 1789 performs a macabre series of charades on the theme of the Crucifixion of Christ, while sounds of the revolutionary mob grow ever nearer. And in both, Barker's characteristic techniques of shock and contradiction reach out to people like the woman whose response is reported in the First Prologue to *The Bite of the Night*: 'Because I found it hard I felt honoured' (2).

Notes

1.	For a complete list to 1988 of the plays of Howard Barker (b. 1946), see *Contemporary Dramatists*, ed. D.L. Kirkpatrick (London: St James Press, 1988). Since *Contemporary Dramatists*, Barker has published: *The Possibilities* (1987), *The Bite of the Night* (1988), *The Last Supper* (1988), *The Europeans* and *Judith* (1990), and *Seven Lears* and *Golgo* (1990). With the exception of *New Short Plays: 3* (London: Eyre Methuen, 1972), all Barker's plays are published by John Calder (London). Page references to the appropriate volumes will be given in brackets after quotations, with date of publication after the first reference to each quoted play. It should be noted, however, that there are often considerable lapses of time between composition, first performance and publication of Barker's texts. In this essay, the plays will be discussed roughly in order of composition.
2.	For accounts of three early radio plays and the unpublished stage

plays produced between *Cheek* and *Claw,* see David Ian Rabey, *Howard Barker: Politics and Desire* (London: Macmillan, 1989) pp. 10–41. This is the only comprehensive study of Barker's work published to date.

3.   Howard Barker, *Arguments for a Theatre* (London: Calder, 1989) p. 29.
4.   Ibid., p. 32.
5.   'The Wrestling School: Nicholas Le Prevost Talks to Kate Kellaway', *Plays and Players* (March 1990) 22.
6.   Quoted in Oleg Kerensky, *The New British Drama* (London: Hamish Hamilton, 1977) p. 243.
7.   See Barker's statement in *Contemporary Dramatists*, ed. James Vinson (London: St James Press, 1977) p. 65.
8.   *Arguments for a Theatre*, p. 52.
9.   Ibid., p. 46.
10.   *New Short Plays: 3* (London: Eyre Methuen, 1972) pp. 17, 34.
11.   *Arguments for a Theatre*, p. 30.
12.   The role of the artist is also a central theme in the radio play, *Scenes from an Execution*, broadcast in October 1984.
13.   Tony Dunn, 'Interview with Howard Barker', *Gambit: International Theatre Review*, No. 41 (1984) 44.
14.   Ibid., pp. 34–5.
15.   Ibid., pp. 33–4.
16.   Howard Barker, 'Oppression, Resistance, and the Writer's Testament' [interview], *New Theatre Quarterly*, No. 8 (1986) 336.
17.   *Arguments for a Theatre*, p. 22.
18.   'Oppression, Resistance, and the Writer's Testament', p. 337.
19.   *Arguments for a Theatre*, pp. 51–62.
20.   'Off-beat track: Howard Barker meets Laurence Marks', *Observer*, 21 February 1988, 24.
21.   *Arguments for a Theatre*, p. 81.

14

The Plays of Pam Gems: Personal/ Political/ Personal

Katherine H. Burkman

Emerging as a dramatic presence on the British stage in the 1970s, Pam Gems has contributed her many talents to that scene and beyond ever since.[1] Lyn Gardner even calls her 'the grand dame of British Theatre',[2] partly because, despite Caryl Churchill's successes in America, Gems is the one who found her way onto the West End stages of the British establishment and has been a prolific contributor to that scene since, writing some twenty plays in ten years for it. As part of what John Russell Brown has called the second wave of contemporary British playwrights, comprising the political, the fringe, and women's theatre, her work has been involved with all aspects of that wave.[3] The politics of her plays are more focused than that of the first wave, ushered in by John Osborne's 1956 production of *Look Back in Anger*, and it is the particular mixture of the personal and the political that marks her contributions to the dramatic scene.

While Gems objects to feminist theatre that is narrowly anti-men and is a believer in marriage and the need for children to have two parents, she dwells in her dramas on the plight of women as it works itself out on both a personal and political level. Indeed, whether writing of the personal and public life of the singer, Edith Piaf (*Piaf*, 1973), of the public and personal life of the ruler, Queen Christina (*Queen Christina*, 1977), or of the struggles of less famous women in plays such as *Dusa, Fish, Stas and Vi* (1976) or *Loving Women* (1984), her work embodies the feminist idea that the personal is in itself political, the other side of that coin suggesting as well that the political is personal.[4]

Although Gems refuses to be categorised as a feminist and does not conform to any particular branch of feminism (radical, bourgeois, socialist),[5] her dramas certainly bespeak the reassessment of gender that has been part of the post-1960s world. From her first major success, *Dusa, Fish, Stas and Vi* (1976), a play that addresses the concerns of four women who share a London flat, to her more recent *Aunt Mary* (1982), in which two of the central characters are transvestite authors, gender issues have been central to her dramas and have been treated with a kind of wit of desperation that gives them their singular power.

In 'Beyond Hellman and Hansberry: the Impact of Feminism on a Decade of Drama by Women', Phyllis Mael mentions Pam Gems as one of many women playwrights of the 1970s whose voice is shaped by a 'developing feminist consciousness'.[6] Perhaps it is because Gems did not write seriously for the theatre until her forties that her feminist consciousness emerged onto the British stage with a mature mixture of empathy and distance. Possibly, too, it is this mix that allowed her to make the transition from the fringe, where her work first appeared, to the established theatres where her plays have been so frequently produced over the last several years.

Gems was born in 1925 of working class parents. Her father died when she was only four, and she was reared with her two brothers by her widowed mother. Although she had won a scholarship to a grammar school, she joined the Women's Royal Naval Service, served from 1944–6, and then took a degree in psychology at Manchester University (1946–9) as an ex-service student. Shortly after earning her degree she married at the age of twenty-four. Keith Gems, a model manufacturer, formerly an architect, took his family to Paris in the fifties and then to the Isle of Wight; they moved to London in the seventies. During these years Gems raised her children, three of whom have thriving careers; her son Jonathan is himself a promising playwright.

After the birth of Jonathan (1952) and Sara (1954), Gems worked for the BBC in London, where she had also worked for a short time before her marriage. Living in a house that she soon discovered was a brothel, she wrote three plays for television, one of which, *Builder by Trade* (1961), was aired. While caring for the children partly inhibited her writing, Gems found that after the birth of a mongoloid daughter (1965), she could make use of the isolation that followed to write. Speaking of her daughter, Gems says, 'She was incontinent for nine years and people didn't want to visit us. You tend to retire into yourself then, and that was very good for me because I wrote'.[7] After the permanent move to London, occasioned by the need to find better educational opportunities for their handicapped child, Gems found the time to get involved in London's fringe theatre; and after preliminary successes with commissioned works by Almost Free, a feminist group, she eventually became established in the London theatre scene with her first great success, *Dusa, Fish, Stas and Vi*.[8]

Gems's strength as a playwright lies partly in her ability to take on feminist issues without writing polemical plays. This feminist stance tends to get her into trouble with some critics who are threatened by her feminism, and with others who find her not radical enough. Susan E. Bassnett-McGuire, for example, admires the way Gems's *Queen Christina* challenges Greta Garbo's romantic film version of the queen, a woman brought up as a man to rule her people and one faced with tremendous gender difficulties. She criticises Gems, however, for giving a single actor such a central role and for allowing her feminist heroine to become too embroiled in personal problems.[9] Sally Aire also criticises what she sees as an inconsistency in Gems's focus on traditional feminine concerns; she dislikes the vanity that emerges along with the character's love of culture and does not wish this 'lesbian' character to weep for her childless state – 'A woman's a woman, "for a' that"', Aire complains.[10]

What some critics find inconsistent, however, may simply be Gems's refusal to create feminist heroines according to some pre-determined ideal. Her first version of *Dusa, Fish, Stas and Vi*, for example, was called *Dead Fish*, a title which gave away the play's ending in the suicide of the political activist, Fish, who seems to be the major force for life in the group of four women who share a London flat. Fish's suicide, which stems from her despair over rejection by her unfaithful fellow activist lover, is the play's central irony. 'I don't feel fertile any more', she writes in her suicide letter to her three friends. 'My loves, what are we to do? We don't do as they want any more, and they hate it. What are we to do?'[11] The irony is not just, however, that Fish has turned out to be less independent than her fellow flat-mates had imagined, but that they have somehow imbibed her strength and fertility. Dusa, the helpless, newly-divorced mother, has retrieved her children, kidnapped earlier by her husband. Vi, who has rejected the world, retreating into a dangerously anorexic condition, has gained weight and found a job, and Stas, who works with brain-damaged children by day, stealing and serving as a call girl at night to save for a career in marine biology, seems to have saved just about enough to get on with her goals. Stas, however, as a scientist, has earlier expressed what is part of the play's scepticism over political change. To Dusa's suggestion that the activists are making some progress, Stas replies: 'I'll tell you what's changing things . . . the last fifty years of physics and the next fifty years of biology. What you're talking about is fashion'. Her even more negative stance puts political change in cosmic perspective as she notes in a somewhat Beckettian tone that the tendency in the physical world is 'for things to collapse. My old man's a farmer. Ask any farmer, he'll tell you' (27).

John Peter is no doubt quite right when he writes that the play is not 'an anti-male tract' but rather 'pulsates with humanity', a humanity that despite the play's sadness is filled with an enabling humour.[12] When Vi asks Dusa to buy her some myrrh on her trip to the store, she explains that she needs it to turn 'fellers into frogs' (14). So much for Fish's knight in shining armour.

Nevertheless, Fish's suicidal question haunts all of Gems's plays, in which she offers no answers but numerous explorations of the question, what are we to do as women in a man's world, or for that matter as men in a man's world? One reviewer who compared *Dusa, Fish, Stas and Vi* with Harold Pinter's *No Man's Land* finds a support of each other in the women, a communal warmth that is lacking in Pinter's male world of four.[13] This support is present to some extent in *Piaf*, Gems's most successful play to date and the one she actually wrote earliest (1973), although it did not reach the West End until 1978 or Broadway until 1981.[14]

If John Osborne's 1956 production of *Look Back in Anger* galvanised a new kind of playwriting, in which there was a turning away from drawing room comedy and its superficial, upper-class banter to plays about the working classes that were critical of society, Gems's *Piaf* is about an angry woman rather than an angry man. Piaf does not look back in anger but angrily straight ahead, making her way in a man's world as best she can.

Brecht rather than Osborne is the major influence on Gems. 'For feminists', writes Janelle Reinelt, 'Brechtian techniques offer a way to examine the material conditions of gender behaviour (how they are internalised, opposed, and changed) and their interaction with other socio-political factors such as class'.[15] Gems uses Brecht's techniques, historicising the incidents of the French singer's life, until *Piaf* becomes, like Brecht's *Mother Courage*, an epic of survival and waste. In the biography, *Piaf*, by Margaret Crosland, the singer drifts off finally into drug addiction and premature old age, a somewhat ridiculous figure, who in her fifties keeps a series of young lovers whom she attempts to control.[16] In the play Piaf clearly transcends her situation even while her behaviour shows how she succumbs to it.

The play begins with an insistence on independence: we see the decaying Piaf at the end of her life, about to collapse at her microphone and struggling with the manager who would help her offstage: 'Get your fucking hands off me, I ain't *done* nothing yet . . . ' (11). Almost exactly the same admonition is one that the young Piaf, whose rise to fame and fortune the play charts, gives in the next scene to Louis Leplée, who discovers her singing on the streets. 'Get your fucking hands off me, *I* ain't done nothing' (11) are her initial words to the man who provides Piaf with a singing career off the streets where she has been surviving as a singer and whore. This time the 'done' in 'I ain't done nothing yet', refers to committing no crime, and the word 'yet' in the sentence at the microphone is omitted. The play explores the entire notion of what it is that Piaf does do with her life, her talent and her womanhood.

Some of the play's comic pathos derives from Piaf's combination of innocence and vulgarity. Impressed by her talent, Leplée wants to know how long she has been singing, and Piaf's answer is, 'Coupla minutes, that's all' (12). But if this remark is a measure of Piaf's naiveté about her own talent, in the scene in which Papa Leplée gives her the name of Piaf, meaning the little sparrow, Piaf shows her other side. When the waiter laughs at her for sipping out of a finger bowl and she realises her mistake, Piaf demands soap and in a fury announces, 'All right, clever cock. Seen me drink – now you can watch me piss' (16), which she proceeds to do on the spot. After an angry exit, Edith returns to give Leplée what she expects he will require of her, sexual favours, which he probably only turns down because of his homosexuality.

Here are all the ingredients of Piaf's very individual sense of integrity – she will do what she must to survive, recognising herself as a commodity, but she is not yet aware of her worth as a commodity; she yearns for a romantic image of herself in that she prefers the name Desirée to that of Piaf, but if she must be Piaf she will accept that; she is not yet aware of her worth as a person, much less a singer, but she has enough of a sense of herself to 'piss' on anyone who does not take her seriously.

In her biography, Crosland takes pains to make it clear that Piaf never sold her favours on the street, only her voice, keeping a pimp at one time as a protector for her singing (44). In the play, Piaf is paired with a friend and fellow-whore, Twoine, and in one scene she passes one of her men on to her friend when she needs to leave for an appointment. The distinction here between biography and play seems unimportant. Piaf is used by men, she is a commodity, whether a sexual or singing one, and the important question is how she can come to own herself and her voice, how she can become self-possessed.

As the play evolves and her career goes forward, Piaf becomes increasingly aware of her power on stage. When Josephine, a fellow singer, discusses Piaf as not needing glamour because 'you're the real thing' (38), Piaf says, 'Nah, it's not the money . . . No . . . when I'm out there – it's got to happen. Doesn't happen . . . terrible' (40).

Gems makes it clear that Piaf's fighting with her fists and with her mouth (her creative vulgarity) are essential to her way of taking on a brutal world so that she can make it happen out there, be the real thing. The playwright telescopes her position as victim and fighter in the scenes in which three of her 'friends' kill her benefactor for his money, trying to use her to entice him. As Leplée becomes sexually interested in one of the men, Piaf breaks the mood with a dirty joke, but, unable to save him, she is left with only a song in response – in this case, 'La ville inconnue'. When questioned by the police, the play's refrain returns – 'I ain't done nothing' (21). After being slapped about, Edith sobs, possibly both over her benefactor's death and her present treatment. As she repeats yet again, 'I ain't done nothing', still another meaning is added. The words have the sadness of her inability to protect her 'guv'nor', to do anything about his situation and also about her own. To survive, Piaf must, like Mother Courage, negotiate terms with the enemy. Slapped by the Inspector, she is slapped by the Manager as well, and she must be told by Twoine that the Manager is working now for her.

Gems allows scenes to run into each other so that, for example, in Scene viii Edith hears of the European middleweight boxing champion, Marcel Cerdan, while Scene ix opens in the midst of her affair with him. This 'shuttling from scene to scene', writes Susan Carlson, 'and the mixture of song and talk provide a shifting, uncertain, unsettling background against which the unity of Piaf's character grows and glows'.[17] While men come and go in Piaf's life, the Champ becomes important in the play, partly as her double – both characters know themselves as used commodities and see themselves as aging and always on the line. Marcel tells of how his greedy father got him started in the ring, unconcerned with his welfare as long as the money was good (35). Piaf's essential loneliness is revealed, however, as the Champ has his own family and she is always and repeatedly left alone.

The further telescoping of scenes with Piaf and a series of young lovers, ever younger as the play progresses, does not accentuate the grotesque aspect of Piaf trying to hang onto her youth, but rather the lonely Piaf, who never found the perfect love of which she felt deprived – as a child Piaf was abandoned by her mother, and her father also was unable to care for her much of the time. Near the time of her death, Piaf talked, Crosland reports, about a song she wished to write: 'It will be the story of an abandoned soul whom passion does not rescue from solitude . . . '[18]

What also emerges in the scenes that conflate her two marriages and many affairs is her treatment of young men as commodities, her merciless training of them so that they could become her singing partners, her rather pathetic turning of the tables so that they become the whores whom she possesses and rules. There is no glorification here, no glamour to the tyrannical scenes: 'Yeah, well, he'll do till I trade him up. Always set up your next trick before you shove in the icepick' (44), she says to one of her entourage about her most recent lover. A moment later she confesses her loneliness, acting despicably one moment, telling a terribly dirty joke the next, injecting herself with morphine, but always singing and giving her audiences 'the real thing' (60). 'Don't worry, love', Jacko, one of her many loves tells her. 'You'll never be a lady' (64).

As a fighter and as a singer, then, Pam Gems's Piaf resists those who would make her become a lady, a controllable commodity, something, some thing. One can hear the Beckettian strains again in the final play on the drama's refrain, 'I ain't done nothing', when there is a replay of the opening scene; once again the manager tries to help Piaf away from a microphone and she cries out, 'Get your fucking hands off me, I ain't done nothing nothing yet' (65). Reminiscing about their pasts in the next scene, Piaf tells Twoine that she 'never could hold on to nothing' (70). Nothing is as palpable as it is in *Waiting for Godot*, where there is 'Nothing to be done' and 'nothing happens'. Yet in another sense Piaf has done everything in this play; she has laughed, loved, lost and sung. After dying, Piaf takes a curtain call, singing one of her major theme songs, 'Non, je ne regrette rien' (72) – No, I regret nothing – which gives to nothing its final meaning. I accept who I am, I am somebody, and I have done everything. All those double negatives that are the play's song join with Piaf's song, so that artist and art merge in this final affirmation of Piaf as no thing, but rather as a triumphant anti-heroine.

The fascination with legendary women continues in other plays. In her excellent discussion of women's images in modern English theatre, Katharine Worth suggests that Pam Gems is one of those writers who 'dig up the old myths about women and reroot them in the new soil of our time'.[19] The demythologising of such legendary characters as Piaf, Queen Christina, or Camille, to name three of the women whom Gems has chosen to treat in her plays (*Queen Christina*, 1977, revised version produced in London, 1982; *Camille*, 1984), does not rob them of their power. In *Camille*, for example, in which the heroine gives coarse descriptions of what has led her to her profession as a prostitute, and in which she gives up her lover only for the promised education of her son. '[Her] passion for Armand has to be seen', Worth writes, 'as something of a miracle, like Piaf's gift of pure song. In reforming the image to give it a new, coarse vigour, Gems is actually claiming more, not less, for her heroine'.[20] Fish has died longing for a child, Marguerite gives up her lover for her child, and Queen Christina bewails missing the experience of having a child. Such, Gems suggests, is part of a woman's predicament, just as the hardness and coarseness of the women in these plays is a part of their means to survival. The Beckettian strain persists as well in *Camille*, as Marguerite asks Armand's father whether he thinks she is 'nothing' (133).[21]

The assertion of the need for motherhood and the celebration of a kind of coarse strength in women takes a somewhat more polemical as well as a comic turn in *Loving Women* (1984). Here the political activist, Frank, is adored by both his fellow revolutionary, Susannah, and Crystal, a hairdresser whom Susannah has arranged as a caretaker for Frank after he has a nervous breakdown. Crystal, whom he marries, confesses that she used him at a time when she desperately wanted a child, and Susannah returns to him after years away, bewailing her childless state and suggesting he father a child for her. At the end of the play, the rather coarse and comic Crystal conspires with the now politically disillusioned Susannah, and the two women plan to live together, with or without Frank. 'He always was an old chauve – well, they all are', Susannah concludes. 'Sod him, who needs him!', Crystal agrees (217).

The play echoes somewhat more polemically and less effectively *Dusa, Fish, Stas and Vi*'s scepticism about political change in a world in which women still want children but tend to run into the kind of chauvinism in men that dooms relationships that might be mutually fulfilling. Frank, who lectures Susannah about the unreality of their work together at a time when Crystal seems more real to him, returns to his political passion (partly because he cannot satisfy Crystal) at the very time that Susannah is exhausted and only craves a garden and motherhood. The final joining of the women at the end of *Loving Women* seems like a sadly comic answer to Fish's question that ends the earlier play: 'We don't do as they want any more, and they hate it. What are we to do?' (42).

Passionaria (1985) and *The Danton Affair* (1986) were not received with critical enthusiasm. *Passionaria*, the drama of Dolores, a peasant who became a force in the Spanish Communist Party in 1936, was apparently too polemical, as its comments on the 1985 miners' strike in Britain and other contemporary issues seemed to undermine its power.[22] *The Danton Affair*, an adaptation of the stage chronicle by Stanislawa Przybyszewska, which took Gems eighteen months to research and write, was also considered, at least by Giles Gordon, to be an 'unastringent script'.[23]

A play that received more mixed reviews, *Aunt Mary* (1982) is a delightful celebration of a marriage among two transvestites and their female friend, Muriel. While Charles Spencer dismissed the play as 'an intense disappointment, an infuriating piece of whimsy which spends two hours going nowhere', Claire Colvin enjoyed it as 'an anarchic and surrealistic comedy that illustrated several points of the Gems philosophy'.[24] What it does illustrate is her belief in marriage as a commitment, whether the marriage is between men, women, or men and women. 'People', she says, 'need to commit themselves to something and someone outside themselves'.[25] Michelene Wandor, who included the drama in Volume Three of her *Plays by Women*, admires Gems for writing wittily about men and 'managing to combine earthiness and sophistication in a highly original and idiosyncratic fashion. . . . Here the author's insight is harnessed into a continually entertaining and serious exploration of the relationship between art and life, appearance and reality and sexual identity'.[26]

Gems had, of course, thoroughly explored the relationship between art and life in *Piaf*, in which she depicts the singer fighting so furiously to refuse to let her art or herself become a commodity. But just as Piaf refuses commodification, insisting on a kind of freedom to control her sexuality and her voice, so too do Aunt Mary and Cyst, two transvestite writers whose pen names have allowed them to work out their gender identities in privacy. Like Piaf, however, they are not wholly successful in freeing themselves from the games of dominance and subservience that inform sexual and social relationships.

Cyst plays the role of Blanche DuBois, almost losing her beloved Aunt Mary to his heterosexual interest in a television worker, Alison, the person who envisions commodifying the two on the tube. The less than ideal dynamics of Aunt Mary's and Cyst's relationship are worked out in relation to Martin, the young poet who brings Alison onto the scene but is unable to get her to leave the men to their own world.

Actually, the exploitation threatened by Alison is already at work in Aunt Mary's idyllic world. She points out to Cyst, 'It never occurs to you that the way you let me exploit you harms me'.[27] Cyst, in fact, learns some new assertiveness through Alison, finally attracting the marriage proposal from Aunt Mary that will exclude her teacher, whose form of assertiveness promises destruction. When Mary and Cyst decide to include the left-out Muriel in their wedding, Mary taking on the two as wives, they agree on banishing fame and fortune with Alison, at least achieving a clear idea of whom they are not. Gems has said of her play and the male enjoyment of feminine fashion: 'Conformity . . . submission through fear . . . can never bring about the just society. The day our clothes submit, we submit'.[28]

As the men affirm their difference, as difficult as it is, the strains of *Piaf* come back to mind: 'Je regrette rien'. Gems may stray at times into overly polemical treatments of our modern dilemmas, but she has managed on the whole to explore the political and the personal in her numerous dramas with a wit, warmth, and humanity that make of her plays a welcome celebration.

Notes

1. For a complete list to 1988 of the plays of Pam Gems (b. 1925), see *Contemporary Dramatists*, ed. D.L. Kirkpatrick (London: St James Press, 1988). Since 1988, Gems has published two novels: *Mrs Frampton* (1990) and *Bon Voyage, Mrs Frampton* (1990).
2. Lyn Gardner, 'Precious Gems', *Plays and Players*, 379 (April 1985) 12.
3. See Roger Cornish and Violet Ketels, *Landmarks of Modern British Drama: the Plays of the Seventies* (London/New York: Methuen, 1985) p. vii.
4. See Susan E. Bassnett-McGuire, 'Towards a Theory of Women's Theatre', in *Semiotics of Drama and Theatre: New Perspectives in the Theory of Drama and Theatre*, ed. Herta Schmid and Aloysius Van Kestereu (Amsterdam/Philadelphia: Benjamines, 1984) p. 448.
5. According to Michelene Wandor, radical feminists hate men as the enemy, bourgeois feminists seek to be equal to men in a man's world, and socialist feminists seek to change the economic and political systems which have fostered gender problems (Cornish and Ketels, p. xx).
6. Phyllis Mael, 'Beyond Hellman and Hansbury: the Impact of Feminism on a Decade of Drama by Women', *Kansas Quarterly*, 12, 4 (1980) 143.
7. Claire Colvin, 'Earth Mother from Christchurch', *Plays and Players*, 347 (August 1982) 9.
8. The play moved from a fringe performance at The Edinburgh Festival in 1976 through a production at Hampstead Theatre Club to become Gems's first West End success at the Mayfair Theatre in 1977.
9. Bassnett-McGuire, p. 452.
10. Sally Aire, 'Queen Christiana', *Plays and Players*, 25 (Dec. 1977) 31.
11. *Dusa, Fish, Stas and Vi* (New York: Dramatists' Play Service, 1977) 42. All quotations are from this edition; hereafter, page numbers are given in the text.
12. John Peter, [Review], *Sunday Times*, 12 December 1976, 35.
13. Rodelle Weintraub, 'Pam Gems', in *Dictionary of Literary Biography: British Dramatists Since World War II*, ed. Stanley Weintraub (Detroit: Gale Research Co., 1982) pp. 192–8. The comparison with Pinter is an interesting one, in that Pinter's plays, *One for the Road* and *Mountain Language*, were greeted critically as a departure from his apolitical drama. With the playwright's own help, however, critics are currently looking back at his more ostensibly 'personal' dramas and realising how their power struggles were always political ones at heart.
14. All quotations from *Piaf* are from *Three Plays: Piaf, Camille, Loving Women* (Harmondsworth, Middlesex: Penguin, 1985). Page numbers will be given in the text.
15. Janelle Reinelt, 'Beyond Brecht: Britain's New Feminist Drama'. In *Performing Feminisms: Feminist Critical Theory and Theatre*, ed.

Sue-Ellen Case (Baltimore/London: Johns Hopkins UP, 1990) p. 150.

16. Margaret Crosland, *Piaf* (New York: G.P. Putnam's Sons, 1985).
17. Susan L. Carlson, 'Women in Comedy: Problem, Promise, Paradox', in *Drama, Sex and Politics*, ed. James Redmond (Cambridge: Cambridge UP, 1985) p. 167.
18. Crosland, p. 179.
19. Katharine Worth, 'Images of Women in Modern English Theater', in *Feminine Focus: the New Women Playwrights*, ed. Enoch Brater (New York: Oxford UP, 1989) p. 6.
20. Worth, p. 13.
21. All quotations from *Camille* are from *Three Plays: Piaf, Camille, Loving Women* (Harmondsworth, Middlesex: Penguin, 1985). Page numbers are given in the text.
22. Gardner, p. 13.
23. Giles Gordon, 'The Danton Affair', *Plays and Players*, 396 (Sept. 1986) 28.
24. Charles Spencer, 'Aunt Mary', *Plays and Players*, 347 (Aug. 1992) 35; Colvin, p. 9.
25. Colvin, p. 9.
26. *Plays by Women: Volume Three*, ed. Michelene Wandor (London: Methuen [Methuen Theatrefile], 1984) p. x.
27. Pam Gems, *Aunt Mary*, in Wandor, *Plays by Women: Volume Three*, p. 27.
28. Wandor, *Plays by Women*, p. 48.

15

Postmodern Classics: the Verse Drama of Tony Harrison

Romana Huk

> To understand this, it becomes necessary to level the artistic structure of the *Apollonian culture*, as it were, stone by stone, till the foundations on which it rests become visible.
>
> Friedrich Nietzsche, *The Birth of Tragedy*

I

Over the course of the last two decades Tony Harrison, the well-known British poet and classicist, has brought his poetry to full power on stage. His metrical arguments, which have always addressed social issues and audiences rather than isolated readers, find their perfect venue there, despite the fact that, as Derek Walcott recently put it, the very idea of metred verse drama has come to summon for most people 'the beat of footfalls down a vacant corridor, a museum, a ruined colonnade'.[1] Reversing those footsteps, Harrison's much-hailed successes in translating and contemporising classical verse drama have led him to invent what critics are now struggling to describe as his own unprecedented sort of politically radical, popular, postmodern poet's theatre.[2]

Harrison's interest in the classics is not, as he has said himself, that of an antiquarian. His work draws attention instead to very contemporary issues concerning the politics of interpretation by deconstructing what he calls the 'prop to the status quo' which culture has made of the classics at various phases of its social and political history.[3] But Harrison's is deconstructive theatre with a twist – one manifested poetically in both his conception and practice of adaptation. On the one hand, his plays' forfeiture of conventional originality for the interrogation of past drama signals his acknowledgement of what has come to constitute postmodern theory's new concept of fate: that all writings and interpretations are always already embedded in the language, and, therefore, the vision of their cultural text, shaped as it is at each juncture between history, politics and art by hegemonic forces of dominance. On the other hand, Harrison resists the paralysis, cynicism or silence that accompanies what deconstructionists describe, in Greek terms, as our 'aporia' (or 'no way out') of intertextual deadlock by adapting for contemporary theatre yet another Greek construct. Like Nietzsche, he believes that this construct allowed the earliest practitioners of drama to face up to fate and still affirm life, with its opposing range of disruptive powers and shaping possibilities.

Nietzsche reconceived it in *The Birth of Tragedy* as the creative/destructive, Apollonian/Dionysian dialectic, which pitted the Apollonian will to construct textual 'illusions' of mythical order, reason and tragic necessity against its opposite: the Dionysian, chaotic and leveling, material life force. The irreducibility of the latter's force to linguistic or rational formulation – symbolised by music and lyric poetry within tragedy, and by satyrical revelling at the end of tragic trilogies – continually called for recognition of the construction's illusion, for a 'new world of symbols', for perpetual adaptation and redramatisation of the myths that exerted their real force upon culture.[4] Thus Apollo's presence in Harrison's plays, whether as himself or in some other incarnation, always represents 'received' or official culture and its exclusive 'high' art. To confront him, Harrison's radical recreation of the Dionysian principle links it to contemporary voices of social, racial, and gendered otherness, whose disruptive presences are also always in danger of being dropped through the fissures of culture's self-creating narrative, or textual tradition, which he believes has a history of selectively inscribing and lexically refining the classics into what Nietzsche called 'a permanent military encampment of the Apollonian' in order to read its western cultural legacy as a Golden Age precedent for its own rigidified social hierarchy and moral order.[5] Retracking and reimaging traces of alternative forces in his new translations, Harrison seems to assume that if there is 'no way out' of textual hegemony there is, perhaps, a way *in*, a way of recolonising foundational texts in order to re-establish another kind of precedent, one of continual implosion and adaptation of cultural illusions by otherness in all of its internal and external forms: the only possible *telos* of his post-Brechtian dialectic operative in a world of texts from which there is no exit.

Poetry as Harrison writes it becomes once again the instrument of such creative/destructive dialectic; all his plays depend upon his unique rendering of its structure, medium and vision. Cocteau's oft-quoted distinction between 'poetry *in* the theatre' (but not fully related to the dramatic action, such as we had with Eliot and Fry),[6] and 'poetry *of* the theatre' becomes an even more provocative one when discussing Harrison's plays, given that his poetry *is* his theatre. It enacts within its metred lines the fundamental conflict between forces that on one level would contain the textual illusion and those that on another would destroy it. At the same time it identifies one with the other in a vision central to his own developing social theory.

On its first working level verse provides the traditional structure to be penetrated by disruptive otherness. In his extra-theatrical poetry, Harrison is known for 'occupying', as he writes in one sonnet, the formal metres of verse with his own 'unreceived' Yorkshire accent and working class perspective in order to both apprehend and renew the tradition that formed him from a position inside it, with a voice its standards were set to exclude.[7] On an expanded scale, his adaptations deploy 'common' versus 'received' voices, interpolations of 'low' art forms, new gendered emphases, and culturally transposed settings with their modern racial issues and sublimated material histories. Thus he seeks to unmoor foundational texts, encouraging ancient and modern representations of class, gender and race to clash, interrogate and revise one another in the course of semiosis made slippery by poetic licence. Poetry therefore not only provides the 'Apollonian' structure which is to be occupied but also, and at the same time, in renewed dialectic, the invasive 'Dionysian' medium necessary to undermine the traditional representations it houses.

That medium once again bears a material counter-force in Harrison's work, noted for its hard-hitting, colloquial delivery, consonantal sound (which he associates with the 'body' of language) and concrete imagery.[8] In dramatic dialogue, its pulse-like iambs, or 'heartbeat', as Harrison describes it, are also capable of taking over the text, undermining the words, and carrying a subverbal counter-rhythm into all but physical collision with the abstract social and moral constructions within which his characters find themselves trapped.[9] Almost all of Harrison's work turns upon such pivotal conflicts between textuality and materiality, or sensuality, which contemporary theory describes as being another kind of *inherent* otherness that can never be fully captured in language or formed by dominance.[10] Allying this internal force with those externalised as 'other' in his plays, Harrison presents social conflict as a kind of psychomachia in which dominant forces and their individual adherents self-destructively constrain their own innate impulses toward disruption and renewal by projecting them upon the socially diminished or outcast. Thus poetry finally becomes not only Harrison's structure and medium but his way of reading culture: its fluid associations and intertextual vision map the repercussions that silence, marginalise, devalue or vilify internal and external forces of rejuvenation.

Therefore, although it is true, as the jacket blurb for the first critical anthology of essays on his work has it, that Harrison is, 'like Brecht . . . both a major social poet and an innovative dramatist', his drama more accurately *revises* rather than 'extend[s] the Brechtian tradition of music theatre'.[11] Music, often of a percussive nature, is an important staple in Harrison's productions, but for reasons quite different from those Brecht might have articulated. Instead of using music and poetry to distance or 'alienate' the audience from the action, and thereby prevent the kind of identification that would interfere with their ability to analyse clearly and see beyond the illusion at hand, Harrison's reimagining of music within what he believes must have been 'operatic' Greek theatre involves his audience on *both* the sensual and rational level – the two different and contradictory ways of knowing operative in his dialectic – thereby also breaking the illusion but not from any position of transcendence. Wary of what Nietzsche called the *'optimistic* element in the nature of dialectic, which celebrates a triumph with every conclusion and can breathe only in cool clarity and consciousness', Harrison engages his viewers in a new sort of hermeneutical enterprise which questions the editorial process of analysis by making that which falls through the lines of 'clarity and consciousness' palpable again, part of the argument on stage as well as in their readings of it, where 'rationality' bears a definition arising inevitably out of the same textual tradition as his script.[12] Therefore his plays become, like Brecht's *Lehrstücke*, 'learning plays', though ones which cultivate not a clearer but a *double*-consciousness, an internal otherness constantly on guard against the coercions of language and its always illusory architectonics of truth.

It is perhaps not surprising, then, that his work is more closely related to the verse plays of his friend Wole Soyinka than to any produced since mid-century by British playwrights. The 'creative schizophrenia' of post-colonial writers, as Derek Walcott describes it, leads in Soyinka's case to the same adaptive drive that promotes an 'electric fusion' or, as the subtitle for his adaptation of *The Bacchae* of Euripides has it, a secular 'Communion Rite' in which poetry brings the materiality of words back down from abstract realms of representation onto the physical stage – the Greek 'orchestron', the 'dancing place', the threshing floor of the cultural text.[13]

II

Although Harrison's first widely-received success came in 1973 with his commissioned translation of *The Misanthrope*, which is suggestively reset in De Gaulle's France and celebrated for its recapture of Molière's demonic satire and colloquial energy in rhyming couplets, it was his adaptation of Aristophanes' *Lysistrata* for Nigerian players nearly a decade earlier that truly set the stage for things to come.

Aikin Mata (1964), like Harrison's later adaptations of comedy, from his trilogy of fifteenth-century English mystery plays to his recent reconstruction of a Sophoclean satyr-play fragment, recovers its place in a tradition of festive/disruptive, 'carnivalesque' texts which Bakhtin traces back to satyric and Aristophanic comedy.[14] Harrison reconstructs within such texts much of what later generations found most objectionable and tended to edit out: the Dionysian element, whose 'concretised sensuality' and 'procreative force' translated all exalted, mythic and authoritative constructions into the material images of the communal body in order to see them in an 'other' light, resist their linguistic abstraction and the power structure that exploits it.[15] By interpolating modern forms of popular comedy from slapstick to music hall within such texts, as well as vigorous modes of popular dance, Harrison both recreates the contra-conventional material energy lost in what he describes as 'effete' European productions of classical comedy, and at the same time revalues the so-called 'low' forms of contemporary comic art.[16]

Such oppositional energies are diversified and magnified in his first comedy (as in his first tragedy) by their settings in nations formerly colonised by the British. Harrison demonstrates in *Aikin Mata* the fruitful violence that is done to classical scripts 'refined' over time by intertextual influences when the tables are turned and they are occupied by those they were meant to 'civilise'. In their preface to the play he and his collaborator James Simmons write that the uninhibited mixture of mime, music and dance which their student players at Ahmadu Bello University in Zaria brought to Aristophanes' play from their experience of performing in Soyinka's *The Lion and the Jewel* restored those elements to what Harrison believes were their integral place in the original play, providing a glimpse at what might have been its unadulterated force.

In *Aikin Mata* that force is literally a material, 'procreative' one, and one which turns Aristophanes' vision of protest for peace through sexual boycott into a carnivalised war with textual hegemony on all levels, fueled by a Dionysian desire for a 'new world of symbols', which gets its way by the end of the play. The title identifies the central transformative symbols and physical counter-rhythms which the play sets into motion against the Nigerian patriarchy and inter-tribal hostility at the time of its production, just before the civil war. Hausa for 'women's work' (represented specifically by the pounding of guinea corn and yams with mortar and pestle), aikin mata also, in 'vulgar' usage, refers to sexual intercourse. Thus the liminal world of the body becomes, in this setting, identified with the marginalised 'working class'; the women's decision to 'strike' involves turning their representation as bodily forces into the weapons they use to fight their way to the centre, where a new reading of priorities from a material perspective inverts and dissolves the social structure that defined them. From the moment that Magajiya (Lysistrata) announces to the Alkali (or magistrate) and the male chorus that women have taken over the palace, the purse, and that ' . . . now we must reverse our rôles:/ You must obey as we did formerly, and *we* / Will give the orders. War is woman's work' (35), war is redefined through its metaphorical conscription into the 'base' worlds of food production and love-making, while 'women's work', conversely, comes to mean the steady take-over of Nigerian government by its 'pounding' rhythms, which travel from their limited associations with the thrusts of pestle into mortar and their ready analogy in the sexual act to newly proposed figural models for social and political intercourse.

The verse embodies this occupying rhythm, which can be intensified through the kind of alliterative pulse heard in Magakiya's lines quoted above. Highly stylised, inter-choral exchanges, dances and mimes also accentuate its pounding to music and drums (whose percussive sound, reminiscent of the heartbeat, remains a constant feature of Harrison's theatre). Perhaps equally importantly they remind us, as Magajiya herself will in a metatheatrical move near the end of the play, that this text is itself as artific(ial) and adaptable as the cultural one 'danced' to daily, which also 'plays a tune/ With words, and if you dance, you dance' (73). That the material body is caught in a cross-fire of textual 'tunes' is acted out in stichomythic fights between the male and female choruses. Through physical movements and gestures, stops and starts they dance out the dislocation, confusion and subsequent transformation occurring due to poetic upheavals in the community's signs and representations, and therefore within the community itself. For example, in the following scene the women, having pantomimically cross-dressed the Alkali in their own role's garb, chant from atop the palace walls in war metaphors, sending the exalted terms of patriarchy down to the level of 'women's work' and the displaced men below:

> Choragos(w): Love's a combat.
> Chorus(w1):   Love's a wrestle.
> Chorus(w2): Love's a mortar . . .
> Chorus(m) (*stop dancing and shout up at women*):
>   . . . and a *pestle*.
>   (*resume dancing except for Choragos (m)*
> Choragos(m): You were born; and you; and you.
> Chorus(m): Out of *pounding* . . .
> Chorus (w) (*jeering.*): . . . *fufu**?
>   (*The drums pause.*)
> Chorus (m): You! . . .
>   (*Yoruba: *cassava*) (43)

While male bellicosity proves itself ridiculous and self-destructive in such translation, the women's wielding of their phallic pestles as weapons in carnivalesque imitation of the men in their world of military dominance makes the same point: such violence with a mutual symbol of production and fertility ultimately strikes back at

'You!' – at Nigeria, impounding life's processes and spending sons in war.

At the same time that such parodic constructions are doing their deconstructive work, Magajiya 'pounds' the dislocated group of signs and violent images, slowly turning the way in which the latter are put to rhythmic use in 'women's work' into an alternative model for the running of the state:

> . . . Oh, you must know
> The to and fro of love, the press of bone
> Upon a bone like grinding stones, the feel
> Of gristle like a pestle softening the flesh.
>
> . . . .
>
> Think how the scattered seed and single yams
> Are blended by such persuasion of hard stone
> And wood. *Persuasion.* Nothing would become
> Another thing delightful in itself
> By crude, ungentle strength. By *gentle* force
> And soft compulsions such as these, we will
> Coerce this split Nigeria into one sweet whole.
>
> (39)

Such 'coercion' is later distinguished from 'co-option' in the preparation of the reconciliatory feast, during which disparate ingredients neither 'lose distinction' nor 'cause indigestion' (68). Uneducated but eloquent Magajiya becomes a voice in the play for several kinds of 'difference', as well as for persuasive, material, common knowledge which demystifies what one tribal ambassador calls the 'theoretical' and 'unreal' pronouncements of statecraft (74).

Thus though this play is the first of several 'sex wars' which Harrison will write, the battle is not strictly between males and females but between dominant forces and their *constructions* of otherness, which the women in this play, in a microcosmic enactment of his own practice of adaptation, implode and recreate in a new world of symbols understood as being only that, and always illusory, reconstructible. Therefore, in a figural departure from *Lysistrata*, 'Reconciliation' is not embodied here as a beautiful naked woman – a problematic image of male repossession of things as they were – but rather as being imminent in the very weapon employed by both sides, the pestle/penis. At the end of its semiotic odyssey between male and female constructions and reconstructions of it, it lands as a comic sign of the word trying again to be made common flesh in the hands of Magajiya, the new leader, who seeing the ambassadors come to truce 'erect, unsatisfied', senses that 'peace is so close/ My fingers seem to touch it; it feels nice' (71). In this utopian vision, 'women's work' actually gets done as such, and the play's concluding non-gender-specific rituals of eating, drinking and uniting bind diverse celebrants in the play's material, 'pounding' counter-rhythm finally universalised in their own image 'Of Africa shaped like a heart' (78).

Tragic texts involve Harrison in a slightly different and more subtle strategy of adaptation. If 'comic presentation and sexual ambiance' release the 'terror' of chaos, with its dislocations from constructed moorings of language and consequent potential for social renewal, then tragedy seeks to contain such forces and con-solidate moral agreement in its different project of imagining and confronting fate.[17] In his tragic adaptations Harrison practices what he calls a kind of 'translator's judo', using the weight of the original plays' constructions of moral order, justice and necessity to throw them into new light, and reveal traces of what their characters must repress or project, both individually and socially, in order to adhere heroically to the script.[18]

Harrison's adaptation of Racine's *Phèdre* (1677) attempts to embody or 'reinterpret physically' those dominating forces at work in the society surrounding the latter's 'absolutist' reading of Euripides' and Seneca's versions of the myth; he does so by relocating the tragic polarities of Racine's text in nineteenth-century British India, which 'herself' becomes his *Phaedra Britannica* (1975).[19] In his preface, Harrison quotes Martin Turnell on Racine's pre-revolutionary France, likening its social dynamic to that of his own setting just before the Indian Mutiny of 1857 when 'reason also had to operate tyrannically and repress by force an uprush of the senses whose indiscriminate way of perceiving, might jeopardise rigid boundaries constructed between 'masters and servants, the rulers and the ruled, royalty and the people' – the only two classes that seem to exist in Racine's work (xix).

Dramatising such divisions in his inter-racial setting, Harrison traces the fates of expelled senses and of the designated 'others', the Indians and even 'half-bred' Thomas (Hippolytus), upon whom such intrinsic forces must be projected. Apollonian illusions of greater 'rationality' and cool, classical order aspired to by the colonisers and claimed as their own Western cultural heritage are continually undermined in Harrison's adaptation by poetry that connects rulers to 'barbarians', masters to 'beasts'. Its sub-layer of hallucinatory imagery is supported by the stage set itself, which calls for a full-length neo-classical façade (reminiscent, Harrison suggests, of Comédie Française productions of *Phèdre*) to represent the Durbar Hall of the Governor's Residency, a Victorian 'construction' equipped with hundreds of blinds to keep out the hot Indian sunlight and alternative, sensual world.[20] The colonisers' own words are also constantly contradicted by the verse's non-verbal rhythm, its 'Heart beat like a tom tom' (11), replete with blood and pulse imagery and even heavy breathing marked out in metrical feet; moving more quickly than Racine's alexandrines, in rhyming couplets whose iambs Harrison calls a 'bloodthrob' (xxv), it roots them in the very sensuality they suicidally would suppress. Caught like mythic Phaedra with no reconciliatory ground between Minos, her father the punitory judge, and her mother Pasiphaë, the transgressive sensualist with a bestial appetite, Harrison's collective protagonist struggles against itself toward destruction before its own exiled Dionysian principles growing into the 'monstrous composite' which appears in new translation at the end of the play.

Harrison's production of this text characteristically and subtly shifts its focus from the title character to the larger social rhythm that creates her plight. In this case there is an eye to its storm – the Theseus figure, the Governor, who represents imperial Britain, survives the play, and in many ways controls its events even in absentia for the first of its two acts. Harrison's interrogation of this paradigmatic hero of reason against disorder, made a moral pillar in *Phèdre* and later apotheosised by the Victorians as a long-surviving clue to their own natures, involves recovering mythology's record of his darker, more lascivious and ruthless aspect, and recasting him in modern mythologisations of imperialism's civilising spread.

Such disruptive notes available in the myth allow Harrison to portray the Governor as leading, by virtue of his position, a double life, thereby escaping the repressive boundaries which will destroy his wife and son (and, by analogy, Britain's future in her colony). At his Residency he maintains an illusion of 'discipline', a 'cleaner air' (39, 34), so that while away for a symbolic half of the year, he may stray into 'areas still unsurveyed', unbounded, where he pursues, undetected, even 'in disguise', what Burleigh (Theramenes) satirically calls his '"scholar's" passion for the primitive' and its dark, sensual gods (1, 2), satisfying the 'other' side of his nature even as he turns swiftly against it in acts of violence, rape and massacre: a hunting down of the 'beast' within him through projection and criminal exorcism.

In his preface Harrison compares the 'Imperial dream' the Governor represents and administers in this way to Goya's dream of reason, which also 'produces monsters' in dark recesses just beyond its unmaintainably saintly light (xx). Retrieving such imagery from Theseus' returning story of phantasmagoric capture by the 'barbarian' King of Epirus (whose wife he had been in the process of abducting with a friend), Harrison turns the Governor's similarly dream-like account of imprisonment in an airless 'hell-hole', chained next to a 'flesh-starved monstrosity' (34) – a reflection of his own unrecognised *alter ego* – into a mirroring illusion for the situation his own hypocritical rule is creating not only within himself but at his Residency, and thus into a key to the tragic events of the play.

Like the 'somethings hungry in a pit' (33) envisioned by the Governor, his wife the Memsahib and son Thomas Theophilus also grow unrecognisable selves in the dark recesses and 'unventilated atmosphere' (34) of the Residency where, having neither the opportunity nor the temperament to live doubly, they construct monsters of their own inescapable and so-called bestial desires. Harrison dramatises the process by which the inherent 'animal' element, here figured in the horses continually associated with Thomas/Hippolytus, becomes the 'beast' when unassimilated, repressed or projected. Thomas, half Rajput, but as strictly bound by the colonisers' code as he is clad in its tight white uniform in the play, 'masters' any 'mutinous passions' he feels with what he calls his 'shibboleths': 'bridle, curb and bit' (38). Such shibboleths – linguistic constructions which by etymology are class-divisive – represent internal divisions that in the end kill him; caught in his chariot's reins in Racine's version and in the stirrups in Harrison's update, he will be dragged to symbolic unrecognisability by the trappings on his own horses as he attempts, in what might be seen as a dream-enactment of the Memsahib's suicide, to destroy his 'beast' – the final apparition of their collectively constructed monster. The Memsahib, similarly divided but more powerfully situated than the boy, reacts like the Governor by projecting her attraction to exactly that which is 'animal' in Thomas upon India and its malevolent, illness-producing forces. She ultimately destroys her Indian *ayah* (Oenone), Thomas and herself in her attempt to exorcise her demons.

Harrison's adaptation thus recreates 'Phaedra' (who has no name in the play, only 'the Governor's Wife') and her step-son as 'victims', in Thomas' words, 'shivering with symptoms in this feverward' (35), though the disease contracted has no more to do with India or congenital propensities, as the Memsahib fears, toward perverse lust than it does with the love Thomas feels for his father's Indian political prisoner, Lilamani (Aricia), who symbolises all he has imprisoned within himself. Instead, it is the Governor's hegemonic, hypocritical and hallucinogenic divisiveness which prevents them from recognising what their servants understand to be 'feelings common to humanity' (6), and turns them into the 'flesh-starved monstrosities' of his own vision. When he returns, assesses the situation, and wishes himself shut up again 'in that hole' (34), the audience absorbs by poetic connection one of the play's most important ironies: that that is precisely where he has brought himself.

He escapes it and the fate of his 'victims' by once again projecting his encaved monsters upon 'others', in this case his own half-Indian boy whom he accuses of being the incestuous

> Animal! [*inhale, exhale*] Now it all comes out!
> The reversal everybody spoke about!
> The lower self comes creeping up from its lair
> out of the dismal swamps of God-knows-where.
> It lumbers leering from primeval slime
> where it's been lurking, biding its own time.
> How could his kind absorb our discipline,
> our laws of self-control, our claims of kin.
> I've expected far too much. It's in his blood.
>
> (35)

The dramatic 'reversal' as well as the beast and the blood are revealed to be the Governor's own as his innocent son, a potential conduit between cultures, rushes against an incarnation of his father's delusions. The 'avenging Siva' the latter calls down upon the boy and then senses, 'like shivering and chill preceding fever' (39) appears in Burleigh's description of Thomas' death, 'and shambles forward through the shimmering heat' (50); this illusion-*breaking* illusion of Siva, the Indian god of destruction and regeneration, comes like the Dionysian forces that Nietzsche believed 'annihilated' tragic illusions at the ends of plays. Thus in Harrison's deconstruction of Racine's lines of causality as well as casuistry the consequences are all that are real; the Governor's imploded myths of self leave him in the same position as Lilamani, whose rebellious family he massacred – a victim of his own self-destructive rule, broken only through connection with the 'other'. The audience joins in that realisation and in destroying the play's illusions when the Governor asks Lilamani to 'ford . . . those frontiers of blood into his heart', and the play ends with the sound of Siva's monsoon rains coming on, as the Memsahib and the final stage directions put it, 'like slow applause' (54, 53).

   Variations on the same judoistic and carnivalesque strategies in adaptation shape Harrison's two trilogies, *The Oresteia* (1981) and *The Mysteries* (composed of *The Nativity*, 1980, *The Passion*, 1977, and *Doomsday*, first performed with the others in 1985). Both trilogies are based on texts in which key foundational concepts find their initial dramatic inscription within culture: Athenian democracy and rational justice on the one hand, and Christian dogma on the other. Such concepts are, once again, like 'patriarchy' and 'rationality' in his first two plays, deconstructed from sensual and 'other' vantage points in order to illuminate, in the first case, what must be sacrificed to the new political/cultural ideal, and in the second case to celebrate the possibility of renewal for official beliefs when the terms of the Biblical 'highest are brought low'. Both are recreated in early English metres, whose heavy-limbed, alliterated stresses bear an even more conspicuously physical impact, and whose popular origins and interpolated balladry allow Harrison to begin his much-noted practice of casting (or *re*casting, in the case of *The Mysteries*) north country words and inflections (and actors) into the classics as well. Each nearly ten years in the making (and each far too vast in scope to treat at length in this essay), the trilogies represent something of a second phase in Harrison's career, during which his characteristic concern with the representation of otherness in cultural inscription is brought closer to home.

   The heroic Anglo-Saxon measure and musculature, reminiscent of *Beowulf*, into which Harrison translates *The Oresteia* not only recaptures something of what he calls the 'craggy' physicality of Aeschylus' use of language, full of neologisms not unlike Old English word-images, or kennings; it also helps disruptive forces of otherness in the trilogy to bring material evidence against the judgments of rationalising, historicising, and juridical forces that attempt to sort out the excesses of the Trojan War and its aftermath of domestic violence. Harrison's presentation of the dramatic argument concentrates on the momentum that connects the two kinds of excess, all of which culminates in the trial of Orestes for murder of his mother, Clytemnestra, who had killed his father, Agamemnon, for making a sacrifice of their daughter at the outset of war. In his interrogation of Orestes' acquittal, which depends upon the sublimation of matriarchy's last surviving forces of vengeance, the Furies (interpreted to date as having led to the triumph of Hellenic 'culture' over 'nature'), Harrison reweights the arguments of both participating forces not, in effect, to side with the 'others', figured forth as feminine throughout the trilogy, but rather to illuminate the agenda that represents them as such.

As Carol Rutter has noted, the women in the plays are the ones who 'hold grudges' like the Furies, remember violent means to political ends like Clytemnestra, prophesy unheard, like Cassandra, and become reimaged in this graphic version as the 'bloodhounds' whose voices full of 'bloodright' and 'bloodguilt' go coursing through the trilogy with a corporeal force that clashes with the interests of statecraft; it was Harrison's adaptation, Rutter writes, that 'made her hear the claimant voice of this she-grudge story'.[21] He accomplishes this in part by highlighting gendered patterns of experience in kenning-like compounds – 'she-gods', 'he-gods', 'she-kin', 'he-child', etc. – so that by the time the Furies, the 'she-gods', arrive in the court of Athens to litigate unsuccessfully against Apollo for the conviction of Orestes, the audience has a new view of the proceedings, one which connects along poetic peripheries a whole line of feminine 'cases' beginning with what serves as a virtual archetype for them all: the gagging and sacrifice of Iphigeneia for 'the war-effort' by her father Agamemnon, whose ships needed wind to sail out for Troy.[22]

The silencing of women in the plays not only allows them to be used as sacrifices or as scapegoats, such as Helen becomes for the male chorus as they struggle with gory memories of the unnecessary carnage of the war; it also allows the dominant masculine community to cast their own sublimated disruptive consciences upon women in order to subduct both at the same time, in much the same way that 'Phaedra Britannica' cast her own disruptive sensual self upon India in order to keep both down. Thus Apollo, instigator of the matricide and spokesman for one half of Orestes (who in Harrison's production is played by a notably small, almost feminine figure, as though to emphasise his 'other' half, the half that sways in a dance of guilt with the Furies), enacts on a godly plane the internal battle of his protégé as he turns to the rather beautifully masked she-gods and, like the Governor in *Phaedra Britannica*, bellows 'Animals! Beast-hags hated by he-gods!'[23]

Pursuant to Apollo's misogynistic argument devaluing Clytemnestra's murder, motherhood, and women in general, whose wombs he calls 'convenient transit' for the father's seed (283), the Furies are literally ruled down, their 'ancient conscience/pushed underground' (287) into the caverns below Athens so that 'culture' may launch, like Agamemnon's ships, its patriarchal and allegedly democratic system. Harrison's translation emphasises the way that system works: Athena, engendered solely by Zeus and thus wont to 'put the male first' (284), decides with an all-male jury to acquit the son of an ally in the war, who 'won [her her] spearspoil' (277). She thereby gains the support of Argos and Apollo *and* the opportunity to appropriate, through threats, bribery, and 'the linctus of language' (288), the power of the Furies installed as the Eumenides, the Kindly Ones, made guardians of Athens alone. Unlike the ideal democracy symbolised in *Aikin Mata*'s reconciliatory feast, the self-serving product of Athena's 'gentler persuasion' (287) at the end of *The Oresteia* depends upon the loss of an ingredient, the voice of the dissentient, destructive, non-partisan, non-forgetful 'Grudges' who vanish in a final procession up into the audience, who are asked to stand to receive it – a dramatic enactment of this text's absorption by the culture that has inscribed it within its own heroic tradition (as Harrison suggests with his verse form). Harrison's adaptation demonstrates that this 'precedent' for seemingly clear-cut progress made through 'rational justice' over 'revenge' carries hidden agendas but, as he says, 'there's a lot of vested interest in the Classics as being a rather aseptic foundation of our culture'.[24]

If in *The Oresteia* Harrison is concerned with what, quoting Engels, he calls 'the historical defeat of the female sex',[25] riding in tandem with that of the disruptive principle, in *The Mysteries* he reverses another kind of defeat, this one local, and accomplished through the production history of the text. The 'others' in this case are, ironically, the authors themselves: the medieval artists/artisans, the ordinary, northern working people who, through a collective process Harrison admires, one which involved the continual revision and adaptation of their own myths, fashioned cycles of liturgical plays for their street pageants only to be first suppressed by the reformed English Church, even destroyed in manuscript, and then relegated in this century to the margins of their own texts by translators invested in maintaining lines of authority. Angered by versions of the mysteries as he had seen them revived in York, where 'God and Jesus were played by very posh-speaking actors from the South, and the local people again played the comic parts', Harrison wished to 'restore Yorkshire's great classic to itself', which first meant restoring its 'homogeneous language' so 'that God, Christ, and everybody else speak in the language of the time, which is also colloquial'.[26]

By so doing, Harrison reactivates the carnivalesque principle that adheres in the leveling drive through which participating townspeople and craftsmen's guilds brought the exalted mysteries of the Church down to earth, translating them into the words and material images of their everyday lives and jobs (just as the word 'mystery' itself can be demystified by its own etymological roots in 'craft' and 'trade'). The figure of Christ the carpenter, who recrafted the mysteries of Old Testament inscriptions into new word-images and homely parables, broke the dead letters of Church laws, and 'preached where people were most present',[27] becomes himself the embodiment of that creative/destructive energy moving between abstract concept and concrete image, word and flesh – or Apollo and Dionysus; Harrison's *Mysteries* demonstrate the catholicity of his adaptational construct.

He rediscovers its rejuvenative power in the original form of the plays: a northern descendant of Old English verse whose heavily alliterated ballad measures, full of mnemonic rhyme, onomatopoeia, monosyllabic images and changing, dance-like counts, offers up words and ideas, as several reviewers have put it, like 'physical objects'. Treating the Bible as poetry, full of relationships that demand continual re-embodiment in the physical world, Harrison emphasises the dynamic most central to the plays' own celebration of the feast of Corpus Christi, one which made 'carnival' all but a commandment: the necessary 'communion' established with divinity in the 'body' of Christ, made like theirs out of 'the simplest part of earth' (15) to which they were to continually return in order to remake him, a project symbolised by the bread he offers, both before and after crucifixion, as an example of 'his corse, no common crust' (102, 189).

Translating that injunction poetically, Harrison, director Bill

Bryden, their company of updated actors/'artisans' and indeed the audience too, given that this is a promenade production which often involves them, collectively 'make God' by recreating the mysteries again in the simplest images of working Yorkshire, using the materials and relationships that inform its daily life. Thus God enters the world of miners, painters, firemen, butchers, bus conductors, mechanics, construction workers (and others) like a good foreman on a forklift truck, a 'maker' like them (11), and Lucifer gets dumped out of his incongruous armchair on another such vehicle while slacking off in self-preoccupation; Mary, first portrayed as a housewife, becomes a familiar figure of old age in a wheelchair before being paraded off to her son by a town band of tuba, banjo and drum – 'to his bigly bliss [her] bones for to bring' (204); Simon of Cyrene, played by one of the production's Anglo-African actors, hurries by in his business suit until stopped to help carry Christ's cross; and a miner last sights Christ through the Good Friday darkness with the light on his helmet, representing the common people who were closest to the events as he (rather than the centurion) concludes *The Passion* by confirming Christ's divinity: 'But since ye set nought by my saw/ I'll wend my way' (156).

Almost no scene passes without laughter, often at its own contrivance. Historically dismissed for such 'intrusive and even blasphemous . . . mixture of comedy and serious action',[28] the mysteries in Harrison's translation foreground all such 'diableries', as Bakhtin calls them, in order to emphasise their central, close-to-classical, illusion-breaking and life-supporting functions.[29] Like the satyr plays that followed tragic trilogies at Greek festivals, comic spoofs, like the famous 'Second Shepherd's Play' which follows and parodies Christ's nativity (and is recreated here as a Keystone Kops chase after Mak the lamb-stealer), throw the plays' constructions up into the air, calling the audience's attention to their provisional nature, and to the need to continually, collectively reconstruct them in 'new worlds of symbols'. With their jubilant dances like Dionysian dithyrambs between tragic scenes and their spillings into the audience, Harrison's *Mysteries* become his fullest demonstration to date of how the Greeks' tragic/comic, dialectical imagination might be translated into an even more 'democratic' method of myth-making for the twentieth century.[30]

On the other hand, Harrison's most recent staged work, his reconstruction of the Sophoclean satyr-play fragment *Satyroi Ichneutai* ('Tracking Satyrs'), offers his most comprehensive view to date of western culture as it actually functions. *The Trackers of Oxyrhynchus* (1988) also combines tragedy and satyrical comedy but disturbingly reverses the order, concluding with his vision of the continuing social tragedy that accompanies textual sublimation of the Dionysian world.[31] Like his as-yet-unperformed theatre works, *Medea: a sex-war opera* and *The Common Chorus* (a trilogy consisting of a new version of *Lysistrata* set at the site of the women's protest at the USAF base at Greenham Common, an adaptation of Euripides' *The Trojan Women*, and a play of his own in progress, *Maxims*, about the invention of the machine gun and chemical warfare), *The Trackers of Oxyrhynchus* becomes part of what might be seen as a new phase in Harrison's work which is characterised by even greater freedom in adaptation and more direct confrontation with current, topical, social and political issues.

At issue in *Trackers* are the consequences of selective memory loss on a cultural scale; Harrison turns Sophocles' only partially exhumed satyrical spoof of Apollo's takeover of the lyre and 'high art' into a dramatisation of culture's literal and figurative burial of satyrical drama's integral role in tragedy, engineered by forces seeking to still the dialectic and divide art into elite and popular categories – a development Harrison views as being both a symptom of and textual tool used to perpetuate the 'deep sickness' still apparent in divisive society.[32] He brings the Greek construction of 'satyrdom', or the inherent Dionysian self whose appearance after tragic constructions reaffirmed shared, elemental life and its 'other' perspective on artificial illusions, through a three-part movement into the present moment, where it finds itself 'homeless' in Apollo's world of high art. In the second of two stunning transitions in the play, the satyrs depart their fragmented script and, symbolically, their place in the imagination's self-portrait, to become representations of real, socially outcast and violent young men who by the end become the real homeless just outside the walls of the National Theatre. They thus enact Harrison's long-playing theme concerning the destination of ostracised aspects of self when what Nietzsche calls 'the alleged reality of the man of culture' forges and fosters deep divisions in art, society, textual traditions and therefore most of the tools with which individuals and cultures come to interpret themselves.[33]

If the second transition moves the action from the play's text into contemporary history, the first dramatic transition in the play moves from history into the text to be reconstructed – all of which becomes

an only half-comic reproduction of the way intertextual forces of
dominance act. It begins at Oxyrhynchus, in what remains of the
ancient Egyptian town's rubbish heaps, where in 1907 B.P. Grenfell
and A.S. Hunt, the Oxonian papyrologists, excavated four-hundred
lines of Sophocles' *Ichneutai*. Their sudden transformation at the end
of the first segment into the *Ichneutai*'s opposing roles of Apollo and
Dionysius' best-known devotee, the head satyr Silenus, is in keeping with satyrical drama's characteristically magical and surprising
changes. But this one, despite its hilarity, also signals the potentially sinister collusion between forces of art that dominate words
and texts (represented throughout by Apollo himself, who goads
Grenfell into finding 'that play where [he] speak[s] the phrases')
(87), and therefore dominate to a great extent the imagination –
particularly Grenfell's, which is 'literally possessed' (81) not only by
Apollo but also by Apollonian illusions of high-minded, Olympian
antiquity, which have taught him to 'prefer/ papyrus poetry and
plays to papyrus *cris-de-coeur*' (85) (from the poor and homeless),
and forces of history, because as Grenfell, turning to the audience,
explains:

> The past is rubbish till scholars take the pains
> to sift and sort and interpret the remains.
> This chaos is the past, mounds of heaped debris
> just waiting to be organised into history. (79)

The forward stage set; composed of the mounds Grenfell points to,
becomes one huge metaphor for culture's processes of selection and
disposal of textual clues to itself. What it does not want to see it
does not see, or 'read'; Grenfell, so 'dazzlingly fast' with ancient
Greek that 'he can actually *read*/ what most people can't decipher'
(81), repeatedly turns away from the many excavated petitions for
shelter and loans with impatience, misinterpreting them or putting
them away without trying: ' . . . the rest I can't read' (82). Hunt
can; in the second published version of this play he verbalises his
different sort of historicising energy more clearly:

> Grenfell, I love literature quite as much
>   as you
> but these petitions have historical and human
>   interest too.

>   (77)

Aside from the 'surreptitious drink' (86) he takes to break from Grenfell's 'military routine' (80), Hunt's Dionysian aspect is less in evidence than his colleague's Apollonian one. Harrison wished that Hunt seem somewhat constrained by his role and even by his lines, just as disruptive satyr-selves are kept down by the social forces that shape Grenfell. But the sympathy he bears for 'the folk in dire need' (84) who surrounded the poets and playwrights, and the connection he makes between them and the Egyptian *fellaheen* Grenfell goads into working faster in the mounds indicates his Dionysian identification with the material experience, suffering, and 'anonymous toil', as Walter Benjamin put it, of those who always underlie and indeed enable, through the appropriation of their energies, the creation of art and the building of great cultural monuments. 'There is no document of civilisation', wrote Benjamin, 'which is not at the same time a document of barbarism'.[34]

Like the *fellaheen* who do the work of 'tracking' down Grenfell's poetry and plays, the satyrs also prove necessary, in their case as men-beasts with 'horse-like sniffers' (94), to the project of tracking down Apollo's beloved lost cattle, newly threaded into Hermes' lyre, and thus to the discovery of what Apollo, after its procurement, will exclude them from – 'high art' (119). But the satyrs vibrate with a power dormant in their Egyptian descendants, thereby extending and deepening the portrayal of loss inherent in culture's gain. Though they expand the identity of the exploited by representing the British working class in Greek translation, speaking in thick north country dialects and substituting wild clog dancing for dithyrambs (a spectacle which reminded many reviewers of Bill Tidy's northern tabloid cartoon strip, *The Cloggies*), they also represent, with their enormous phalluses standing for disruptive sensuality, and their phenomenological 'surprise at everything' – which 'reassess[es]/ from basic principles all [we] possess' (60) – one half of the art impulse, one charged pole in its dialectic, the integral regenerative principle without which Apollo's new lyre will conventionalise refinements, 'will create that sort of elite/ that will never get caught out tapping its feet' (119).

But the satyrs' 'staccato clatter' defies (at least for the length of the fragment) the possibility of their exclusion from art by demonstrating its vital link to the life and beat of the verse which they (like Apollo) deliver to its rhythm. The satyrs are even connected by numerous images to the lyre itself, made of a tortoise shell and the cattle with whom they, 'as part goat or horse, . . . identify'

(118). Thus they are in part the very 'gut' of the music by which they too, or their 'two-thirds human part, s'impressed' (118); they compose and understand the sacrifice made for its making, serving as a reminder of the necessary relation of celestial to bestial, 'high' to 'low'.

As such, they constitute the original dialectic's Dionysian threat to what Nietzsche calls the *principium individuationis* of Apollo: the drive to develop 'beautiful illusions' in art, 'dreams' of high culture that edit out the suffering of the communal body. The play fell into that dream when Grenfell passed out, after a tussle with internalised Apollo, at the end of the first segment; the reconstituted fragment cast him, with his dominating biases, into the role of the god. There is a 'delicate boundary', Nietzsche writes, 'which the dream image must not overstep lest it have a pathological effect (in which case mere appearance would deceive us as if it were crude reality)'.[35] In Harrison's adaptation that line defines the end of the satyr-play fragment and its Dionysian opposition to Grenfell/Apollo's self-realising dream – which then swiftly climaxes within the play's final 'crude reality': contemporary history.

Just as the satyrs voice both choral wonder and objections to the new sound, singing in newly invented melody that 'summat's been flayed / for this sweet serenade' (111), and asking where a satyr will 'start drawing the line' (118), Apollo draws it first along a militant 'desatyrised zone' (121) within which any satyr attempting to play the lyre or flute, as did the legendary Marsyas whose story Silenus bitterly retells, will be flayed of their skin like the brutes with whom they sympathise. Thus Apollo, who has dropped his own discernible accent and 'refined' his image in the course of the play, turns dialectics into 'a fixed scale in creation' (117) which sets high against low and makes the preservation of the former justification enough for any inhuman action taken against the latter. In a chilling conflation of time periods and imagery (not unlike Titian's *The Flaying of Marsyas*, reproduced in the playbill, which depicts a violinist present at the gruesome event), Silenus forecasts that

> You'll hear the lyres playing behind locked
> doors
> where men flay their fellows for some abstract
> cause.

. . . .

Some virtuouso of Apollo's ur-violin
plays for the skinners as they skin.

(126)

As the victims of the new system become its literal scape*goats*,
Apollo makes his own projections: that the position the men-beasts
assume at the Theatre of Dionysus in Athens (whose stage with its
'illusions' is propped on the marble shoulders of bent-over satyrs),
will manifest itself in real terms, in the famous 'Cardboard City'
made by the homeless just below the National Theatre, where many
in the audience spotted them on their way in to see Harrison's play.
There their disruptive force will be sublimated like that of the Furies
'pushed underneath' Athens in *The Oresteia*:

While I am the one with the lyre and the wreath
satyrs will always be pushed underneath.

I prophesy that they'll track through the ages
and end up where you saw them, underneath stages.

(121)

As Apollo delivers such fulfilled prophecy to an audience he
'assumes . . . are all Apollonian' (120), the satyrs step off the
network of split-open papyrus crates from which they had, at the
outset, and in response to the audience's own solicited chanting,
burst into the satyr-play-within-the-play as representations of the
audience's 'other' selves. Having danced and 'tracked' down the
origins of the lyre for them and for Apollo along these crate-backs
painted like lines of text, their exit symbolises their being dropped,
like the '*différance*' against which culture must always define itself,
through lines of textuality into the oblivion that has absorbed almost
every trace of the satyr-play tradition.

In the play's dénouement their ineradicable otherness degener-
ates first into the violence of those who, as Harrison writes in his
preface, 'will sooner or later want to destroy what they are not
allowed to inhabit' (xiv), and finally into homelessness, as the
former satyrs turn their papyrus crates into makeshift shelters.
Though Silenus begs the audience to either chant them into the
new 'social text' or back into their original Greek one, the audience
of course cannot respond – practically speaking, because 'no one
reads Greek' (134); symbolically and more importantly because

they have lost the ability to exercise their double-consciousness in order to assimilate the satyrs, having lost too, like their victims, the ability to interpret for themselves what the textual tradition, as edited by forces of dominance, once had to offer or warn them of – what has been wilfully 'lost in the translation'. The play ends with a terrifying image of that loss as Silenus, in one last effort to mount the tragic stage, is apprehended by Apollonian forces/flayers whose approach, signalled only by a 'burst of Apollo music' (136), narrows his spot-light until he vanishes with a silent scream.

That image, coupled with the sound of Marsyas' cries produced in the play as 'the tuning up of a large string section of an orchestra' (124), offers a key to Harrison's theatre works, as discussed in this essay. His method of replaying the classics involves making his audiences hear both the music and the scream: the cost of what is rendered beautifully by his poetry. He 'levels the artistic structure of the *Apollonian culture*', as my epigraph from Nietzsche has it, 'stone by stone' until we see that 'the foundations on which it rests' are, as at the Theatre of Dionysus, our own satyr-selves caught in a double-edged image of culture's need to build illusions on the backs of self-destructive suppressions, as well as of its inherent potential for disruption and renewal. If otherness is always 'pushed underneath' then continual deconstructive reconstruction, or adaptation as he practises it, becomes Harrison's *poros* in *aporia*, his way out. 'Above all', he writes, 'I love the ephemerality of the theatre!';[36] his own theatre becomes a place of opposing selves coming together, if only to see that nothing gets written in stone.

Notes

1. Derek Walcott, 'The Poet in the Theatre', Ronald Duncan Lecture No. 1, 29 September 1990, South Bank Centre (London: Poetry Book Society, 1991) n.p.
2. For a complete list of Harrison's theatre works to 1991, see *Tony Harrison*, ed. Neil Astley (Newcastle: Bloodaxe Books, 1991) pp. 507–9. Further references to this volume will appear as *TH*.
3. John Haffenden, 'Interview with Tony Harrison' in *TH*, p. 245.
4. See Friedrich Nietzsche, *The Birth of Tragedy and the Case of Wagner*, trans. Walter Kaufmann (New York: Random House, 1967) pp. 46, 40 *et passim*.
5. Ibid., p. 47; Haffenden, op. cit., pp. 242–3.
6. Harrison has said that 'the trouble with Eliot and Fry is that they brought the lyric into drama' instead of vice versa (Richard Hoggart,

'In Conversation with Tony Harrison', *TH* 45).
7. See 'Them & [uz]' in Harrison's *Selected Poems* (Harmondsworth: Penguin, 1987) p. 122.
8. Harrison writes: 'It's not the percussiveness of consonants but their sensuality, their sexuality if you like. Vowels are spirit, consonants body, people say. Then I'm for bodies . . . ' (*'The Oresteia* in the Making: Letters to Peter Hall', *TH* 279).
9. Richard Hoggart, op. cit., p. 43.
10. See, for example, Randy Martin's *Performance As Political Act: The Embodied Self* (New York: Bergin and Garvey Publishers, 1990), and Fred McGlynn's 'Postmodernism and Theater' (in *Postmodernism: Philosophy and the Arts*, ed. Hugh J. Silverman [New York/London: Routledge, 1990]).
11. *TH* [book jacket].
12. Nietzsche, op. cit., p. 91.
13. Derek Walcott, 'What the Twilight Says: An Overture' to *Dream on Monkey Mountain and Other Plays* (New York: Farrar, Straus and Giroux, 1970) p. 17.
14. M.M. Bakhtin, *Rabelais and His World*, trans. Hélène Iswolsky (Bloomington: Indiana University Press, 1984) p. 28n.
15. Ibid., pp. 255–6.
16. Tony Harrison and James Simmons, *Aikin Mata* (Ibadan: Oxford University Press, 1966) p. 5. All quotations are from this edition; hereafter, page numbers will be given in the text.
17. Wole Soyinka, *Myth, Literature and the African World* (Cambridge: Cambridge University Press, 1976) p. 155. Soyinka adapts Nietzsche's ideas to discuss the birth of Yoruban tragedy in this chapter.
18. Haffenden, op. cit., p. 240.
19. Tony Harrison, *Phaedra Britannica* (London: Rex Collings Ltd., 1975) p. xx; cf. Racine's absolutism as described in Haffenden, above. All quotations from *Phaedra Britannica* are from this edition; hereafter, page numbers will be given in the text.
20. Haffenden, op. cit., p. 240.
21. Carol Rutter, 'Men, Women, and Tony Harrison's Sex-war *Oresteia*', in *TH* 296.
22. Tony Harrison, *The Oresteia* (in *Theatre Works: 1973–1985* (Harmondsworth: Penguin, 1986) p. 195. All quotations are from this edition; hereafter, page numbers will be given in the text.
23. *The Oresteia*, p. 282. Harrison remarks upon the fact that in Greek art the Furies are 'always depicted as beautiful, but they're described horrendously'; the discrepancy in views betrays a complex inner conflict (Haffenden, op. cit., p. 245).
24. Haffenden, op. cit., p. 245.
25. Ibid., p. 241.
26. Hoggart, op. cit., p. 44.
27. Tony Harrison, *The Mysteries* (London: Faber & Faber, 1985) p. 117. All quotations are from this edition; hereafter, page numbers will be given in the text.

28. David Bevington, *Medieval Drama* (Boston: Houghton Mifflin, 1975) pp. 239–40.
29. Bakhtin, op. cit., p. 15. Bakhtin writes: 'Laughter penetrated the mystery plays; the diableries . . . have an obvious carnivalesque character. . . . '
30. Harrison's description of *The Mysteries* as being created by a 'democratic' process of collective adaptation is quoted from the introduction to Channel Four's television production of the plays, 22 and 29 December 1985, 5 January 1986.
31. Tony Harrison, *The Trackers of Oxyrhynchus*, the National Theatre Text (London: Faber & Faber, 1990) p. xiv. All quotations are from this edition; hereafter, page numbers will be given in the text.
32. Oliver Taplin, Harrison's friend and fellow classicist, makes this diagnosis in 'Satyrs on the Borderline: *Trackers* in the Development of Tony Harrison's Theatre Work' (*TH* 463).
33. Nietzsche, op. cit., p. 61.
34. Walter Benjamin, *Illuminations*, ed. Hannah Arendt, trans. Harry Zohn (New York: Schocken Books, 1969) p. 256.
35. Nietzsche, op. cit., pp. 35–6.
35. Letter to the author, 19 June 1991.

Index